Series: Studies in World Christian History

The present reality of Christianity is that it has become a diverse world-wide phenomenon which extends beyond the traditional European and North American imperial/established national ethnic churches. The conditions that led to this reality are less clearly understood. The ways Christians have and do relate to other Christians have become crucial to understanding the past, present and future of World Christianity. How have churches, often divided by ethnicity, culture, nationalism, and, therefore, theology, related to one another? How are the newer churches developing intellectual and Christian cultural frameworks related to their experiences and cultures? How have the colonial religious patterns of the sixteenth to twentieth centuries as part of Western commercial and military expansion been questioned, or are these being reinforced or reinterpreted as part of neo-colonialist religious "globalization"?

The Studies in World Christian History Series publishes texts and studies that illumine the historical, cultural and ecumenical structures of World Christianity and the interactions among Christians.

The following essays are presented in honor of Larry D. Smith, longtime editor of *God's Revivalist*. They focus primarily on the Radical Holiness Movement of which *God's Revivalist* and God's Bible School have been a key center for almost 125 years, and its impact on World Christianity is inestimable.

—David Bundy, Series Editor

The Radical Holiness Movement in the Christian Tradition

A Festschrift for Larry D. Smith

William Kostlevy and Wallace Thornton, Jr., Editors

Series: Studies in World Christian History

EMETH PRESS
www.emethpress.com

The Radical Holiness Movement in the Christian Tradition: A Festschrift for Larry D. Smith

Copyright © 2016 William Kostlevy and Wallace Thornton, Jr.
Printed in the United States of America on acid-free paper

All rights reserved. No part of this book may be reproduced, or stored in a retrieval system or transmitted in any form or by any means, electronic, mechanical, photocopying, recording, scanning or otherwise, except as permitted by the 1976 United States Copyright Act, or with the prior written permission of Emeth Press. Requests for permission should be addressed to: Emeth Press, P. O. Box 23961, Lexington, KY 40523-3961. http://www.emethpress.com

Cataloging-in-Publication Data

The radical Holiness Movement in the Christian tradition : a festschrift for Larry D. Smith / William Kostlevy and Wallace Thornton, Jr., editors – Lexington, KY : Emeth Press, ©2016.

    xii, 181 pages : illustrations, portraits ; cm -- (Studies in world Christian history)

    Includes bibliographical references.
    ISBN 9781609471019 (paperback)

    1. Holiness movement -- History. 2. Methodism -- History. 3. Smith, Larry D., 1942- I. Studies in world Christian history. II. Kostlevy, William, 1952- III. Thornton, Wallace, 1968- IV. Smith, Larry D., 1942-

BX7990.H6 R32 2016
287/.6

                      2016942300

Cover Photo
Photo of Larry D. Smith on the cover by Robert A. Flischel.
Used by permission of God's Bible School and College

Contents

Foreword / vii
 Donald W. Dayton

Preface / ix
 Michael Avery

Introduction / xi
 William Kostlevy

Chapter 1. A Wesleyan Theology for Governance of Seminaries / 1
 Kenneth J. Collins

Chapter 2. "Purposeful Living": Images of the Kingdom of God in Methodist Sunday School Worship / 11
 Jennifer Woodruff Tait

Chapter 3. The Establishmentarian Turn in the Wesleyan Methodist Church / 27
 Barry W. Hamilton

Chapter 4. Luther Lee: Social Reformer, Editor, and Church Leader -- 1843-1855 / 39
 Paul L. Kaufman

Chapter 5. Radical Holiness Becomes a World Christian Movement: The Influence of Isabella Sarah Leonard in Great Britain, Australia and Singapore, 1881-1892 / 53
 David Bundy

Chapter 6. Radical Holiness Evangelism: Vivian Dake and the Pentecost Bands / 69
 Howard A. Snyder

Chapter 7. "Planning and Prevailing for the Children": E. E. Shelhamer and Julia Arnold Shelhamer on Children and Parenting / 85
Gari-Anne Patzwald

Chapter 8. Single Vision, Separate Spheres: Iva Durham Vennard and the Methodist Episcopal Church / 97
Priscilla Pope-Levison

Chapter 9. Dr. Tenney, the Free Methodist Church, and the Twentieth Century Wesley Revival / 111
William Kostlevy

Chapter 10. David P. Denton: Evangelist of Truth / 123
William Snider

Chapter 11. Born in the Fire / 135
Edwin Woodruff Tait

Chapter 12. Reckoning with Babylon: G. T. Bustin and Radical Holiness Interaction with Catholicism / 149
Wallace Thornton, Jr.

Contributors / 167

Foreword

I have visited God's Bible School (GBS) many times, but it took me quite a while for its significance to sink in. When I was in seminary in 1968 my denomination, the Wesleyan Methodist Church, which was comprised of members pushed out of the Methodist Episcopal Church in response to antislavery agitation, merged with the Pilgrim Holiness Church (PHC) to form today's Wesleyan Church. The PHC had taken shape largely out of the circles of GBS and its organ *God's Revivalist.*

Over the next decade or so, while I was working on my dissertation on *The Theological Roots of Pentecostalism* in which the theology of GBS played a key role, I often dropped by to visit the library and bookstore or serve as an informal adviser to key figure H. E. Schmul on his important project of reprinting out of print holiness classics to support the "Radical Holiness Movement" centered at GBS and call the mainline movement back to its increasingly neglected heritage.

By the end of the century I was visiting more often to explore the major impact of GBS on Korean Christianity--and to view the plaque describing the impact of alumni Charles and Lettie Cowman of the Oriental Missionary Society and other GBS missionaries to Korea in the early 1900s. But increasingly the highlight of my visits would be the chance to stop by the office of Larry Smith, editor of *God's Revivalist* and author of the massive illustrated centennial history of GBS.

Larry Smith is a bigger than life figure, physically, intellectually and spiritually. Only as I began to have the honor of participating in the production of this Festschrift did I realize how profoundly this is true. He was a cofounder and later president of John Fletcher College. His early experience as a high school drama teacher no doubt helped shape his skills as a camp meeting orator. But the crowning achievement of his career has been his long tenure as editor of the *Revivalist* and professor at GBS. I have always been impressed with many features of Larry's personality, but I have specially appreciated his ability to find that delicate balance between representing with full integrity the thrust of his tradition while managing to transcend it at the same time.

This last characteristic was manifested in an event that I fondly remember. For a quarter of a century I represented the holiness movement (via the Wesleyan Theological Society) in the theological dialogue of the Faith and Order Commission of the National Council of Churches. It was often the case that we would tour religious sites in the area of our meetings. I was often frustrated that members of the more traditional churches with European roots were often satisfied with what seemed to me to be pale imitations of European institutions. When we met across the Ohio River from Cincinnati in Covington, Kentucky, I intervened and insisted that we include a visit to an "American original" by taking in God's Bible School on the "Mount of Blessing" above the city of Cincinnati. Larry helped me organize that visit.

The visit seemed to go well. President Avery addressed the group. I lectured briefly on the importance of GBS for Korean Christianity. We toured the campus and then hit a crisis. Larry badly wanted to report on the visit with a photograph in the *Revivalist.* The NCC group consisted largely of women not accustomed to the rigorous dress patterns of GBS. (As I remember the issue was that several of the women were wearing pantsuits.) Finally Larry came up with a solution. He subtly and artfully arranged the visitors so that any offending dress patterns were hidden behind those more in accord with GBS standards. I was impressed by the fact that he was openly hospitable and proud of the NCC visitors and yet found a way to honor the tradition of GBS.

With such fond memories and genuine appreciation for the gifts of Larry Smith I am honored to be asked to be involved in this homage to him and his career. We wish him God's blessing on his life.

—Donald W. Dayton

Preface

The first time I heard Larry Smith speak, I had the same reaction that thousands of others experience. It was as if I had been transported back in time and was listening to one of Methodism's greatest orators. His rich vocabulary made every sentence a descriptive work of art. His broad understanding of Methodist theology and history breathed through every word he spoke and made his illustrations sparkle with life. His writings for *God's Revivalist* were no different. His distinctive style made reading his editorials a literary delight, while his remarkable insights into the great doctrines of Methodism made each one of them a must-read. Larry Smith is not just a good writer; he is an eminent one.

Larry was born on the plains of Nebraska in a humble parsonage in 1942. He was dedicated to God and baptized a Free Methodist. He grew up surrounded by the godly influence of his parents and the earnest, careful living of the holiness people in the Free Methodist Church. These influences awakened his need for God at a very early age and led to his conversion as a four-year-old boy at a Free Methodist camp meeting.

Larry's formal training prepared him to teach, but it was his love for both teaching and writing that brought him to God's Bible School and College in 1995, where he joined the Bible faculty as a part-time professor and was appointed the eleventh editor of *God's Revivalist*. In his role as editor he made *God's Revivalist* a premier holiness periodical where the great truths of the Methodist holiness tradition have been faithfully proclaimed. His editorials were powerful essays that challenged us to be "earnest Christians" who strove to manifest "perfect love" towards God and man—a doctrine his own life beautifully exemplified.

The essays included in this Festschrift are a true tribute to a man who so deeply loves the movement whose history they proclaim.

—Michael Avery

Introduction
William Kostlevy

This book of essays honors the remarkable career of our friend and colleague Larry D. Smith. Known best in wider Wesleyan circles for his remarkable twenty-year career as editor of *God's Revivalist*, Larry has always been first and foremost an educator. Beginning as a high school English and drama teacher with a freshly minted college degree from Kearney State Teachers College in Nebraska (B.A., 1963; M.A., 1965), at the age of 27, Larry became a cofounder of Fletcher Bible College, of which he was later president. After the College closed in 1979, he continued as headmaster of Fletcher Christian Academy until 1994.

Larry's classroom teaching career continued at God's Bible School and College where in addition to editing the *Revivalist* he taught courses in the history of Christianity and Methodism from 1995 to 2015. In the classroom Larry was noted for a passion for excellence, love of his students, and deep reverence for the pioneering spirit of the saints of church history, for Methodism, and for his own roots in the Free Methodist Church on the Nebraska prairie.

Larry was raised in a Free Methodist parsonage, and, with his father, was one of the founders of the Evangelical Wesleyan Church. In fact, his ministerial career began as a 19-year-old pastor of the Ansley (Nebraska) Free Methodist Church. He later served as pastor of the Kearney Evangelical Wesleyan Church. From 1972 to 1994, he was pastor of the Salem Methodist Church in Axtell, Nebraska.

As only one of the thousands of Holiness Movement traditionalists who separated from Wesleyan denominations, such as the Church of the Nazarene, Wesleyan Methodist Church, and Free Methodist Church, in the two decades after World War II, Larry desired to uphold standards of piety and discipleship consistent with earlier Wesleyan and Christian practice. However, as with many products of Holiness spirituality, Larry rapidly came to have a concern that many of us share, that an authentic Wesleyanism required a return not only to the Methodism of Wesley but beyond it to traditions rooted in the New Testament and the Scriptures of ancient Israel. Given Larry's catholic vision, the words of tribute for Larry given by God's Bible School and College president Michael Avery are especially appropriate. President Avery wrote that Larry "has challenged each of us to be 'earnest Christians' who seek the 'narrow way' without developing a narrow spirit."

The essays that follow are reflections by Larry's friends, acquaintances and noted scholars on portions of the broader Holiness and Wesleyan tradition. The essays by Jennifer Woodruff Tait and Kenneth J. Collins deal with pedagogical concerns in the Wesleyan tradition. The essay by Barry Hamilton focuses on classical Methodist concerns. The essay by Paul Kaufman looks at the role of Luther Lee in founding the Wesleyan Methodist Connection, while the essays of Howard Snyder and William Kostlevy look at aspects of Larry's Free Methodist heritage. Gari-Anne Patzwald deals with the interesting careers of Julia and E. E. Shelhamer and unites Free Methodist, Holiness Movement and pedagogical concerns. The continued role of Methodism in the larger twentieth century Holiness Movement is the focus of Priscilla Pope-Levison's essay on the remarkable Iva Durham Vennard. David Bundy's contribution highlights the important but neglected subject of the career of Holiness Movement missionary Isabella Sarah Leonard. The essays by Wallace Thornton, Jr., and William Snider look at the careers of two interesting figures in the come outer movement of the 1950s and 1960s, G. T. Bustin and David P. Denton. Edwin Woodruff Tait's essay on Lillian Harvey tells the story of the transcontinental impact of the Holiness Movement in the twentieth century. In the end these essays are presented as a tribute to Larry D. Smith, educator, editor, friend and colleague.

Chapter 1

A Wesleyan Theology of Governance for Seminaries[1]

Kenneth J. Collins

Mission and Purpose

The principal mission of a Christian seminary is to serve the Church (in both ecclesial and academic settings) by preparing students for effective ministry in their witness to the world of the resplendent love of the Father in giving the gift of the Son, a gift that is attested to and received by the presence of the Holy Spirit. By means of this mission, seminaries are necessarily committed to pursuing and expounding the truth of the Lordship of Christ ("For Jesus said, 'I am the Way, the Truth and the Life'" [John 14:6]), a task that represents both corporate and personal endeavors, and always includes not only transformation in being, in accordance with increasing Christ-likeness, but also the importance of speaking the truth in love. Indeed, plain speaking that is free, accurate and helpful has always been a part of the Wesleyan tradition.

In particular, Asbury Theological Seminary's mission statement identifies the seminary as a community called by God "to prepare theologically educated, sanctified, Spirit-filled men and women to evangelize and to spread scriptural holiness throughout the world through the love of Jesus Christ, in the power of the Holy Spirit and to the glory of God the Father."

Scriptural holiness or the holy love of God and neighbor embraces both sound learning and vital piety, the life of the mind and the heart of the soul. It has both personal depth, transforming the hearts of people, and social extent, revitalizing the communities in which they live. In inculcating scriptural holiness, a seminary actively and intentionally fosters the intellectual, emotional, moral and spiritual health of its students, faculty, staff, administrators, trustees and alumni. Holiness, in other words, is holistic and is indicative of the balance and harmony that re-

---

[1] I composed this essay at the behest of Provost Leslie Andrews at Asbury Theological Seminary. I then modified it in light of several formal conversations with trustees, administrators, faculty and staff. Special thanks are in order to Drs. James Thobaben and Fred Long who were especially helpful in their recommendations.

sults from being in a proper relationship to both God and humanity. Accordingly, although Asbury Theological Seminary aims at the highest levels of academic excellence, it never considers such excellence to be sufficient preparation—apart from significant moral, spiritual, and emotional growth—for the increasing challenges of ministry in a complicated and hurting world.

Theological Reflection on Scriptural Holiness or "Holy Love"

Current word studies of the term "holy" reveal that it is the opposite of the word "profane" and that it, therefore, entails a movement of separation, precisely for the sake of purity. Such an understanding falls hard on contemporary ears with their preference for inclusion. During the twentieth century, however, Emil Brunner, Swiss dialectical theologian, expressed this same idea of separation in his observation, "The Holiness of God is therefore not only an absolute difference of nature, but it is an active self-differentiation, the willed energy with which God asserts and maintains the fact that He is Wholly other against all else."[2] Or as the late Richard Taylor put it more recently, "there is a moral intensity in God's holiness that makes tolerance of unholiness an impossibility."[3]

And yet love, on the other hand, involves a movement of revelation, engagement, and at its highest levels, communion. Again, love is outgoing, embracing, and inclusive. It is "the movement which goes-out-of-oneself, which stoops down to that which is below: it is the self-giving, the self-communication of God."[4] Consequently, as Wesley, Brunner, Taylor and others have known so well, the term "holy love" is not a simple and straightforward expression, but involves a conjunction that is expressed in the ideas of separation for the sake of purity and communion for the sake of love. Both therefore must be held in tension, not one to the neglect of the other. As such the best and most accurate summarizing word or phrase and Wesley's ultimate hermeneutic is not *love*, as has sometimes been argued, but *holy love*.

Secondly, just as holiness informs love, so too love informs holiness. Indeed, according to Wesley, "no true Christian holiness can exist without the love of God for its foundation."[5] Thus, in his sermon, "The Witness of the Spirit, I," Wesley maintains that we must love God first "before we can be holy at all; this being the root of holiness."[6] And this love of God that is so intimately connected to holiness,

---

[2]Emil Brunner, *The Christian Doctrine of God*, trans. Olive Wyon (Philadelphia: Westminster Press, 1949), 160.

[3]Richard S. Taylor, *Exploring Christian Holiness: The Theological Formulation* (Kansas City: Beacon Hill, 1985), 16.

[4]Brunner, *The Christian Doctrine*, 187.

[5]Thomas Jackson, ed., *The Works of John Wesley*, 14 vols. (Grand Rapids, Michigan: Baker Book House, 1978), 8:290. (Minutes of Several Conversations).

[6]Albert C. Outler, ed., *The Works of John Wesley*, Vols. 1-4. *The Sermons* (Nashville: Abingdon Press, 1984), 1:274. (The Witness of the Spirit, I).

giving it form, is implanted in human hearts and is evident among the community of the faithful through the gracious agency of the Holy Spirit. That is, believers are "led into every holy desire, into every divine and heavenly temper,"[7] Wesley points out, by the Holy Spirit who "sheds the love of God abroad in their hearts, and the love of all mankind."[8]

Identity and Mission: Dynamically Related

Asbury Theological Seminary has its identity in undertaking its distinct mission. By way of analogy, the seminary is not a noun but a verb. That is, its essence is comprehended in the love of God manifested in the worship of the Most High, and in *service* to others. The kenotic passage of Philippians 2:6-8 charts the way, and reveals the substance of that service in both humility and love. In one sense, humility entails not only lowliness but also being open to giving love *to* and receiving love *from* all people. As such this grace, this mark of mature Christians, listens to and genuinely hears "the other."

Precisely because of the meekness of Christ, His taking on the form of a servant, the gospel necessarily highlights the universal love of God and neighbor. Therefore the constitution of a seminary community (in terms of students, faculty, staff, administrators, trustees, and alumni) as well as the constituencies it serves will be inclusive and diverse, representing the broad reach of humanity.

Since all people bear the *Imago Dei*, their dignity and preeminent worth do not utterly arise out of their particular group identifications, but emerge out of a consideration of the *relation* of men and women to a God of holy love. Indeed, implicit in the *Imago Dei* are the elements of accountability, responsibility, and other-directedness. God has created humanity, in other words, through Christ as those beings made for a relationship with the Most High and with others through the presence of the Holy Spirit. Therefore, the members of a community who bear the impress of the divine being will watch over one another in love, foster a Christ-like spirit, and exercise care and judgment in all of their service.

Theological Reflection: Universality of the Gospel

Seminaries may rightly rejoice in their diversity and appreciate all the many cultural variations in their midst, for they are greatly enriched in many ways by such diversity. They, nevertheless, do not find their unity *in* their diverse populations nor in some ideological script that makes diversity itself the overarching value, but *in* Jesus Christ whose Lordship is the highest value, transcending particular group identifications, and through whom the community enjoys "one faith, one hope, one baptism."

Reacting against a few of the maxims of the Enlightenment, some recent trends in postmodernism have suggested that little basis exists for affirming common

---

[7]Ibid., 1:236. (The First Fruits of the Spirit).
[8]Ibid., 1:262-63. (The Spirit of Bondage and of Adoption).

elements in the human community. Various group identities that are informed by ethnicity, race, socioeconomic status, religion, sexual orientation, and language are supposed to create structures of affiliation and identity that make a universal narrative for humanity virtually impossible. Beyond the logical contradiction of maintaining that all grand narratives are henceforth precluded, a claim that actually functions as yet another universal script, some current postmodern perspectives not only fail to grapple seriously with what common elements actually remain in human communities (such existential concerns as guilt, the question of meaning, and death), but they also fail to appreciate how religion in general, or Christianity in particular, actually functions in human lives.

Although some in the Church today encourage members of their congregations to draw their identities largely from their particular group commitments, and in doing so call this the "gospel," such a move in the end is largely divisive and does not represent the genius of a gospel ethic. Mistaking a particular polarity (whether poor/rich or black/white) as the locus of valuation, thereby making it virtually ultimate, fails to see the "evil" in one population—among the poor, for example—or what good may characterize the "rich." Nor is such an analysis improved by substituting any of the other popular polarities (female/male, for example) if they become, once again, the very center of valuation. Granted universal Christian values will be, and should be, expressed in a culturally specific manner, but the form of that expression should never take priority over being a "new people" in Jesus Christ who remains the common and celebrated Lord of the community of faith.

Beyond critiquing the sectarianism and factionalism of the polarizing approaches that are so popular today at educational institutions, the gospel indicates, to the consternation of some postmodernists, that a universal dimension does indeed remain in the human community regardless of different social locations. Men and women, black or white, rich or poor are best defined not in terms of the provincial groups in which they participate, but with respect to their relation to a God of holy love. Thus, to call poor people sinners, which by the way John Wesley often did, is not to detract from their dignity as human beings (as some leaders in mainline denominations claim today) but is actually to affirm it. That is, such a judgment reveals that the most important thing about human beings is not their economic status, no matter how severe it may be, but that they are beings *made for God*, created to enjoy a *relation* with the Most High that is marked by the richest love. Put another way, all human beings, regardless of their group commitments, are united in their sin; they are also, therefore, joined in their need for grace. Again, the gospel is universal, despite some postmodern protests to the contrary, and it has a word of hope and liberation for *all* people. The narrative of God's reconciling action in Jesus Christ (neither Jew nor Gentile, slave nor free, male nor female) does not mistake what is penultimate (ethnicity, race, economic status, etc.) and make it ultimate.

The Variegated Nature of Seminaries

Theological seminaries are not the Church *per se* but are institutions, parachurch structures that serve the Body of Christ. Simply put, a seminary is not the local church, and to treat it as such is to fail to recognize the distinct promise that such an institution holds for both leadership and service. Nevertheless, a seminary is composed of a community of Christian believers united by worship, by participation in the sacraments, and by a statement of faith, among other things. As such, a seminary is a multidimensional institution that integrates ecclesial, spiritual, and academic purposes. A seminary becomes unbalanced when it fails to hold all of these elements in their proper place or when its structures of governance do not evidence the mutuality and concern of responsible, accountable leadership at every level.

Seminaries are made up of members whose functions in the institution are distinct (students, faculty, staff, administrators, trustees and alumni) but who are united in the goals of theological education. A seminary community must, therefore, be governed by leaders who understand the complex nature of the institution, with its many levels and dimensions, and who are able, therefore, to think in terms of a number of different frameworks. Ongoing study by seminary leaders with respect to the nature of theological education is therefore vital.

Theological Reflection:
The Apostle Paul's Analogy of the Body

Just as a seminary is a multifaceted institution in its labors, so also is it composed of people who serve the institution in a variety of ways, in accordance with clearly defined roles. The analogy of the body, utilized by the Apostle Paul to affirm the interdependent nature of the Church while confronting mentalities of divisiveness and superiority, readily comes to mind. In 1 Corinthians 12 Paul reasons:

> Just as a body, though one, has many parts, but all its many parts form one body, so it is with Christ. For we were all baptized by one Spirit so as to form one body—whether Jews or Gentiles, slave or free—and we were all given the one Spirit to drink….But in fact God has placed the parts in the body, every one of them, just as he wanted them to be. If they were all one part, where would the body be? As it is, there are many parts, but one body. (TNIV)

In the same way, the seminary community is marked by one Spirit, that of Jesus Christ who is the Head of the body, and He unites the various organs in their service. Again, just as the organs of the body, in fulfilling their distinct roles, are united, a part of a unity that transcends them, so too the members of a seminary community, connected in so many ways by the life-giving arteries of grace and love, are united in their common mission of serving Jesus Christ. Such service occurs in the context of differentiation of function and is informed by responsibility, accountability, and mutuality.

By way of analogy, under healthy conditions the cells of an organ are in communication with the other cells in their immediate environment. The cues offered are both chemical (proteins) and physical (membrane ruffling). Now when cells of a particular organ of the body, let's say the lungs, sever themselves from the community and are no longer a part of the cellular communication system, things quickly go awry. As Natalie Angier points out, "A cancer cell is a cell that is deaf to the chemical tutelage around it and indifferent to the slings and ruffles of its neighbors."[9] These aberrant, self-willed cells set about to do the work of cells heedless of the information and response of other members in the environment. Their task is simply to divide, divide, divide until, if left unchecked, the cancerous cells not only destroy organs, but the entire body as well.

In a similar way, the gracious harmony of a seminary community is torn asunder when particular components fail to receive the communications of other members of the environment. With the loss of communication comes the loss of genuine community as well—and the larger good it serves.

Our Particular Theological Tradition

Asbury Theological Seminary represents the best of the Wesleyan-Holiness, Evangelical tradition. It is mindful of the past, of the legacy of tradition, and open to the future, that is, to the challenges of an international community in the twenty-first century.

Although the seminary is one of the principal institutional guardians of the Wesleyan-Holiness, Evangelical tradition, it remains ecumenical in outlook and drinks deeply of a broad and rich catholic spirit. It clearly recognizes that vibrant Christian communities exist in other traditions, denominations, and parachurch structures. The seminary and its leaders, therefore, will be in dialog with other theological institutions in order to understand the current challenges of theological education in a thoroughgoing way and to be ready to profit from the wisdom and counsel of others.

Theological Reflection: Wesley's Sermon, "The Catholic Spirit"

In his sermon "The Catholic Spirit," Wesley maintains that love is due to all humanity, but a special love is warranted for those who love God. Two hindrances that sometimes prevent this love, resulting in various levels of narrowness, self-isolation, and in the worse cases outright bigotry, are differences with respect to both thought and practice. That is, in the Church, constituted as it is by several communions of faith, believers will not all think alike, having various opinions that do not strike at the heart of the faith, nor will they all engage in the same modes of worship.

Given such diversity, in this sermon Wesley does not recommend either speculative or a practical latitudinarianism. Unsettledness in thought and practice (es-

---

[9]Natalie Angier, *The Canon: A Whirligig Tour of the Beautiful Basics of Science* (New York: Houghton Mifflin, 2007), 210.

pecially in terms of worship) is not a blessing but a curse. A truly catholic person, then, is as "fixed as the sun" in his or her judgment of fundamental truths, distinguishes essentials from opinions, and extends the hand of fellowship in love to all whose hearts are right with God. In other words, believers can be firm in their judgments while recognizing that other real Christians, animated by the love of Christ, differ both in thought and practice.

In a similar way, Asbury Theological Seminary, representing a distinct tradition in the universal Church, can prosper by being in an appropriate relationship with seminaries of other theological traditions since all—when viewed in their best sense—share common goals. A spirit of humility, marked by love and teachableness, should therefore characterize the leadership of these institutions as they dialog with one another in their service of Jesus Christ.

The Importance of Narratives that Inform Mission

Wesleyan seminaries are orthodox communities that seek to embody a Trinitarian understanding of God in their daily lives and practices. The Christian Godhead whereby three distinct persons are one, and whereby the mutual relations of love characterize the divine being, should inform the seminary's life in general and its structures of governance in particular. Put another way, each person of the Trinity is other-directed and is ecstatic (in the best sense of the word) in loving and celebrating the other. Such mutual relations are marked by humility (openness to love) and the richest expressions of love in celebrating the other. And in terms of the relation of the Trinity to humanity, what theologians call the "economic" trinity, the Father freely gives the gift of the Son, the Son delights in being given, and the Spirit attests to the precious gift that is Jesus Christ. Here then is not the reign of self-will but an outpouring, a generous giving of the divine being, for the sake of humanity in an embracing, inclusive love.

In light of these preceding theological understandings, seminaries must be governed in such a way that the love of God, manifested in Jesus Christ through the Holy Spirit is and remains the central narrative of the community. This narrative is held in place by the pre-eminent and normative authority of Scripture which is received by the Wesleyan community of faith, reflected upon by reason, and fleshed out in vital Christian experience. Accordingly, the seminary must take special care that the gospel of grace that animates and gives substance to her vision is actualized in structures of governance that are in harmony with that vision.

Other narratives from social science, the business community, and academia, for example, are vital to seminaries and should be consulted, but such stories are always secondary. What is called for, then, on the part of the seminary community is a critical appropriation of the insights from a diversity of sources whereby the gospel of the universal love of God and neighbor remains the normative pattern.

A seminary runs the risk of having its stated purpose and mission weakened, if not undermined, by elevating a secondary narrative and making it the principal script of the institution. For example, although seminaries obviously have business and financial dimensions, to carve the institution principally along these lines (whereby students are deemed "consumers" and faculty and staff are considered "employees") is to fail to take into account the spiritual and ecclesial dimensions through which students, faculty and staff view their own labors as the gracious and divinely empowered exercise of a vocation.

Moreover, the structures of governance that are created by the seminary must be in harmony with its identity and mission as a servant of Jesus Christ who is the one, supreme head of the community. Indeed, a community that testifies to the beauty of holy love in its highest expression of entire sanctification should be marked by the gracious behaviors and practices that are consonant with this witness.

Summary of Theological Elements Necessary for the Governance of Seminaries

Christ-like governance of a seminary entails the following elements:
- Attentiveness to the mutual relations of love that characterize the Trinity and that should be emblematic of vibrant Christian communities
- Lowliness and service to others in spreading scriptural holiness, in inculcating holy love
- Recognition of the universal love of God manifested in Christ through the Holy Spirit as well as the dangers of being diverted into egoism, sectarianism or a party spirit.
- Understanding that in the fulfillment of its mission a seminary is multidimensional in function and diverse in population and constituency
- Given such diversity, care must be taken that the seminary does not forsake its *common* mission or the universality of the gospel itself.
- In a similar fashion, the genius of the Wesleyan theological tradition, in particular, must be held in a catholic spirit and one that is animated by the love of Christ. This is evidenced by dialog with other institutions.
- The principal narrative of the love of the Father in giving the gift of the Son and attested to by the Holy Spirit that informs the seminary must be intentionally held and fostered by students, faculty, staff, administrators, trustees and alumni. Otherwise some other narrative will be unintentionally held and could possibly skew the mission of the seminary.
- Responsibility and accountability at every level of governance (since all are servants of a risen Lord); teachableness in receiving and developing the gifts and talents of others; and a bracketing out of self-interest and provincial concerns in order to pursue the larger good of the institution in its witness to a God of holy love—all of these elements represent appropriate ways in which a seminary can and should pursue its goals.

Conclusion

A theology of governance from a Wesleyan-Holiness, Evangelical perspective underscores the goodness of divine authority that is mediated to the servants of the body of Christ. Only those who are and remain *servants* are a part of the community that is knit together by the cords of accountability, responsibility, and gracious affection. As stewards of the gifts that find their source not in human attainment but in the beneficence of God, all servants of the seminary community, whether students, faculty, staff, administrators, trustees, or alumni will seek to grow in those graces, especially humility and love, that will help them to keep their eyes focused upon the love of the Father, the grace of the Son and the enabling power of the Holy Spirit as they actualize the mission of the seminary.

Moreover, a theology of governance from a Wesleyan vantage point is realistic and critical enough to offer suitable checks and responsible balances when either individuals or groups, at any level of the seminary's institutional life, seek to pursue their own self-referential will as if it were the general good of the seminary. In such instances various levels of pretense may have to be unraveled in the name and for the sake of holy love. Egoism, a party spirit, and power seeking have no place in a community that glorifies and celebrates a crucified Lord. This vital truth must constantly be brought before the community in the pulpit, classroom, and boardroom.

It is therefore incumbent upon the seminary to craft and articulate polices of governance that will operationalize these important truths in particular practices—practices that can and should be measured in terms of clear biblical and theological principles. In this way, greater light will be focused on the labors of the community, especially in terms of mutual relations, such that the larger good of the seminary, that is, spreading scriptural holiness throughout the world, will thereby be fostered through the witness, the very life, of the gracious and peaceful community itself.

Chapter 2

"Purposeful Living": Images of the Kingdom of God in Methodist Sunday School Worship[1]

Jennifer Woodruff Tait

From the outset, the primary aim of Sunday School has been to mirror essential images of the Kingdom of God to its pupils. One of the most effective ways of doing this has been through acts of worship.[2] This essay outlines those images of the kingdom, as portrayed through Sunday School worship in the Methodist Episcopal Church and the Methodist Episcopal Church, South, through official hymnals, songbooks, published orders of worship, and prescriptive literature. Sunday School personnel have sought to integrate pupils into the kingdom through a variety of means—by encouraging them to be civilized, educated, inspired, converted, challenged, molded, patriotic, enriched, deepened, enlightened, consciousness-raised, motivated, nurtured, and entertained—but they have never, ever ignored them!

1784-1844: Laying the Foundations

1790s-1820s

Although Methodists have always enjoyed pointing to Biblical and post-Reformation Christian education as their models, the modern Sunday School movement was really inaugurated in England in the 1780s by Robert Raikes.[3] In 1781, he founded four Sunday Schools in Gloucester, in which poor, uneducated children were to be instructed in reading and the catechism on Sundays—their only

---

[1]This paper was originally presented at the Eleventh Oxford Institute of Methodist Theological Studies, Christ Church, Oxford, June 2002.

[2]The Sunday School movement has also been known as Sabbath school, church school, and Christian education, for varying theological and social reasons.

[3]Thomas Walter Laquer, *Religion and Respectability: Sunday Schools and Working Class Culture*, 1750-1850 (New Haven: Yale University Press, 1976), 21-22. Also see Anne M. Boylan, "Sunday Schools and Changing Evangelical Views of Children in the 1820s," *Church History* 48 (Spring 1979), 320-333.

day off—by "decent, well-disposed women" in the neighborhood, and perpetually examined and disciplined by a local clergyman.[4] While Raikes was not the first who attempted to teach poor children to read and write in a "Sabbath School" environment, his example became a paradigm for the later movement.[5]

In a pastoral letter written in 1791, Francis Asbury addressed American Methodists regarding his desire to establish Sunday Schools on the Raikes model. Children were to be given religious lessons to memorize; in addition, boys were to engage in "manly exercises, as working in the garden or field, walking, reading, or speaking in public, or [swimming]," and girls were to learn to "read, write, sew, knit, mark, and make their own cloathing [sic]."[6] Asbury also recommended that "the worship of God in the school-house, should be reading the word of the Lord, singing and prayer, every morning and evening."[7] Apparently some followed this advice, for his 1792 postscript spoke of a school directed by "a godly woman, where all were solemn and quiet, and regular prayer both morning and evening."[8]

Until around 1820, Sunday Schools primarily concentrated on civilizing their young charges through teaching "proper behavior, enforcing cleanliness, providing Sunday clothing, and reprimanding children." This model proved a precursor to the modern concept of public education offering free education to all.[9] Little is known, however, of Sunday School worship during the early days of American Methodism.

1820s-1840s

Around 1820, a shift took place in the aims and purposes of Sunday School. Children were beginning to be considered as "candidates for evangelization, perhaps even conversion"; Sunday School began to welcome churched as well as unchurched children; and finally, free public schools had been founded where poor children could receive non-religious instruction.[10] By the time the Methodist Episcopal Church (MEC) divided in 1844, Sunday Schools had been transformed from "a temporary experiment for teaching the poor reading and religion to a permanent means of religious training for all Protestant children."[11]

The founding of both the American Sunday School Union (1824) and the MEC's Sunday School Union (1827) heralded this new approach. The Sunday School Union published a curriculum that divided students by age, culminating in a "Bibe class" for adolescents that stressed conversion and invited them to serve

---

[4]Laquer, 21-22.

[5]Laquer, 24.

[6]Edward J. Wynne, "Bishop Asbury and the Sunday School," *Methodist History* 18 (July 1980), 273.

[7]Wynne, 273.

[8]Wynne, 274.

[9]Anne M. Boylan, *Sunday School: The Formation of an American Institution, 1790-1880* (New Haven: Yale University Press, 1988), 322; Wynne, 275.

[10]James E. Kirby, Russell E. Richey, and Kenneth E. Rowe. *The Methodists*. (Westport, CT: Greenwood Press, 1996), 181-182.

[11]Kirby, 181-182.

as teachers for the younger children. The curriculum emphasized "sin, repentance, and regeneration," and catechisms were used extensively.[12] In 1840, General Conference enacted legislation which gave the Sunday School Union official sanction in the church, required the establishment of Sunday Schools under the control of the pastor and the quarterly conference, obliged bishops to appoint agents to promote the cause of Sunday Schools in the conferences, and instructed the Methodist publishing house to begin a new Sunday School periodical entitled the *Sunday School Advocate*.[13] The 1844 General Conference further initiated a plan for the funding of Sunday Schools.[14]

Worship in this era probably did not vary much from the earlier-established pattern of singing and prayer. Hymns were one of the main ways in which images of the kingdom were communicated to children. "Happy deaths for saintly children" were a primary focus. For example, an 1835 Sunday School Union hymnbook listed titles such as the "Death of a Pious Child" and "Death of a Scholar." Judgment day was also a common theme. "The Wicked Child Judged" and other similar hymns pointed to a conversion experience as an entry to the kingdom and a means of escape from the terrors of judgment.[15]

1844-1939: Achieving the Ideal

1850s-1900s

After the 1844 split, both branches of episcopal Methodism inaugurated themes and images that would later come to fruition in the "golden age" of Methodist Sunday Schools. The greatest stimulus to change was the publication of *Christian Nurture* (1847) by Congregationalist Horace Bushnell. Contrary to the conversionistic emphasis of the early nineteenth century, Bushnell proposed a theory and method of Christian education suggesting

> *that the child is to grow up a Christian, and never know himself as being otherwise*....the aim, effort, and expectation should be, not, as is commonly assumed, that the child is to grow up in sin, to be converted after he comes to a mature age; but he is to open on the world as one that is spiritually renewed, not remembering the time when he went through a technical experience, but seeming rather to have loved what is good from his earliest years.[16]

Influenced by Romantic currents in theology, Bushnell thought Christian educators should teach young children "rather...a feeling than a doctrine. . ." and

---

[12]Kirby, 182-184; John Q. Schisler, *Christian Education in Local Methodist Churches* (Nashville: Abingdon, 1969), 33

[13]Boylan, *Sunday School*, 11-20.

[14]Robert W. Lynn and Elliott Wright. *The Big Little School: Sunday Child of American Protestantism* (New York: Harper & Row, 1971), 42.

[15]Quoted in Lynn 42-43.

[16]Horace Bushnell, *Christian Nurture* (n.p.: Scribner, 1861; reprinted by Grand Rapids, Baker Book House, 1979), 10. Italics are Bushnell's.

bathe the child in their own feeling of love to God, and dependence upon him, and contrition for wrong before him...then, as the understanding advances, to give it [the child] food suited to its capacity, opening upon it, gradually, the more difficult views of Christian doctrine and experience.[17]

Catechisms became less popular, and the uniform-lesson series (which taught the same lesson for all grades with separate take-home material for various ages) was used more widely.[18] Conversion remained a goal, but it was more likely to be approached gradually. Mid-century leader of Sunday School reform (and eventually MEC bishop) John Vincent thought the Sunday School had three functions: promotion of growth in divine life, preparatory education in Christian truth, and mission to the disadvantaged, all three combining "conversion, spiritual culture, and the formation of character.[19] Vincent and other Sunday School educators favored standardizing and professionalizing the Sunday School through the use of uniform lessons and the proper training of teachers, and expanded its reaches to young adults who might otherwise be lost to the church.[20] The dividing of students into grades by age—primary/infant (5-8), intermediate (8-10), junior (10-15), and senior (15-20)—became more common,

This standardization of the Sunday School was inevitably reflected in its worship.[21] An opening assembly for all grades was introduced in which "Scripture readings, remarks, songs, and prayers" revolved around one topic.[22] This pattern would become hugely popular for all forms of Sunday School worship until well into the twentieth century. Since opening and closing exercises often involved the reciting of "Golden Texts" from the week's lessons, a further opportunity was provided in which approved images of creation, salvation, and piety could be emphasized.[23]

Another development of this era was the increasing use of music in Sunday Schools, although controversy frequently erupted over types of music and the underlying worldviews associated with them.[24] The popular gospel hymnody of the day sometimes conveyed images of God's creation that were at odds with official doctrine, and the Methodist bureaucracy frowned upon the use of secular tunes of "folk's lore and border minstrelsy" and the employment of doggerel-like lyrics in

---

[17]Bushnell, 51.

[18]Kirby, 190-192, 209-211. The Uniform Lesson Plan was introduced by the National Sunday-School Convention in 1872.

[19]John H. Vincent, *The Modern Sunday-School* (New York: Eaton & Mains, 1900), 14, 73.

[20]In 1860, the MEC General Conference legislated that the Sunday School should train adults as well as children (Kirby, 202).

[21]It was also supposed to be supported by an organized, regularized library; see "Our Sunday School Literature," *Methodist Quarterly Review* [MEC], April 1876, 324-347.

[22]Kirby, 211; Vincent, 121.

[23]Kirby, 212.

[24]"Sunday-School Hymns and Music," *Methodist Quarterly Review* [MEC], May 1885, 431.

gospel hymns.[25] Both official Methodist publications and gospel songbooks now focused less on "happy deaths for pious children" and frightening images of judgment, and more on enjoying the love of Jesus and witnessing about the Christian life. Hymnody emphasized familial and social bonds, the importance of being good citizens, a knowledge of the social causes of the day (temperance and abolition), and an awareness of the future glories of eternity.[26] However, there were still plenty of hymns about heaven. One example by Fanny Crosby, "Fading, Slowly Fading, Sweet Sabbath Day," ties in the image of the Sabbath day's closing with that of heaven and eternal life.[27]

After the turn of the century, images of the kingdom in Sunday School worship would begin to focus even less on the afterlife and more on practical Christianity in the here and now.

1900s-1930s

The early twentieth century saw an explosion of church school literature and a greater degree of complex organization.[28] In most large churches, classes worshiped separately and would ideally include a Cradle Roll and nursery department (children under 4), beginners (4-5), primaries (6-8), juniors (9-11), intermediates (12-14), seniors (15-17), young people (18-23) and adults (23+).[29] Guided by new studies in psychology regarding how children learned, educators published lessons graded and adapted to differing educational requirements of each age.[30]

Sunday School educators continued to emphasize the teaching potential presented by worship:

> The worship period is a vital part of the educational process. The singing, the reading of the Scripture, the offering of prayer, the bringing and dedication of gifts, and the inspiration of pupils through an address are vastly more than introductory activities.…Worship trains the feelings and is at once the product and the producer of action.[31]

---

[25]"Sunday School Hymns and Music," 429-430.

[26]Heather D. Curtis, "Children of the Heavenly King: Hymns in the Religious and Social Experience of Children, 1780-1850," in *Sing Them Over Again To Me: Hymns and Hymn Books in America*, ed. Mark A. Noll and Edith L. Blumhofer (Tuscaloosa: University of Alabama Press, 2006), 214-234.

[27]Phoebe Palmer Knapp, *Notes of Joy, for the Sabbath School, the Social Meeting, and the Hour of Prayer* (New York: Biglow & Main, 1869), 53.

[28]This era also saw the beginning of the term "church school," meant to tie the Sunday School more fully into the life of the church.

[29]Children were enrolled in the Cradle Roll shortly after birth, an action that had no particular relation to baptism. See *Church School Literature: Its Proper Use and How to Order It* (Nashville: General Board of Christian Education of the MECS, 1932).

[30]See E.B. Chappell, ed. *Introduction and Use of the Graded Lessons: General Manual* (Nashville: Smith & Lamar, 1914).

[31]Chappell, 134-135.

The aim of children's worship was to prepare the way for "the corporate worship of adults—the fulfillment of individual Christian nurture and of reverent group worship for the young at each age. Such beginnings will produce a revival of real worship in our churches."[32] Scripture reading was inclined to be "liturgic and not didactic," although Scripture memory verses were still used.[33]

The superintendent's opening address was intended to be inspiring, and the need for inspirational topics prompted an explosion of available materials. These continued to put a strong emphasis on building the Kingdom through good conduct and moral behavior, "interpreting...current events in the light of an overruling Providence or in the light of duty or of opportunity for service," which "may be one of the truest and best modes of spiritual teaching, for spiritual teaching is aiding the pupil to solve his moral problems."[34]

Accessible resources also attempted to guide the Sunday School leader, pianist, and musicians in the proper selection and performance of Sunday School music.[35] Hymns were to be adapted to the age level of the learner; furthermore, they should be "good literature and the tunes must be good music….nothing that is cheap and belittling…the entire worship must be marked by dignity, grace, and orderly beauty."[36] Again, popular hymnody was challenged: "A careful examination of one of these ['insipid popular commercial books'] shows that the great hymns of our faith are generally relegated to odd corners of the book...while the veriest trash is given prominence."[37]

Special days or festivals of the Sunday School, the nation, and the local church became popular.[38] Children's Day (which featured performances by Sunday School pupils) and Decision Day (which challenged children to conversion) were important events in the church school's "Christian year." Decision Day—the climax of the year's work of confronting children with the challenge of the Christian message--hoped to lovingly lead children who were "already [children] of God" into making a public declaration of their faith.[39] Preparation through prayer and talks culminated in a worship service that featured "a simple, brief, clear ap-

---

[32]Reginald McAll, "Training for the Worship of the Young," *Methodist Review* [MEC], May 1927, 366.

[33]Chappell, 135-136.

[34]Chappell, 136.

[35]Reginald McAll, *Practical Church Music: Methods and Training for Successful Piano, Vocal, and Platform Leadership* (New York: Abingdon, 1932).

[36]Chappell, 135; McAll, *Practical Church School Music*, 145-146.

[37]According to McAll, the "veriest trash" included such phrases as "blossom bells," "lily bells," "Look him in the eye and smile," and "the darling little birdies are singing, glad and gay" (156).

[38]McAll, *Practical Church School Music*, 157-162.

[39]Christian S. Reisues, "Church Members from the Sunday School," *Methodist Review* [MEC], March 1915, 242; F. Watson Hannan, *The Sunday School: An Evangelistic Opportunity* (New York: Methodist Book Concern, 1920), 103.

peal to the young people to surrender their lives in perfect loyalty to Jesus Christ both for his sake, and in order that they may help him save the world."[40]

After the merger in 1939, both branches of episcopal Methodism continued to emphasize this image of a kingdom constituted through good citizenship, moral behavior, reverence, and personal experience of God. But change was on the horizon.

1939-1968: Settled and Sure; Coping with Change

1940s-1950s

In the 1940s, Sunday Schools peaked in attendance, resources, and confidence in their own ability. They were strictly graded (at least in larger churches) and grounded in the psychology of education. They made ample use of published curricular resources, attempted to include "high" types of art and music, connected with other expressions of Christian education (vacation church school, weekday religious education, and Christian camps), and focused on nurturing and challenging children and adults to a relationship with Christ. All this would, educators hoped, produce a lifestyle closely allied to the current culture and possessing a decidedly upper-middle-class orientation.

Sunday Schools emphasized the value of American citizenship as never before. A dedication litany for the Christian flag, the American flag, and the armed forces service flag was introduced in 1942 for these items' use "as sacred symbols in the church."[41] The affiliation of the church with the American way of life would hopefully result in a wider vision of good conduct, service to others, avoidance of frivolous entertainment, and middle-class achievement. A stained glass window designed by Michigan youth in 1941 illustrates these aims through images of "the various things that make life worthwhile" including: "Education and an Appreciation of All Good Literature," "Easter, Immortality, Purity, and the Love of Nature," "Boy and Girl Friendships," "The Christian Home," "God and Home and Every Land," "Creative Arts," "Dramatics," "Recreation," "Hope, Faith, Ideals," and "Inspiration, Strength, Co-Operation."[42] According to one educator, the Sunday School, after encouraging a relationship with Christ through both nurture and decision, should also cultivate right attitudes and form right habits…develop

---

[40]Hannan, 114.

[41]C. Blaine Duncan. "A Litany of Dedication: The Flags," *The Church School*, September 1942, 708. See also James W. Sells, "An Order of Thanksgiving for Harvest, Land, and Liberty," *The Church School*, November 1944, 481; Elesha Coffman, "Do You Know the History of the Christian Flag?" *Christian History,* http://www.christianitytoday.com/ch/asktheexpert/jul13.html, posted August 8, 2008.

[42]"Youth Enriches Worship," *The Church School*, October 1941, 40-41.

loyalty to the church...and develop a sense of obligation for civic and social righteousness, community service, and interracial friendships.[43]

The physical environment of worship and visual images of the kingdom became a growing concern: "If one chooses a worship theme such as the 'Word of God,' an open Bible on the table or altar surrounded by candles or flowers will give weight to the content of hymns, prayers, and remarks concerning the subject."[44] Encouraged by such a philosophy, "worship centers" became common in which a picture or symbol such as a Bible or cross, or Warner Sallman's *Head of Christ*, was placed to illustrate an aspect of Christian life.

Singing, still a prominent aspect of church school worship, continued to be an area of tension, due for the most part to its effect on the emotions.[45] Youth caused problems through their preference for "pep" and the popular music of the day.[46] Educators' desired qualities of worship music included dignity, facing "realities of life as it is today," and "as much beauty and quality as it is possible to obtain."[47] One teacher wrote, "The old so-called 'gospel songs' with their familiar tunes and swinging rhythms are too frequently what people want to sing. But this is not worship. Sentimental words and undignified music are not worthy to sing to the glory of God."[48] Teachers were encouraged to lead students to "love good hymns and good worship music," such as were contained in the *Methodist Hymnal* and sung in adult worship, because it would prepare them for discipleship.[49] Educators disapproved of sentimental, nostalgic, and pietistic or individualistic songs despite (or perhaps because of) their commercial success: Teachers should even avoid encouraging students to sing with gusto, an act more appropriate to "old time singing schools" than "services of worship."[50] How well all of these recommendations trickled down to the actual Sunday Schools, or how well they were liked when they did, remains a question.

Leaders were encouraged to use special days to teach religious truths: New Year's Day, Easter, Memorial Day, Independence Day, Labor Day (as long as it

---

[43]L.F. Sensbaugh, "The Sunday School 'Menace,'" *The Church School*, October 1945, 433-434.

[44]Henry M. Johnson, "New Techniques in Worship," *The Church School*, May 1943, 295.

[45]Rowena Ferguson, "Worship is Communication," *The Church School*, November 1945, 486.

[46]One author wrote against gospel, "Is it not part of our responsibility to introduce young people to the fact that pep, after all, is not the highest good either in life itself, or in music?" (Edwin Michael Hoffman, "When Is a Hymn Truly Worshipful?" *The Church School*, January 1947, 4ff).

[47]Hoffman, 4.

[48]Hoffman, 4.

[49]Clarice M. Bowman, "Music and Intermediate Worship," *The Church School*, November 1943, 585.

[50]Bowman, 585.

did not promote "division and class feeling"), Thanksgiving, and Christmas.[51] The Sunday School continued to develop and change its own liturgical year as well. Decision Day was no longer popular, but Children's Day remained, along with Promotion Day and Rally Sunday. Promotion Day involved the "promotion" of students from one class group to another, usually at the beginning of the school year in conjunction with Rally Day. As time went on, they were brought together in a "Christian Education Week."[52]

Rally Day now became the focal point of the whole Sunday school year, and was intended "for the purpose, first, of informing and challenging the people of the community with regard to the Church's program of religious education; and second, for receiving an offering for the Annual Conference Board of Education."[53] Worship services—particularly dramas that explained the aims and purposes of the church, Christianity, and the Sunday School—served to get the Rally Day message across. Numerous examples appeared in resource magazines, and students were also encouraged to write their own worship materials.[54] The importance Rally Day assumed revealed a shift in what Sunday school and its pupils were intended to be and do. Changes to this well-oiled educational machine were, however, just around the corner.

1960s

The 1960s transitioned from the peak of "traditional" Sunday School to the experimental, questioning focus of the 1970s—from a church that sought to uplift youth with Mendelssohn to one that wished to reach them with Janis Joplin.[55] In 1965, the Methodist Church's second *Book of Worship* was published, marking "the virtual conclusion of a process of liturgical revision, common to most Protestant denominations, which had attempted to recover worship practices promoted by the sixteenth-century Reformers." But "by the end of the decade, that process had been abandoned altogether" in favor of an ecumenical hearkening back to the traditions of the early church.[56]

Vatican II, specifically the *Constitution on the Sacred Liturgy* (1963) and later directives as to its implementation, played a large role in initiating this change in Methodist worship.[57] Vatican II-influenced reformers emphasized early church

---

[51]Clarence Edwin Flynn, "Special Days as Teaching Opportunities," *The Church School*, November 1945, 483ff.

[52]John C. Millian, "Starting the New Year through Christian Education Week," *The Church School*, September 1944, 398.

[53]*Discipline*, 1940, 1183, quoted in *The Church School*, May 1942, 458.

[54]Mabel Keboch, "Preparing for Promotion Day," *The Church School*, September 1944, 388-389.

[55]Kenneth G. Fansler, "What If All the Arts Were Used to Communicate the Gospel?" *The Church School*, December 1970, 21-27.

[56]Robert B. Peiffer, "How Contemporary Liturgies Evolve: The Revision of United Methodist Liturgical Texts (1968-1988)," (Ph.D. diss.: University of Notre Dame, 1992), 3.

[57]James F. White, *New Forms of Worship* (Nashville: Abingdon, 1971), 16.

patterns of worship, worship's communal nature, the centrality of the sacraments, contemporary relevance, and horizontal as well as—sometimes more than—vertical dimensions of worship.[58] At the same time, cultural assumptions from the last hundred years that the morality, opinions, and lifestyles "congenial to forty-year-old middle-class whites [were] to be normative for all society" were now being "rudely questioned and found wanting by many elements of society," liturgical reformer James White noted.[59] He cited a splintering of society, a new sense of freedom in many areas, alternative lifestyles which rejected "suburban values of security and comfort," changing moral standards, growing racial consciousness, and the acceptance of the "generation gap."[60] "Our services," he emphasized, "reflect the values, modes of perceiving reality, and life styles with which a forty-year-old middle-class white person feels familiar, especially one with a college education...We can no longer say 'Like it or lump it.' There is another alternative. They can leave. And many have."[61] Middle-class morality was nowhere more evident than in Methodist Sunday Schools, with their emphasis on Christian conduct, moral uplift, obedience, and good citizenship. Educators focused on how to transform them overnight.

After the merger, Methodists faced the challenge of developing an identity as a new denomination and puzzled over how the various aspects of worship could be reformed and given new life and vision. Sunday School literature of the time witnesses to this reformation, even though Methodists were still working within the parameters of the 1964 *Hymnal* and 1965 *Book of Worship* (*BOW*) which was an updated but not radically altered version of the 1945 *Book of Worship for Church and Home*.[62] Like its 1945 predecessor, the *BOW* laid out models and patterns for Sunday services, supplied a number of written prayers and litanies for various occasions, and provided orders for admitting children and adults into the church and for recognizing church school officers, church school teachers, and choristers. It eliminated some services related to family worship and others for rural communities that had been included in the 1945 book, and added a Psalter, Biblical canticles, and greater overall attention to the Sundays of the Christian year. Among its seasonal prayers was one for "Christian Education Sunday, formerly called Rally Day."[63]

Congregations, however, were beginning to expand their vision of the kingdom into one that was more experimental, free-flowing, culturally aware, and racially inclusive. The suggested pattern for worship, while often still based on a prayer-song-inspirational-talk, more frequently drew its inspiration from the

---

[58] White, 55.
[59] White, 17.
[60] White, 16-21.
[61] White, 21.
[62] *The Book of Worship for Church and Home, With Orders of Worship, Services for the Administration of Sacraments and Aids to Worship According to the Usages of the United Methodist Church* (Nashville: Methodist Publishing House, 1965), "Preface" (no page number).
[63] *Book of Worship for Church and Home*, 157.

Images of the Kingdom of God in Methodist Sunday School Worship 21

broader Christian tradition. One Lenten curriculum unit quotes Origen, John Wesley, Thomas Aquinas, Martin Luther, Peter Abelard, and an anonymous Scholastic theologian as springboards for meditations.[64]

Sunday Schools now showed more willingness to perform secular plays (such as Thornton Wilder's *Our Town*),[65] and discuss non-mainstream movies—such as *Midnight Cowboy*, "a movie that says God means man to be brother to the neighbor he meets."[66] Television was growing in influence. Since "there are more TV sets than bathtubs in the United States," one husband and wife team recommended that Sunday school could "take advantage of some of the better programs as content for class discussion."[67] Another church's Christian education art show rose out of a criticism from a group of Black Panther youth who, on witnessing the Warner Sallman *Head of Christ* painting in the church school building, remarked, "All your pictures of Christ are stereotypes of sweetness. You are seducing the minds of your youth with Sallman."[68] The completed art show included not only Old Masters, but also modern art, West African paintings, Byzantine icons, and others "showing Christ in agony, contemplation, love, joy, anger, meditation, and other moods" and picturing him in a way "few had ever seen"—as "a Chinese, a Mexican, a Negro."[69]

Music, too, was undergoing a change. The *Hymnal* was still considered to be the center of the Sunday School's musical life, but there was less focus on youth songbooks (authorized or otherwise) and more on teaching children to sing the hymns of the church and short worshipful responses.[70] Rather than eliminating music with "pep," educators began to suggest that youth be reached *through* their music: "The bouncy, bossa nova beat of the Doors...Music that speaks relationship....LAAW wahhh gahhhh OOOOOHHH oooooo wwwwooo, as Janis Joplin wails a new language of communication...and those who see and hear, feel!"[71]

An early 1970s publication sponsored by the Board of Discipleship (a significant name change from the Board of Education) sought to express these new visions involving mass media, holistic learning, and contemporary context. Some of those who contributed vision statements wrote of such hopes and visions for kingdom education as:

> Intergenerational learning centers: where children and youth become teachers as well as learners....Increased sensitivity to the fine arts....Integration and close inter-relationship between worship, education, evangelism, and action...Video and audio cassettes...active involvement...festivals and celebrations...The "good,

---

[64]*The Church School*, January 1969, 39-46.
[65]A. Argyle Knight, "A Drama Council in the Local Church," July 1969, 6-7.
[66]Fansler, 24.
[67]William and Marie Pearce, "What If...You Used Resources?" *The Church School*, December 1970, 9.
[68]John W. Boretoes, "Try an Art Show...We Did," *The Church School*, July 1969, 8.
[69]Boretoes, 9.
[70]"Hymn of the Month," *The Church School*, December 1969, 20.
[71]Fansler, 21-22. He adds, "One man's Bach may be another's 'Old Rugged Cross,'... graffiti are valid as a vehicle, and cassettes can catalogue community" (26).

moral, ethical, social justice" plan for living must be replaced with a living, working commitment to Christ...

—and finally, added a telling statement:

> The death of the Church/Sunday School: the end of a system in which 'students' grouped in age levels meet under the supervision of a 'teacher' to digest curricula packages of content material and then spew them back, being rewarded by gold stars for knowing such essentials of the Christian heritage as the shortest verse in the Bible.[72]

Not all of these visions came to pass, but it was not for lack of trying.

1968-2002: Experiencing a New Thing

1970s-1980s

The Sunday School of the 1970s introduced balloons, dance, contemporary and folk songs, and a blurring of distinctions between "worship" and what was beginning to be called "Christian education"—a term that no longer limited "Sunday School" or "church school" to Sunday, or even to the church. The emphasis was now on action, participation, and celebration: "Worship as celebration is something one does; it is not done *to* him, or *for* him." Sanctuary spaces were encouraged to switch from "immovable furniture, fixed pews ...that efficiently keeps the congregation from experiencing one another, and separated from the minister" to spaces characterized by utility, simplicity, flexibility, and intimacy.[73]

A United Methodist pastor claimed that "contemporary celebrative worship coupled with creative teaching styles creates a climate for increased attendance, commitment, and enthusiasm."[74] His church turned their entire Sunday morning service into a "celebration-study happening," combining elements of worship and education. Weekly topics for his "happenings" included Communion or Holy Community, Rally Day—Festival of a New Beginning, World Peace and War, Searching for a Meaningful Lifestyle, and "I'm OK, You're OK."[75] Worship and study included multimedia, "game playing," "encounter-rap group," music, drama, role playing, and arts and crafts. Church members were involved in creating prayers, poetry, and banners, making films and slides, and writing "contemporary" affirmations such as:

---

[72]*Visions: A Collage of Hopes for the Future of Church Education* (Nashville: Board of Discipleship, 1973), 3ff.

[73]L. Paul Neufer, "Equipping for Celebration," *The Church School*, July 1973, 1. (The four criteria come from James White).

[74]Wesley D. Taylor, "New Models for Study and Worship," *The Church School*, March 1973, 31.

[75]Taylor, 31-32.

The church often means different things to different people. Some find no need for it; others go to it when they have nothing better to do. But the church can be much to you and me! It is a time to try out the Christian life, knowing that if we fail at it, and we will, we will find support, encouragement, and a word: "Try Again."[76]

Sunday School structure and worship reclaimed a strong intergenerational component. Students were still usually organized into classes for learning, unless the church was very small, but Sunday or Wednesday evening fellowship included worship and arts in intergenerational groups. The "opening exercise" model essentially died out almost overnight, although vestiges of it remained in unusual places. (Many older Sunday School classes retained opening and closing exercises into the early twenty-first century.) There was a push for more involvement of children in church proper, rather than "segregating" them into "children's church" or letting them subsist only on a diet of Sunday School worship.[77] However, many children still did not attend the entire sanctuary service—or sometimes any of it.

Images of God in prayers, litanies, and other resources varied from previous decades. One "Litany of Shared Leadership" begins, "God, you started this business of shared leadership when you made us in your own image."[78] A UMC program for "Sunday School Growth and Renewal" commissioned contemporary songwriters to write songs about the Sunday School. One responded with:

God doesn't ask us to know every answer/ And doesn't expect us to heal every pain./ All God wants us to do is feed the people,/ And through God's grace we know love will remain./...We're reaching and teaching, learning new ways to grow;/ We're caring and sharing, there's so much more to know;/ We're yearning and learning; the seeds are ours to sow;/In living, we're helping each other grow. (Brent Holmes)

An anonymous author contributed a litany of thanksgiving for welcoming a new child to a class; it begins: "LEADER: Good morning everyone! I want you to know that a few years ago God created [name]. CHILDREN: And that is good! LEADER: This child of God has joined us today....We will play, study, and share in this friendly place...We will learn about one another, and discover God's world in many ways...We will laugh, sing, and pray together."[79]

Music now focused on self-expression rather than moral uplift. Teachers were encouraged to "help children communicate their feelings, especially those which they are unable to put into words...help children learn about God and Jesus through their musical experience;" learning and worship centers (still emphasized) might now contain a place for children to listen to music on their own.[80]

---

[76] Taylor, 32.

[77] Elayne Shults, "Youth Sunrise Service: Journey to Jerusalem," *Church School Today*, Winter 1985-86, Q18-19.

[78] Mary Alice Douty Edwards, "A Litany of Shared Leadership," *The Church School*, October 1972, 3.

[79] "A Litany of Thanksgiving," *Church School Today*, Fall 1985, 10.

[80] Peggy D. Bridgers, "Music in the Classroom," *Church School Today*, Winter 1986-87, 32.

In a complete reversal from recommendations of forty years previous, the General Commission on Archives and History even released a pamphlet instructing churches in how to have an old-fashioned singing school.[81]

The Christian year as experienced in Sunday School was changing, too. More and more attention was paid to the historic Christian year and the festivals of the church: Advent, Epiphany, Lent, Easter (including an Easter Vigil), and Pentecost. All Saints' Day was emphasized rather than Halloween.[82] Rally Day, now Christian Education Sunday, put less emphasis on evangelizing the community and more on the dedication of teachers and the presentation of Bibles. Christmas pageants and programs remained popular and Vacation Church School/Vacation Bible School played an ever-increasing role in the Christian educational year.

The publishing of the updated *United Methodist Hymnal* in 1989 (followed by the 1992 *Book of Worship*) signaled further new trends. Vatican II reforms were now apparent in the revised orders of worship and theological emphases of these new service books, which contained a greater number of ethnic and global resources than ever before. They also included choruses and songs from the ever-more-popular contemporary Christian music movement—rooted in church growth principles and the continued quest for relevance.

1990s-2000s and Beyond

Sunday School worship is still evolving in the twenty-first century, but some changes in emphasis are visible.

New orders and forms for worship

Vatican II continues to influence how Methodists worship. Questions are raised about the relationship of Christian education to catechesis and Christian initiation, the meaning of church membership for baptized but unconfirmed children, and the purpose and implication of worship in all aspects of the church's life. The lectionary, growing in prominence since the 1960s, now is the primary organizing force in both weekly Christian education and worship, proving a means of linking the two together.

The growth of youth culture

Meanwhile, the contemporary Christian music and youth culture that grew out of the "Jesus Movement" and folk music of the 1960s and 1970s also continues to exert a huge influence. This influence, together with the general perception

---

[81]R. Kenneth Lile, *Guidelines for an Old-Fashioned Singing School* (Madison, NJ: General Commission on Archives and History, 1986).

[82]Nancy Sorenson, "Something is Happening at Church," *Church School Today*, Winter 1985-86, 42-43. See also Jan Sutermeister Edwards, "Celebrate the Saints on Halloween," *The Church School*, Fall 1986, Q3. Some of the saints suggested for commemoration included Moses, Paul, Martin Luther, Susanna Wesley, John Wesley, and Mary McLeod Bethune.

of adolescents as an extremely specialized marketing niche, has led churches to encourage youth to develop their own culture and vision. Often presided over by a separate youth minister, the youth program often bears little resemblance to the wider Christian education in its aims and purposes, and its worship has developed in new directions often only tangentially related to the denomination's stated approaches.

Encouraging children to participate in worship

Children are encouraged to *experience* worship as part of the larger community of faith. Christian educators emphasize what children add to corporate worship and how it benefits them in ways adults do not fully understand: "The whole of worship is for everyone present to be fed, to be in the presence of God, to rejoice as one of God's people...to recommit to a life of loving God and loving neighbor, and to leave worship renewed and ready for life."[83] However, some churches still keep children and the sanctuary quite separate.

Attract or disciple?

Finally, there is a tension between differing visions of the primary purpose of worship and education and how they work together to create the Kingdom of God. Is that kingdom a contextualized version of the faith adapted to secular culture which has a broad appeal, or a countercultural movement practiced by a few with a first-century vision? Does worship and church organization exist to attract the unchurched, disciple the faithful, or both? And how best are those goals to be accomplished?

This is a continuing debate in the church, expressing itself at every level—from General Conference resolutions on the place of Baptism and Eucharist, evangelism and catechesis, to local church attempts to start new worship services (or stop them being started).

Sunday School worship has moved in many unexpected directions since Francis Asbury wrote his letter in 1791. However, it still possesses the same goal: to teach Christian truth to learners and make them members of Christ's Kingdom. But the definitions of teaching, learners, and the Christian faith and Kingdom have altered greatly in two hundred years. They are likely to alter even more in the next two hundred.

---

[83]MaryJane Pierce Norton, "How to Welcome Children in Worship," in *Worship Matters, Vol. II: A United Methodist Guide to Worship Work*, ed. E. Byron Anderson (Nashville: Discipleship Resources, 1999), 124.

Chapter 3

The Establishmentarian Turn in the Wesleyan Methodist Church

Barry W. Hamilton

After the death of John Wesley (1791), Methodism's enemies unleashed a furious attack on evangelical Christianity in England.[1] When Britain feared an impending invasion of Napoleon's army (1811), these attacks culminated when Henry Addington, Lord Sidmouth, introduced a bill in Parliament to regulate the licensing of nonconforming preachers and to insure their legitimacy. This bill threatened to rob Wesleyan ministers of their liberties.[2] If it had been enacted, Methodist preachers would have been humiliated and suppressed, and preaching would have been effectively outlawed in Methodist chapels.[3] Taking the warning, Methodists and their friends in the Established Church sought legal protection for their faith,

---

[1] For example see Robert Nares, *On the Influence of Sectaries, and the Stability of the Church. A Charge, Delivered to the Clergy of the Archdeaconry of Stafford, on the Days of Visitation at Cheadle, Stafford, and Walsall, in June, 1812*. London: Law and Gilbert, 1813. For a pamphlet that expressed comparable sentiments see *The Monstrosities of Methodism, Being an Impartial Examination into the Pretensions of Our Modern Sectaries, to Prophetic Inspiration, Providential Interferences, and Spiritual Impulse. With a Preliminary Notice of Dr. Walker's New Sect, and the Disputing Society in Stafford Street. By a Curate of the Church of England*. London: J. Charles, 1808. These are only two examples of a voluminous literature of calumny toward the Methodists.

[2] "Each would have been required to obtain a certificate signed by 'six substantial and reputable householders... specifying his competency and character.' The bill proposed to screen unsuitable people from preaching, e.g. the illiterate and immoral. The practical effect would be to rob most, if not all, Dissenting ministers of their preaching licenses. The magistrates, especially those unfriendly to Dissenters, would have been at liberty to refuse licenses for trifling reasons. And magistrates were often known to be particularly hostile toward Methodists." Barry W. Hamilton, *The Role of Richard Watson's Theological Institutes in the Development of Methodism after John Wesley* (Lewiston, NY: Edwin Mellen Press, 2014), 99-100. See also Thomas Jackson, *Memoirs of the Life and Writings of the Rev. Richard Watson, Late Secretary to the Wesleyan Missionary Society* (New York: B. Waugh and T. Mason, 1834), 83-84.

[3] See George Smith, *History of Wesleyan Methodism* (London: Longman, Brown, Green, Longmans, and Roberts, 1858), 2: 494.

resolving to defend Methodism from the ravaging hailstorm of malicious attacks and false accusations.[4]

While British Methodists claimed "no difference" with the Church of England, they surely equivocated, as they shared John Wesley's ambivalence toward the Established Church. They regarded themselves as loyal Anglicans separated by providential circumstances.[5] They championed independence yet respected the Established Church.

Jabez Bunting and Richard Watson were two young men on their way home from preaching appointments, when they chanced to meet on a road near Manchester in 1811 and began discussing Lord Sidmouth's Bill.[6] The former was a rising star in the Wesleyan Methodist Church (WMC), the youngest minister to be welcomed into the esteemed Legal Hundred.[7] The latter was an obscure itinerant who, mistreated by his parishioners, abandoned the WMC for the New Connexion. Eventually Watson regretted his decision and sought an honorable return to his former denomination. That opportunity came through Bunting.[8]

In 1813, after Watson had rejoined the WMC, Bunting, always the cunning politician, saw talent in Watson that could facilitate their mutual ascendance, and he presented Watson with exceptional chances to advance through the ministerial ranks of the WMC.[9]

---

[4]For a defense of Methodism published shortly after the death of John Wesley see *Methodism Vindicated, from the Charge of Ignorance and Enthusiasm. Being a Reply to a Sermon, Preached by the Rev. Samuel Clapham, M.A. at Boroughbridge in Yorkshire, September 2, 1794. Intitled, How far METHODISM conduces to the Interests of Christianity, and the Welfare of Society: and Published by Command of the Right Reverend Father in God, William, Lord Bishop of Chester. By a Member of the Church of England.* Margate: W. Epps, 1795. *Resolutions of the Methodist Ministers of the Manchester District, Assembled in Liverpool, May 23, 1811, on the Subject of a Bill Introduced into Parliament by the Right Hon. Lord Viscount Sidmouth: To Which is Annexed, an Abstract of the Debate in the House of Lords, on Tuesday, May 21st, 1811, When the said Bill was rejected.* Liverpool: Thos. Kaye, [1811].

[5]*The British Critic and the Rev. Richard Watson: Strictures upon the British Critic, no. xxxi., article 1, Review of Jackson's Memoirs of the Life and Writings of the Rev. Richard Watson* (London: Simpkin and Marshall, 1834), 41-42. The Anglican author acknowledged that the Church of England drove out and persecuted Methodists.

[6]See Smith, *History of Wesleyan Methodism* 2: 497-498.

[7]See Bernard Semmel, *The Methodist Revolution* (New York: Basic Books, 1973), 164-166.

[8]See Jackson, *Memoirs*, 108.

[9]After Watson's return to the WMC and his subsequent meteoric rise in the ranks of the preachers, Watson's enemies accused him of ambition. With regard to his leadership in Methodist missions, observers pointed out how this took place at the initiative of Jabez Bunting. "In that most important work, Mr. Bunting secured the able and masterly advocacy of Richard Watson, and by thus introducing him into the foremost ranks of Methodism, both in the pulpit and on the platform, there Mr. Watson found the most ample scope for the exercise of all the genius which his piety and intellect could command." PLP III.7.2, 76-77. [Watson Manuscript Collection/John Rylands Library University of Manchester"]

While it was Bunting who devised strategy, it was Watson who moved crowds and painted the "big picture" of Christian teaching.[10]

Watson and Bunting took charge when the WMC experienced crises in leadership, theology and finances. They presented the WMC as the actual true English church that had been unfairly forced against its will into separation from the Established Church, and argued that as a result Methodists should not be regarded as Dissenters.

Richard Watson was recruited to write a theology textbook for the training of Methodist preachers. The result was *Theological Institutes, a View of the Evidences, Doctrines, Morals and Institutes of Christianity*, popularly known as "the *Institutes*." Through the *Institutes*, Watson brought young preachers to grips with the English Church's evangelical tradition by recasting Methodist theology in Establishmentarian terms.[11]

From the beginning one of Watson's primary concerns in the *Institutes* was the theological improvement of the young ministers, Local Preachers and even missionaries. As Bunting later noted, the primary reason for Watson's departure from the WMC had been "the glaring defect of that *system* which leaves young men so situated without due protection against hazards so serious." To Watson, it was exposure to theological speculation and the absence of adequate training and guidance that had driven him into the New Connexion in his early ministry.[12]

In opposing rational dissent and establishing Athanasian Trinitarianism as the touchstone of a faithful Methodism, Watson solidified Methodist ministers' loyalty to traditional Christian doctrine. As Bunting's right-hand man, an invincible debater, and stern examiner of ordinands, he was buried beside John Wesley. In the *Institutes* he equated the doctrines of Methodism with "primitive Christianity" and engaged in thoughtful reflection on the major issues that had vexed the English Church since the sixteenth century. In spite of the fact that the *Institutes* included large extracts from scarce works of divinity that made it tedious and dry and tested readers' patience, and that at times it exhibited an authoritarian de-

---

[10]For Bunting's assessment of Watson as a theologian in terms of his ability to grasp the "big picture", see Jabez Bunting, *Memorials of the Late Rev. Richard Watson: Including the Funeral Sermon, Preached in the City-Road Chapel, London, on Friday, January 18, 1833; An Enlarged Account of His Character and Death; and Brief Biographical Notices* (London: John Mason, 1833), 25-26.

[11]Richard Watson, *Theological Institutes, a View of the Evidences, Doctrines, Morals and Institutes of Christianity* (New York: Band and J. Emory for the Methodist Episcopal Church, 1825-1828). See *Methodism Vindicated*, 39-40. After quoting extensively from Anglican sources, the author argued that Methodism consisted in the renewal of the doctrines of the Church of England. The Established Church had in large measure neglected the doctrines of Scripture and its own originating reformers.

[12]Bunting, *Memorials of the Late Rev. Richard Watson*, 41, 43. "One of the important objects to which Mr. Watson directed his attention, after he became one of the resident Secretaries to the Missionary Society, was the theological training of the Missionaries. Some of them resided in his family; and the greater part of them were put upon a course of reading and study under his direction." Jackson, *Memoirs*, 354.

meanor, the work became required reading for all ordinands seeking service in the WMC. The price for rejecting the *Institutes* was exile from the denomination.[13]

Depicting humanity as depraved, and most people as doomed to misery, the *Institutes* favored British Conservatism.[14] Strongly supportive of the British monarchy, the *Institutes* were resoundingly anti-revolutionary and gave critics no basis for accusing the Methodists of plotting to overthrow the British government. Since Methodism's enemies called her a separatist sect, Watson scarcely dared mention John Wesley's name or write a distinctly "Wesleyan" or "Methodist" systematic theology textbook. By contextualizing Methodism as part of the Evangelical Revival that began with the Puritans and aimed to restore apostolic Christianity, he made Methodism the logical product of the English Reformation.[15] He cited the formative thinkers of the English Church such as Isaac Barrow, Robert Boyle, Edward Stillingfleet, Daniel Waterland, Hugo Grotius and James Arminius.[16] Steeped in scripture, he defended the *a posteriori* epistemology of the traditional English Church against the *a priori* thought of modernists and Calvinists.[17] Thus Watson renounced absolutist and anthropocentric knowledge in favor of probabilistic knowledge, a "knowing" that mixed faith and sensate evidence.[18]

---

[13]Hamilton, *The Role of Richard Watson's* Theological Institutes, 147.

[14]For example, see Part Second, Chapter VI, "Attributes of God—Goodness," in which Watson blamed humanity for its miseries. Redeemed people would submit to God with respect to their place in which Providence had placed them. See Watson, *Theological Institutes*, vol. 1, 465. Watson quoted extensively in this chapter from William Paley's *Natural Theology*, and this would have favored a traditional view of British society. This appeared to be a common sentiment among the defenders of Methodism.

[15]For more on the relationship of the Evangelical Revival to John Wesley, see Stanley J. Rodes, *From Faith to Faith: John Wesley's Covenant Theology and the Way of Salvation* (Eugene, OR: Pickwick, 2013), 131.

[16]"He was also an *evangelical* Arminian; --an Arminian, that is, of the school of ARMINIUS himself, and of Mr. WESLEY, rather than of the very different one in which some of the *professed* disciples of those great men, and especially the later followers of the eloquent and learned leader of the Dutch Remonstrants, have been disposed to take up their position." Bunting, *Memorials of the Late Rev. Richard Watson*, 29.

[17]See Bunting, *Memorials of the Late Rev. Richard Watson*, 29-30. "Modern" thinkers who employed *a priori* metaphysics included Samuel Clarke and Isaac Newton. Bunting attributed Watson's inclination toward *a posteriori* theology to his immersion in the Bible, i.e. Watson reasoned from his knowledge of scripture rather than metaphysical presuppositions. Thus he regarded scripture's authority above that of reason.

[18]Such Scholastic epistemology characterized the thought of Anglican divines, e.g. Edward Stillingfleet. Without such realist concepts as "substance," Watson feared that "the doctrine of the Trinity would collapse." Rationalistic knowing could be supported by external evidence, but it could only be probabilistic. See Philip Dixon, *Nice & Hot Disputes: The Doctrine of the Trinity in the Seventeenth Century* (London: T&T Clark, 2003), 153. Reedy mentions a type of reason, often employed by the Anglican divines, "disposed toward a full acceptance of the full contents of Scripture... This wider sense tolerates less strict proofs based on probabilities, particularly proofs based on testimony." See Gerard Reedy, *The Bible and Reason: Anglicans and Scripture in Late Seventeenth-Century England* (Philadelphia: University of Pennsylvania Press, 1985), 36; Hamilton, *The Role of*

His *Institutes* reflected a seventeenth-century Christian worldview that affirmed God's role in limiting human reason.[19] Since fallen humanity could never obtain knowledge of God *a priori*, Watson presumed with his sources that God had given a revelation.[20]

Raising Methodist theological literature to a new level, in part by drawing on the evidentialism of John Hutchinson, Watson devoted the first part of the *Institutes* to proving that the Bible was a divine revelation.[21] While exuding authoritarianism Watson synthesized biblical, natural and human history to attest the Bible's truth. His evidence vouchsafed the credibility of testimony, the antiquity of the Bible, prophecy and miracles as supernatural events, and the correspondence of biblical and secular history.[22]

For the Established Church biblical authority ultimately rested on faith. Yet evidence did not prove the veracity of the Bible—this still required faith. Further, Watson's sources often had a homiletical quality that preached Eurocentric presuppositions about humanity's need for revelation. Faith and reason were thor-

---

Richard Watson's Theological Institutes, 278-279. "For the most part, Anglican divines held that once the laity used their reason to discern the truths of the Bible, they would submit to the Established Church and adhere to its beliefs." See John Spurr, "'Rational Religion' in Restoration England," *Journal of the History of Ideas* 49:4 (Oct. – Dec. 1988), 569.

[19]At points the *Institutes* mirror the seventeenth-century worldview of thinkers like Robert Boyle, whose theological volunteerism affirmed God's creation of limited human reason.

[20]He summarized his "presumptive arguments" in favor of the opinion, "that almighty God in his goodness has made an express revelation of his will to mankind." See Watson, *Theological Institutes*, 170-171, 214-215.

[21]See John Friesen, "Hutchinsonianism and the Newtonian Enlightenment," *Centaurus* 48:1 (January 2006), 41-42. Friesen is citing Geoffrey N. Cantor, "Revelation and the Cyclical Cosmos of John Hutchinson," in J. Jordanova and R. Porter (eds.), *Images of the Earth: Essays in the History of the Environmental Sciences* (Chalfont St. Giles: British Society for the History of Science, 1979), 3-22.

[22]Watson "relied heavily on testimony to establish the credibility of Scripture. His argument dressed up faith in a reasoned discussion that appealed to thoughtful Christians, a strategy to inoculate them from skepticism." Hamilton, *The Role of Richard Watson's* Theological Institutes, 283. Moral certainty had been the legacy of William Chillingworth's *The Religion of Protestants* (1687) which advised readers not to look for greater certainty in scripture than warranted. The Bible revealed enough to support faith in the "hearts and minds of such as are not obstinate." Mountains of evidence could not create faith in stubborn hearts; faith could be nourished only in people with right dispositions. See Robert Todd Carroll, *The Common-Sense Philosophy of Religion of Bishop Edward Stillingfleet, 1635-1699* (The Hague: Martinus Nijhoff, 1975), 9-10. See also Hamilton, *The Role of Richard Watson's* Theological Institutes, 263-264, 281. "The external evidence consists of miracles and prophecy; the internal evidence is drawn from the consideration of the doctrines taught, as being consistent with the character of God, and tending to promote the virtue and happiness of man; and the collateral evidence arises from a variety of circumstances, which, less directly than the former, prove the revelation to be of Divine authority..." Watson, *Theological Institutes*, 252.

oughly mixed to create the "facts" the *Institutes* assumed. By uniting Biblical authority with faith and reason Watson had accomplished his purpose.[23]

Drawing primarily on theological commitments of seventeenth-century Anglican divines, Watson urged his readers to affirm a religious faith that transcended reason. As previously observed, in rejecting Socinianism and other forms of skepticism associated with republicanism, Watson drew his interpretive principles largely from theologians who placed scripture over reason and privileged a literal sense of scripture. Preserving the mysteries of the gospel that stood above reason and incorporating traditional rules of logic concerning scripture, they disassociated themselves from the logic of the radical Enlightenment.[24]

As Gerard Reedy argued in his study of seventeenth-century biblical interpretation, Isaac Barrow (1630-1677), Robert South (1643-1716), Edward Stillingfleet (1635-1699), and John Tillotson (1630-1694) who favored a literal reading of Scripture set the parameters for orthodoxy in the Church of England.[25] These English church leaders shared a common assumption about divine revelation. If God had indeed given a revelation essential for human salvation, this knowledge would not be obscured in mysteries but be readily available to human perception.[26] These divines enabled Watson to present reasonable arguments in defense of the evangelical faith of the English Church. As Reedy points out, the Anglican divines often oscillated between two types of reason and failed to distinguish them. This revealed both their predisposition toward faith (in a traditional sense) and their concern to sound reasonable (in a modern sense). While the divines used a narrow sense to connect with philosophical reason, they often allowed a "wider sense" to predominate—and made room for faith. They strained to overcome Spinoza's intractable split between reason and faith set up in the *Tractatus*.[27] As a result no matter how reasonable their theology sounded, the moderate Anglicans subordinated reason to faith, convincing only those already convinced. As Watson argued, readers should approach the Bible with reverence and receptivity,

---

[23]See *The British Critic and the Rev. Richard Watson*, 19-20. According to this author, a member of the Anglican clergy, British universities by no means offered training superior to that given to Methodist preachers like Watson. If true, this meant that the *Institutes* offered theological literature far above that offered to the Established clergy.

[24]These divines "retained much more of an older view of the limits of human reason and of man's [sic] essential nature than their opponents were ever willing to acknowledge." W. M. Spellman, *The Latitudinarians and the Church of England, 1660-1700* (Athens, GA: University of Georgia Press, 1993), 9.

[25]See Reedy, *The Bible and Reason*, 13.

[26]See Carroll, *The Common-Sense Philosophy of Religion of Bishop Edward Stillingfleet*, 40.

[27]See Reedy, *The Bible and Reason*, 37, 40; Hamilton, *The Role of Richard Watson's Theological Institutes*, 280. For more on reading scripture from a faith perspective see Richard Watson, *Remarks on the Eternal Sonship of Christ; and the Use of Reason in Matters of Revelation: Suggested by Several Passages in Dr. Adam Clarke's Commentary on the New Testament. In a Letter to a Friend.* 2nd ed. (London: T. Cordeaux, 1818), 80-81. See Watson, *Theological Institutes*, 303; Hamilton, *The Role of Richard Watson's* Theological Institutes, 282.

hoping to find truth in its pages. Even as they carried out extensive "historical investigations," to establish the validity of miracles, doubt always loomed in the background.[28]

By Watson's time popular deism had challenged the viability of traditional Christian doctrine for more than a century. One of the earliest attacks upon special revelation was Matthew Tindal's *Christianity Old as the Creation* (1730-1733) which sought to discredit the idea of special revelation by simply pointing out the obvious, that most people had never heard—and would never hear—the message of Christianity. Rather than revelation, reason could discover God's truth through observation of the natural world. Others charged the early church with corrupting apostolic teaching by means of Greek philosophy, rejecting irrational and seemingly mysterious teachings from Christian doctrine.[29] As a result this primitive gospel closely resembled Islam at several points including no concept of the Trinity and no confession of Jesus as both "fully God" and "fully human."[30]

In the 1790s, orthodox English divines launched a fierce counterattack. During the English Reformation, Athanasian Trinitarianism stood at the heart of Protestant teaching as embodied in the Thirty-nine Articles. With the separation from the Church of Rome, the English Church advocated reform through reason and anathematized fideism. The Bible would be the religion of Protestants, interpreted by reason and inspired by the Holy Spirit. For many English divines this experiment had largely been discredited by the unfortunate events of the English Civil War. After the Restoration of 1660, the English Church minimized inspiration and harbored a deep-seated aversion to "enthusiasm."[31] As exemplified by

---

[28]No one who followed the example of the Anglican divines could ever question miracles or prophecy. "The possibility of miracles wrought by the power of God, can be denied by none but Atheists, or those whose system is substantially Atheistic." Watson then mentions the name of Spinoza. Watson, *Theological Institutes*, 256.

[29]Sarah Mortimer, *Reason and Religion in the English Revolution: The Challenge of Socinianism* (New York: Cambridge University Press, 2010), 165. As Mortimer has written, "All the English anti-Trinitarians viewed the clergy as the promoters of mysterious and esoteric religious doctrines designed to conceal the truth from the people and to increase their own power. By constructing their own language and metaphysics around the scriptural text, the clergy were able to elbow out other Christians from their Church."

[30]See Dietrich Klein, "Hugo Grotius' Position on Islam as Described in *De Veritate Christianae, Liber VI*," in *Socinianism and Arminianism: Antitrinitarians, Calvinists and Cultural Exchange in Seventeenth-Century Europe*, ed. Martin Mulsow and Jan Rohls. Brill's Studies in Intellectual History 134 (Leiden: E. J. Brill, 2005), 149-173. In the conclusion on page 170, Klein observes that "Grotius is concerned with reconciliation of the dogmatic christological differences between Christianity and Islam." He also notes that this interest originated with Nicholas of Cusa, who sought to facilitate "possible integration" of the Ottoman Empire into the Christian West.

[31]With regard to the effects of the Civil War on the nation, Sutcliffe observed: "In England, we suffered more from variation than the Protestants abroad. The Episcopalians, the Presbyterians, and the Independents could never be united either in faith, or worship; and the rupture which followed between the King and Parliament made the breach wider and wider still. The effects, in a moral and religious view, are lamentable to the present

the Great Tew Circle, theological discussion turned to reason as the criterion of divine truth. Thinkers like Hobbes and Chillingworth sought a "more rational and scriptural basis" for Christianity. Any doctrine that could not be grasped by reason was not to be believed and people were encouraged to interpret the Bible for themselves in "more rational and scriptural terms."[32]

As this popular Arianism infiltrated the Church of England and dissenting bodies such as the English Presbyterians, moralism replaced "supernatural" doctrines including justification, regeneration and sanctification, and opposition to enthusiasm transformed the Holy Spirit into a figurative expression. In answer to those who accused Methodists of "schism" or denied the credentials of the Methodist ministry, Sutcliffe observed that the Anglican Church had done the very same thing when it broke with Rome and appealed to the Bible alone as the rule of faith. When established clergy accused the Methodists of doctrinal irregularities, they failed to admit to the serious doctrinal declension in their own ranks. In support of his contention Sutcliffe cited John Overton's *True Churchman Ascertained*. As Overton had noted, if there had not been "defect of faith, why is all this obloquy cast on the Athanasian Creed? Its damnatory were not intended to bear on the indulgence of a scruple or doubt; but on the enlightened enemies of the Saviour's Godhead. And as to its peculiar forms of expression, they were dictated by the logic of the age, and then necessary as strong palisades to guard the house of God."[33]

Arianism named the Father as "true God" worthy of worship, confessed Jesus as the Messiah and dismissed the Holy Spirit. In 1763, in this environment some Anglican ministers sought to reinterpret the Athanasian Creed on their own terms. Gathering in London at Feathers Tavern they petitioned Parliament to abolish the requirement that Anglican ordinands subscribe to the Thirty-nine Articles.

---

day. The profligate part of the nation became *free-thinkers*, and found employment for the pens of the clergy by daring attacks of revelation." Joseph Sutcliffe, *The Divine Mission of the People Called Methodists to Revive and Spread Religion, Illustrated and Defended in a Sermon Preached before the District Meeting Assembled in Macclesfield, May 27, 1813* (London, 1814), 11-12. In England after he "had returned from studies abroad," Robert Boyle observed a large number of new religious opinions flourishing under the tolerant policies of Oliver Cromwell. See Jan W. Wojcik, *Robert Boyle and the Limits of Reason* (New York: Cambridge University Press, 1997), 14-19.

[32]See Frederick C. Beiser, *The Sovereignty of Reason: The Defense of Rationality in the Early English Enlightenment* (Princeton, NJ: Princeton University Press, 1996), 86.

[33]Methodists often accused the Anglican clergy of moralism and the subsequent neglect of the gospel of salvation by faith alone. For an example of this charge see *A Dialogue Between a Clergyman, and One Who is Called a Methodist, Occasioned by a Former Dialogue Between a Churchman and a Methodist*. London: M. Lewis, 1770. Sutcliffe, *Divine Mission of the People Called Methodists*, 41-43. See John Overton, *True Churchman Ascertained: Or, An Apology for Those of the Regular Clergy of the Establishment, Who are Sometimes Called Evangelical Ministers: Occasioned by the Publications of Drs. Paley, Hey, Croft; Messrs. Daubeny, Ludlam, Polwhele, Fellowes; the Reviewers, &c. &c.* 2nd ed. York: T. Wilson, and R. Spence, 1802.

When this measure failed, the petitioners left the Church of England to form the Unita-rian Church.

Citing scholars whose works formed the backbone for the defense of traditional Anglican teaching, Watson sought to defend Methodism through a vigorous defense of traditional Anglican teaching. In effect, in the *Institutes* Watson grappled with issues that had vexed England's establishment divines for at least two centuries. Citing scholars Methodism's enemies dared not attack, the *Institutes* vigorously affirmed the Thirty-nine Articles and the "faith of the Bible." The centerpiece consisted in a defense of Athanasian Trinitarianism, with the Father, Son and Holy Spirit confessed as three eternal Persons in one divine essence. It was absolutely crucial, in this context, that Jesus Christ be pronounced the Eternal Son of God.

But if affirming classic Anglican doctrine met Watson's primary and immediate political goals it angered many in the WMC. In the WMC, conflict surrounded Adam Clarke's view that the term "Son of God" was synonymous with "Messiah." According to Clarke, Jesus Christ became Son of God at his Incarnation.[34] Furthermore, Clarke, following Hooker, the Great Tew Circle, and particularly William Chillingworth, insisted that no one should accept a doctrine that could not be reconciled with reason. In this Clarke was affirming a view that even John Locke cautiously embraced. As Locke argued, some things in revelation were "above reason."[35]

In fact, Clarke's Christology was consistent with a long line of English Protestant biblical scholars, and many Anglican vicars held similar views. Following the biblical texts closely and eschewing systematic theology, Clarke, as previously noted, identified the term "Son of God" as equivalent to "Messiah." This rational hermeneutical principle was widely held by Anglican vicars including some who were openly Arian.[36] Such a principle skirted Socinianism and presaged the rise of modern biblical scholarship. Of course, Adam Clarke was no Socinian: he stoutly

---

[34]Clarke advocated the co-equality of the Second Person of the Trinity on account of the term *logos* in John 1:1. He certainly was not the first or only scholar to embrace this argument. For example, Thomas Davies, Vicar of Queen-Street, Cheapside, London supported the full divinity of Jesus Christ on the same basis. Like Clarke, Davies was strongly influenced by Enlightenment rationalism and thought that the "begetter" could not be co-eternal with the "begotten." "We cannot allow the self-contradicting idea of an unbegotten birth, and the begetter and begotten co-eternal." Thomas Davies, *The Eternity, Personality, and Divinity of the Word, Proved and Defended from John 1.-1* (London: T. Plummer, [1805]). Davies contended for the equality of the three persons of the Godhead, and strongly denounced Sabellianism. Davies and Clarke subscribed uncompromisingly to Athanasian Trinitarianism. Those who called them "Socinian" or "Arian" were grossly unfair—they failed to grasp Davies' and Clarke's opinions.

[35]Beiser observed that the Great Tew Circle joined skepticism and Protestantism, since without an infallible Pope there only remains "the fallible judgment of individual reason." See Beiser, *The Sovereignty of Reason*, 111.

[36]See John Locke, *The Reasonableness of Christianity as Delivered in the Scriptures*, A New Edition (London: C. and J. Rivington, 1824), 52.

defended the divinity of Jesus Christ. Unfortunately, even contemporary scholars regard Clarke's views on the Sonship of Christ as heretical. However, Clarke's refusal to speculate on the ontological relations of the Trinity came dangerously close to a voluntarist conception of God that was held by many who identified with Socinianism. This view defined God in terms of dominion or rulership.[37] Many feared that Clarke's opinions could have influenced ordination candidates into considering the plausibility of Arianism. Although Watson was younger than Clarke and far less influential, his defense of Athanasian Trinitarianism was first published as a pamphlet in 1818 on the Eternal Sonship.[38] In the WMC his argument replaced Clarke's position and established Watson's reputation as Methodism's greatest theologian. While Clarke never publically responded and kept his dignity in silence, he seemed to regard Watson's and Bunting's authoritarianism with contempt, and in a conversation with William Pollard, Clarke referred to Bunting and Watson as "the Inquisitors at Manchester."[39]

In the political and cultural climate inspired by the defeat of Napoleon, the nation's military power and commercial wealth birthed the opportune moment for the global expansion of the gospel. At this pivotal time the Wesleyan Methodists who spurned Jacobinism and affirmed loyalty to crown and nation via Athanasian Trinitarianism united a restored gospel with nationalism and postmillennialism. Although courting embourgeoisment with the Establishment, these clearly political motives fail to account for the immense sacrifices the WMC made for foreign missions. In truth, the primary motivation seems to have been the burning desire to share the gospel.[40] Regardless of the international situation or the British

---

[37]Unfortunately even contemporary scholars regard Clarke as heretical on the Sonship of Christ. This view is undoubtedly mistaken, for Clarke affirmed the equality of the Persons of the godhead. See Stephen David Snobelen, "Isaac Newton, Socinianism and 'The One Supreme God,'" in *Socinianism and Arminianism*, 257. These similar opinions did not make Clarke a Socinian; however, they could have been taken further by ordination candidates.

[38]See Richard Watson, *Remarks on the Eternal Sonship of Christ; and the Use of Reason in Matters of Revelation: Suggested by Several Passages in Dr. Adam Clarke's Commentary on the New Testament. In a Letter to a Friend.* 2nd ed. London: T. Cordeaux, 1818.

[39]See "He was distinguished by a placable temper, a forgiving disposition; and, instead of resenting injuries, he, like his Divine Master, prayed for his enemies, and sought to do them good." [J. B. B. Clarke], *The Life and Labours of Adam Clarke, LL.D. to which is added an historical sketch of the controversy concerning the Sonship of Christ, particularly as connected with the proceedings of the Wesleyan-Methodist Conference* (London: John Stephens, 1834), 442. See also Hamilton, *The Role of Richard Watson's* Theological Institutes, 163. William Pollard, [unpublished diary], 93-95 [available from Methodist Archives, Oxford Brookes University (Oxford, UK)]. See also Samuel Dunn, *The Life of Adam Clarke, LL.D., Author of a Commentary on the Old and New Testaments, Etc.* (London: William Tegg, 1863), 231-232. Dunn pointed out that the treatment of ministerial candidates at this time (under Bunting's and Watson's leadership), with regard to the hardline position on the Eternal Sonship, persuaded Clarke's son to enter the ministry of the Church of England.

[40]See John Ward, *A Brief Vindication of the Wesleyan Methodists, in Their Doctrine*

Methodist passion for missions, the seventeenth- and eighteenth-century English divines dominated Watson's *Institutes*. Evangelical Anglicans could have readily agreed with their exposition of Christian doctrine. Watson made a particular effort to demonstrate John Wesley's teachings on assurance as belonging to the evangelical Christian tradition in the Church of England.[41] The contents of the *Institutes* lined up squarely with the teachings of the Established Church. And this is as far as Watson dared tread: he never overreached the boundaries of the Establishment.[42] Without mentioning its name, the *Institutes* implicitly defended Methodism as the restoration of New Testament Christianity. A treasure-trove that embodied the legacy of evangelical Arminianism, they became a staple of denominational courses of study for British and American Methodists. Yet Watson's establishmentarian strategy muted John Wesley's theological contributions and passed over John Fletcher's. In the twentieth century, Methodism began to rediscover its Wesleyan heritage as a profound resource for renewal.

---

and Discipline, or What Some Would Call Their Church Government; With a View to Condemn the Inconsistent Churchman, Out of His Own Mouth. Being Some Strictures upon the Writings of Mr. Exton, and His Second. Wherein they have tried to defame the Methodists, and have thereby brought Reproach upon the true Church of England (Northampton: W. Cooper, 1820), 23. See Hamilton, *The Role of Richard Watson's* Theological Institutes, 105-106. See also Semmel, *The Methodist Revolution*, 152-157. On page 157 Semmel states: "With the defeat of Napoleon, many of the pious of Great Britain saw one remaining imperial Adversary—the Devil himself—and sensing the approach of the last days, enlisted the power, the pounds, and the prayers of England to hasten the second coming." See also Jackson, *Memoirs*, 144. Around the time of Watson's death, some Anglican statesmen supported anti-Establishment legislation. An Anglican author accused them of presenting a greater danger to the Established Church than the Methodists. See *The British Critic and the Rev. Richard Watson*, 43. While Thomas Coke had inspired the WMC with his missionary zeal, Bunting brought vision and administrative skill to the denomination—especially financial management. See John Telford, *A Short History of Wesleyan Methodist Foreign Missions* (London: Charles H. Kelly, 1870), 38-39; Hamilton, *The Role of Richard Watson's* Theological Institutes, 106-107.

[41]See Jackson, *Memoirs*, 372-374. On page 372 Jackson states: "He wrote some valuable papers on that direct witness which is borne by the Holy Spirit, in the hearts of believers, to the fact of their personal adoption. The reality of this witness was generally held by Protestant Divines in some former ages; but it is now regarded by many as a mere peculiarity of Methodism… Mr. Watson… has shown that this great blessing of Christianity is distinctly recognized in the writings of the highest authorities in the Church of England."

[42]See Humphrey Sandwith, *A Reply to Lord John Russell's Animadversions on Wesleyan Methodism. In His "Memoirs of the Affairs of Europe, from the Peace of Utrecht"* (London: John Mason, 1830), 27-28. Early British Methodism compared itself with the Protestant Reformation in significance, e.g. "Review of the Life of Dr. Adam Clarke," *The Methodist Magazine and Quarterly Review*, Vol. XVI, New Series 5:1 (January 1834), 175-176.

Chapter 4

Luther Lee: Social Reformer, Editor and Church Leader - 1843-1855

Paul L. Kaufman

One of the great paradoxes that faced abolitionists in the early nineteenth century was the fact that slavery constituted a moral wrong, yet few churches were willing to condemn it as a moral evil. Even more frustrating to them were the Scriptural arguments that southern apologists for slavery hurled at the abolitionist Northerners.[1]

While most churches were willing to live with the status quo, the abolitionists within those churches would not let the issue of slavery alone. In the Methodist Church, public discussion of the issue was suppressed and the issue festered. Finally, in 1844, northern Methodists could no longer abide the slaveholding members in the South. With thousands of members seceding from the Church, the bishops had no choice but to open the General Conference for debate on slavery. By the end of the session, the Church had split into the Methodist Episcopal Church and the Methodist Episcopal Church, South. Among the most prominent of those who were responsible for the split was Luther Lee, a minister and reformer from Upstate New York.

Born on the eastern periphery of the "burned-over district" of New York, Lee underwent a religious conversion at twenty-one, and subsequently served several pastorates in the Genesee and Black River Conferences of the Methodist Episcopal Church (MEC). In 1837, following the murder of abolitionist Elijah P. Lovejoy, Lee became an abolitionist, and in 1839, he became a general agent for the Massachusetts Antislavery Society.

The idea of secession from the MEC had been discussed between Lee and Orange Scott as early as 1841. For almost two years Scott had reflected on the idea, but his health and other reasons of expediency had kept the matter in check. Lee would not leave by himself. Then in the fall of 1842, Scott quit hesitating and called for a meeting at Albany at which he, Jotham Horton, La Roy Sunderland, and Cyrus Prindle agreed to withdraw from the MEC.

---

[1]Prominent among the few churches that did condemn slavery were the Society of Friends and the Moravian Church.

Luther Lee had not been notified of the Albany meeting because Scott feared that some features of the plan might not win Lee's endorsement, and he did not want to get into potentially abortive arguments. Simultaneously, the seceders agreed that Scott should initiate a publication, the *True Wesleyan,* in which they would publish their reasons for leaving the MEC. Lee finally learned of their actions through the press.²

Lee received a letter from a spokesman for the Boston Preachers' Meeting of the MEC. Hoping to convince Lee to remain loyal, the writer promised: "...you shall have any position in the Church you desire if you will come out and wield your vigorous pen against secession."³ Lee dashed off a reply in a letter stating that his services were not for sale.

Lee finally met with Scott and confronted him for not notifying him of his intention to leave the Church. Scott frankly admitted to him: "I was afraid of you; I did not know that you would agree with me, and I knew if you did not . . . you would sound the alarm before I could get a document before the people."⁴

Lee was first and foremost a Methodist. While offers from other denominations appeared tempting, he knew he must remain in the Methodist milieu, although the thought of a new denomination intrigued him. While he had no reason to question the sincerity of the offer of the brethren in Boston, Lee could never bring himself to turn on his abolitionist colleagues. To remain in a church that tolerated slaveholding bishops while it prohibited the free discussion of slavery made no sense to him. Thus, he took the only logical step; he also seceded.

The *True Wesleyan* of January 7, 1843, contained the reasons for the withdrawal of the first secessionists. It also published the announcement of an antislavery convention to be held in Andover, Massachusetts on February 1 for the purpose of "the ultimate formation of a Wesleyan Methodist Church, free from Episcopacy and Slavery."⁵ That call was issued over the signatures of Lee, Horton, Scott, and Sunderland.

The second issue of the *True Wesleyan* contained Lee's reasons for seceding from the MEC. Slavery headed the list. He called attention to recent proslavery statements by Reverend J. C. Postell of South Carolina, and complained of the "principles" of government that had developed since abolitionism surfaced in the church. He concluded his reasons by citing the "uncharitable and bitter spirit" of the church leaders, editors, and others. The article closed with a defense of Scott, Horton, and Sunderland, arguing that those men should not be held as traitors, but as men with vision who had no other option but to secede.⁶

---

²Donald G. Mathews, *Slavery and Methodism: A Chapter in American Morality 1780-1845* (Princeton, N.J.: Princeton University Press, 1965), 230; Whitney R. Cross, *The Burned-over District: The Social and Intellectual History of Enthusiastic Religion in Western New York, 1800-1850* (Ithaca, N.Y.: Cornell University Press), 296, 310.

³Luther Lee, *Autobiography of the Rev. Luther Lee, D.D.* (New York: Phillips & Hunt; Cincinnati: Walden & Stowe, 1882), 238.

⁴Ibid, 238.

⁵*True Wesleyan,* January 7, 1843.

⁶*True Wesleyan,* January 14, 1843.

While the leaders of the new "Scottite" movement awaited the Andover meeting, they received word of individuals and entire congregations that also had voted to secede. Among them were several churches in Michigan, and a large MEC congregation at Providence that wanted the distinction of being the first Wesleyan Methodist Church in New England. In the West, Edward Smith of Pittsburgh had endured the ignominy of suspension from the MEC, and he also seceded. The *True Wesleyan* urged each seceder to notify the editor so proper promotional advantage could be secured.[7]

Finally the day of the Andover convention arrived. The Methodist Episcopal Church in Andover, of which Lee was the pastor, had been selected as the location for the Wesleyan Anti-Slavery Convention. The Honorable Seth Sprague Jr. of Duxbury was chosen president with Lucius C. Matlack elected secretary. A committee composed of Lee and eight others was formed to organize the business of the meeting. The convention unanimously agreed that the episcopal form of government was "anti-republican,...an encroachment upon human rights," and "subversive."[8] Resolutions establishing a committee of correspondence between the newly-formed societies and a committee to create and publish a discipline passed easily. Curiously, in a move that reflected badly on the MEC, the group also approved a resolution stating that Wesley never intended to establish an episcopal form of government when he appointed Francis Asbury and Thomas Coke as superintendents in America. The final resolution invited interested brethren to send delegates to a "General Convention" to be held in Utica, New York.

In the April 22 issue, the *True Wesleyan* announced the convening of a General Convention for the purpose of organizing the Wesleyan Methodist Church. At Lee's behest, the following issue of the paper carried a political announcement addressed "To the Liberty Party Abolitionists throughout the United States," in which it announced a United States Anti-Slavery Convention at Buffalo, the purpose of which was to nominate a presidential candidate.[9]

The long-awaited convention of all seceders, Methodist Episcopal and otherwise, finally commenced in the Bleecker Street church in Utica on May 31, 1843.

Approximately 150 delegates had arrived; almost twice that many people, including a number of blacks, crowded into the galleries. The eclectic group included delegates from sixteen states and about half that number of denominations. A youthful looking Irish preacher, recently arrived in America as a missionary to Irish immigrants, appeared as a delegate from Ireland.[10]

Jotham Horton called the session to order. Orange Scott was appointed chairman and La Roy Sunderland secretary. A nominating committee that included Lee

---

[7]Smith is a significant figure in the early days of Wesleyan Methodism. He served as president of Allegheny Conference, one of the six original conferences. L. C. Matlack, *The Anti-Slavery Struggle and Triumph in the Methodist Episcopal Church* (New York: Phillips & Hunt, 1881; repr., New York: Negro University Press, 1969), 318-19.

[8]*True Wesleyan*, May 13, 1843.

[9]*True Wesleyan*, April 22 and 29, 1843.

[10]Joel L. Martin, *Wesleyan Manual, or History of Wesleyan Methodism* (Syracuse, N.Y.: Wesleyan Methodist Publishing House, 1889), 20-24.

was formed. To no one's surprise, Scott was elected president with Edward Smith and Horton as vice-presidents. The elections completed, the session moved to the business of organizing a new church.[11]

The most important discussion focused on the adoption of a discipline that contained doctrinal views, moral principles, and rules of government. The new denomination would be Methodist in theology. Wesley's Twenty-Five Articles of Religion, a carryover from the Anglican Church, formed the nexus of the new organization with some articles slightly revised; others that had only faulted Roman practices, but said nothing positive, were deleted.

The delegates spent considerable time debating the form of church government. Smith advocated a strong episcopacy; Scott favored a modified episcopacy with limited and "well-guarded" powers; others leaned toward a congregational form. Lee's influence pushed the convention toward a mixture of presbyterian and congregational organization. Then, also influenced by Lee, the delegates agreed to use the term "Methodist" in the name because it expressed a principle. They chose the term "Connection" to establish that "all these Christian congregations, collectively, are not a Church, but being connected by a central organization they are a connection of churches."[12] In opting for a system of church government that placed sovereignty at the level of the laity, the Wesleyan Methodists, in fact as well as theory, defined the culmination of an egalitarian process that originated with the American Revolution. By so doing, they institutionalized a social movement built around social reform and antielitism.

In actuality, the Utica delegates were organizing a church with which to shape their society. Wesleyan Methodism demonstrates the process by which popular culture became Christianized and institutionalized, and gave new meaning to *novus ordo seclorum* in freeing itself from the authoritarian episcopacy. Lee, as chairman of the committee that produced the Pastoral Address and the chief architect of the new church's polity, must be viewed as a leader of the *avant garde* of Jacksonian social reform. Therein is his significance. He represented much more than an antislavery agitator, a spokesman for women, and an opposer of drink: he was the personification of all that his father had fought for in the American Revolution.

The strength of the Connection lay with the local churches. These were to meet in a quarterly conference as the means for each congregation to conduct business on the local level. Each church elected its own pastor and no power at the conference level could impose a pastor on a congregation without its concurrence. The churches elected their own officers and received their own church members, according to the rules of the *Discipline.* There was no appeal on such local issues. In this, then, the republicanism of America is mirrored; sovereignty resided in the people.

---

[11]Martin, *Wesleyan Manual,* 9-17; Matlack, *American Slavery and Methodism,* 333-45.

[12]Luther Lee, *Wesleyan Manual: A Defense of the Organization of the Wesleyan Methodist Connection, with an Introduction by Cyrus Prindle* (Syracuse, N.Y.: Samuel Lee, 1862), 155-57.

The annual conference was the next higher level above the local church. Every elder and stationed preacher under appointment had a duty to attend. Lay delegates were selected at the local level. At the annual conference equal representation was to be strictly observed: one lay delegate for each elder. This made certain that it would not be a clergy dominated church.

Each conference elected officers according to the *Discipline.* At these sessions, men who had completed the prescribed course of study were ordained to the office of elder. A stationing committee reviewed all local pastor-church agreements. While it might make recommendations to local churches, it had no legal authority to negate the local church's wishes concerning its pastor. The annual conferences also conducted trials involving elders or churches when necessary.[13]

General conferences met every four years and were made up of one ministerial and one lay delegate for every five hundred members. The annual conferences elected those delegates. The president of the General Conference, elected by its delegates, presided over the business sessions and remained in office for the following four years although he had little to do unless a General Conference was in session. The General Conference had full power to make rules and regulations for the churches, so long as no Article of Faith or General Rule was violated.

In organizing their new church, the Wesleyans rejected *in toto* the episcopacy of the MEC. While not enacting a presbyterian polity, the delegates utilized some of its concepts. The Church could not, on the other hand, be identified as purely congregationalist, since rules did come down from the General Conference, although the delegates who formulated the rules were elected at the local level.

On the second day of the proceedings an aged mulatto with white locks, known only as "Reverend Dungy," addressed the convention. While his manner of speech lacked polish, his bearing conveyed enough sincerity to move most of his hearers to tears. After he had learned of the MEC's attempts to silence several abolitionist clergy in 1838, Dungy had feared that he would be next, and he had left the Church. Recently quite ill, he forced himself to attend the convention that he might look "upon the face of Orange Scott and Luther Lee: O, how my heart rejoiced to see these men that have been so slandered and abused!" The audience sat transfixed as he spoke; Lee later observed that the eloquent address so influenced him that although he had intended to take notes, "our pencil soon fell from our fingers, and our vacant page caught nothing but our tears ... [and] the whole convention was overwhelmed by the address of Br. Dungy."[14] In the afternoon five fugitive slaves were presented to the convention, just to remind them of the major *raison d'etre* for the new organization.[15]

Other matters necessary in forming a denomination were addressed, such as accepting the *True Wesleyan* as its official organ. The delegates agreed to observe only two sacraments: baptism and Holy Communion. After discussion, infant

---

[13]Lee, *Manual,* 158-59.

[14]*True Wesleyan,* July 29, 1843.

[15]Letter of William S. Sullivan, June, 1843, a delegate from Michigan, to his wife in Martin, *Wesleyan Manual,* 20-24.

baptism was retained, although many argued that the adult believer's baptism was the only one authorized by Scripture. In keeping with Wesley's practices in England, all three modes of baptism, sprinkling, affusion, and immersion, were retained; the candidate for the rite could choose his or her desired mode.[16]

The General Rules, as passed, reflected the Wesleyan position on social reforms of the era. Two of the most obvious rules prohibited drunkenness, or the manufacturing, buying, selling or using intoxicating liquors, unless for mechanical, chemical, or medicinal purposes, or, in any way, intentionally and knowingly, aiding others so to do; and the buying or selling of men, women or children, with an intention to enslave them, or holding them as slaves, or claiming that it is right so to do.[17]

The only requirement for membership in the new church was "a desire to flee from the wrath to come, and to be saved from their sins." Applicants manifested their desire by keeping the general rules. After admission had been granted, members were required to continue to observe the rules or face expulsion by the quarterly conference. Business went well and a general spirit of unity was present until Smith raised an issue that would prove to be divisive until the end of the century: secret societies in general, and the Masons in particular. It is necessary to look more closely at this issue.

Masons tended to define theirs as a system of morality that operated independently of any organized religion. Heavy in the use of allegory and symbolism, it rooted itself in antiquity, as far back as Hiram, the builder of Solomon's temple according to legend, whose scriptural description involved craftsmanship, and who had somehow evolved into a stone mason. The essential tools of masonry— the square, the trowel, and the compass—became stylized symbols in modern Masonry.

In 1717, speculative freemasonry came into being as several craft lodges met at a tavern in London and drew up a Constitution for Free and Accepted Masons. Before long, however, a knowledge of stonemasonry and bricklaying counted for nothing and the membership evolved into a type of middle class club for those who had the time and the financial means to join. In America, many prominent leaders in the late colonial and early national periods were Masons, among them Methodists, Baptists, Presbyterians, Congregationalists, and Episcopalians.[18]

Whitney Cross observed that in the burned-over district of Upstate New York, Masonry tended to center in the larger towns and cities, inciting rural resentment of urban superiority and the controlling classes. Furthermore, its rituals and oath-taking were performed in secrecy, and that alone caused adversaries to deem membership morally wrong. Even more troublesome to opponents of Masonry was the issue of taking an oath to show partiality to fellow lodge members in mat-

---

[16]*The Discipline of the Wesleyan Methodist Connection of America* (Boston: O. Scott, 1843), 72ff.

[17]*The Discipline,* 22.

[18]William J. Whalen, *Christianity and American Freemasonry* (Milwaukee, Wis.: Bruce Publishing Company, 1958), 1-13.

ters of law. This subverted justice in society and smacked of class and privilege. In addition, its oaths took the Lord's name in vain and its titles and rituals had the appearance of monarchy and infidelity. Charles G. Finney, a former member of the Masons, wrote a lengthy treatise against true Christians holding membership in secret societies. He claimed that the membership was sworn to persecute its opponents, used profanity in its oaths, profaned the Scriptures, had a false appeal to antiquity, boasted a benevolence that was a sham, constituted a false religion, and in general was to be avoided by all true believers in Christ.[19]

Cross observed that about a fourth of all Protestant clerics and only a twentieth of the laity belonged to Masonic lodges in antebellum central New York. While many clerics could not afford entry fees, Dorothy Lipson's research into a Connecticut lodge found that membership fees had frequently been waived for the clergy.[20]

In an era when an egalitarian wave was rolling across the social landscape, however, Masonry had the potential of being divisive. Then in 1826, the supposed murder of William Morgan, as a consequence of his threatening to expose Masonic secrets, unleashed social forces that had been kept submerged, and a wave of anti-Masonic sentiment swept across the nation, resulting in the formation of the Anti-Masonic Party, and putting many otherwise obscure men into places of leadership within state houses and federal offices. All of this was well known to the deliberating body at Utica.[21]

Edward Smith asked the convention what it planned to do regarding the Masonic question. Such a question might otherwise appear innocuous enough, until it became known to the delegates that Lee, Scott, Horton, and Sunderland belonged to the Masons. The effect was electrifying. Several men threatened to withdraw on the spot. How could men of such stature be involved in such a nefarious organization?

Smith, a large man and a ferocious debater, bore the sobriquet "The Lion of the West." He insisted on a rule in the *Discipline* that would forbid membership to any belonging to a secret society. The Easterners, Scott, Horton, and Sunderland, had significant support, along with the prestige that they carried as leaders in the movement. Smith had his support as well, and he was adamant. Lee had been a Mason since 1821, but as he later wrote: "I was a Mason, but did not feel myself under a masonic obligation to make myself its champion on that occasion." He chose not to reveal his position during the debate, maintaining that it was better to remain neutral so he could offer a compromise. When an impasse developed, Lee offered a mediating rule:

---

[19]Cross, *Burned-over District*, 113-25; C. G. Finney, *The Character, Claims, and Practical Workings of Freemasonry* (n.p.: Western Tract and Book Society, 1869; repr., Chicago: Ezra A. Cook & Co., 1879).

[20]Cross, *Burned-over District*, 113-25; Dorothy Ann Lipson, *Freemasonry in Federalist Connecticut* (Princeton, N.J.: Princeton University Press, 1977), 312-40.

[21]Cross, *Burned-over District*, 113-25.

Question. Have we any advice to give respecting secret oath-bound societies?

Ans. We leave that matter with the several Annual Conferences and *individual* churches.²²

Even though a compromise had been reached, everyone knew that the issue would raise its head again at the next General Conference.

Before concluding business, it only remained to establish the boundaries of the annual conferences. Other than attempts to send missionaries into North Carolina in the middle 1840s, the new denomination focused on New England, the Middle States, and the Old Northwest.

During the Utica convention a Pastoral Address, prepared by Lee and several members of a committee, conveyed to the delegates a general description of the character, condition, and prospects of the organization. Within the body of the lengthy document were references to benevolence, Sabbath-schools, missions, temperance, and an exhortation for all to seek holiness of heart, one of the peculiar doctrines of the followers of Wesley. The delegates were urged, "... above all, brethren, we exhort you to make holiness your motto." Also known as the doctrine of Christian perfection, this fit well in the context of the Second Great Awakening, and the postmillennial desires of many of its leaders to seek to live holy lives, a process that had the potential to bring the Kingdom of God to Earth. Wesleyan Methodists were leaving Utica with the clarion call to lead holy lives.²³

An *ad hoc* committee assigned conference presidents and made pastoral placements until duly elected delegates could meet in their respective annual conferences. Lee was appointed president of the New York Conference and assigned to pastor in Syracuse, New York. When the convention adjourned in the second week of June, Lee hurried back to Andover, packed his belongings, and moved his family to Syracuse.

When he reached Syracuse, Lee discovered that the little band of seceders had no place of worship. For the first few weeks, the group used the facilities of the Congregational church. In time they located a hall that could be used until a permanent solution was found. As things worked out, the Unitarians were just completing a new house of worship, and the Wesleyans were able to purchase the old one. Thus, Lee and his congregation felt ready to face the world in general and certain Methodist Episcopal opposition in Syracuse in particular. Lee's new church enjoyed steady growth as long as the antislavery issue appealed to people in the area.²⁴

---

²²*Discipline of the Wesleyan Methodist Connection,* 1843, 93; See also, William H. Brackney, "The Fruits of a Crusade: Wesleyan Opposition to Secret Societies," *Methodist History* 17 (July 1979): 239-52, for an overview of the role of anti-Masonry in the new denomination.

²³See *True Wesleyan,* November 25, and December 2, 9, 1843, February 22, 1845, for a clear statement of Lee's doctrine of Christian Perfection.

²⁴*True Wesleyan,* May 17, 1845, reported the Syracuse church as having fifty-six members; Lee, *Autobiography,* 252-53.

In addition to building up the Wesleyan congregation in Syracuse, Lee traveled into the surrounding area where he organized other churches. As the appointed president of the New York Conference, Lee constantly recruited new preachers to lead the small congregations that were proliferating in the state. The *True Wesleyan* of July 29, 1843 contained an announcement, "Fifty Preachers Wanted, . . . [men] of suitable qualifications . . . can find immediate employment." The notice was signed by Lee and each of the other five conference presidents. It is not surprising that Methodist papers charged Lee and his preachers with stealing "sheep" from the old church.[25]

On July 19, 1843, the Black River Conference of the MEC, Lee's old organization, met in Syracuse. In their deliberations, the delegates adopted resolutions that addressed the issue of slaveholding. Already passed by other conferences, these resolutions would be presented to the 1844 Methodist Episcopal General Conference. This action followed events in the New England Methodist Episcopal conferences where the bishops had begun to permit antislavery resolutions to be introduced and debated. Those positive steps, however, came too late to stop Wesleyans from secession in 1843, and too late to avoid a split with the slaveholding Methodists.

Lee continued to write articles for the *True Wesleyan* on a variety of topics. One, entitled "Colorphobia," described the symptoms of the malignant disease: "a haughty demeanor towards others, [and] a disregard to character and talents when enveloped in a skin tinged by the Creator a little darker than is agreeable to certain tastes."[26]

Once secession had taken place, relations with the MEC were less than cordial. The two denominations tended to meet in conflict in two formats: in the columns of their respective papers, which Lee seemed to delight in doing, and in public debates. Edward Smith wrote a lengthy article describing his debate in Leesville, Ohio, with a Methodist preacher on whether or not the old church was proslavery. The other favorite debate topic focused on Methodism's arbitrary episcopal government. Lee managed to get himself into a series of such debates in the western borders of the New York State.

In the fall of 1843, Lee received a letter from members of the Methodist Episcopal Church in Jamestown, New York. Trouble over the matter of musical instruments threatened to destroy the congregation. Some opposed using instruments in worship; others did not. While the matter awaited a business meeting for a full airing, their preacher arbitrarily claimed sole authority for making a decision on the matter. Subsequent appeals to the presiding elder and to the bishops were equally unavailing. Someone suggested that the aggrieved members turn to the Wesleyans. Knowing nothing about Wesleyans, they sent a spokesman to Syracuse to consult with Lee. He responded that he would consider such a lengthy trip, only if antislavery lectures could also be arranged in the area. The delegate agreed to arrange for a series of such lectures. Shortly thereafter, Lee headed west in the

---

[25]*True Wesleyan*, July 29, 1843.
[26]*True Wesleyan*, August 5, 1843.

cause of antislavery and church recruitment. When he reached Jamestown, people from the area had been expecting him, and some came from as far as twenty-five miles away to hear him speak.

On the national evangelical scene, churches were feeling the pressures of two sections of the country slowly drifting apart. At the 1844 General Conference of the MEC, Lee, Scott, and Smith were in the galleries as reporters for the Wesleyans. The ideologies of the northern and southern camps had firmed since they had met four years previously. The northern wing was tired of being pushed around by the southerners; the proslavery clergy had an aggressiveness that did not bode well for a harmonious convention. In addition, the Methodists had watched as one congregation after another had seceded, with many going over to the Wesleyans. When the issue of Bishop James O. Andrew's slaves surfaced in the middle of May, the breach opened. By the time they adjourned, the Few Amendment of 1840, which disallowed testimony by blacks in church trials in states in which blacks could not testify in court, had been rescinded and the southern delegates had seceded from the church. The main thing that bothered the Wesleyans in the galleries was the fact that the delegates had not acted out of moral outrage but for purposes of expediency. As soon as the new seceder church had threatened to impact Methodist membership, the delegates had suddenly seen slavery for the evil monster that it was. That, of itself, probably ended any hope of reuniting on the part of the Wesleyan Methodists.[27]

The Wesleyans' New York Conference opened on June 19, 1844. Lee was elected president of the Conference and corresponding secretary of the Board of Missions. He was not stationed as pastor at Syracuse, a move that placed him in a position to be selected for work in the General Conference. Not surprisingly, he was also elected as a delegate to the first General Conference scheduled to meet in Cleveland that autumn. The Methodist periodicals, still referring to the new church as "Scottites," reported on Lee's New York conference. Calling him "The 'Logical' Lee," they interpreted his assignment to be that of traveling the area in an effort to get more Methodists to secede, as well as to raise funds for his own salary, scoffing "Such a Missionary Work!!"[28] Undaunted, Lee continued his travels, stopping in Fulton, New York, where he had served as pastor six years previous, and where he dedicated the new Wesleyan meeting house.

Lee's labors of writing and traveling consumed his energies until the first week in October, when he journeyed to Cleveland for the new denomination's first General Conference, at which he was appointed president *pro tem* by a nominating committee. Scott was elected president, but declined to serve for a variety of reasons, and on the second ballot, Lee was elected president. Again, as at Utica, the secret society issue surfaced; this time in the form of a request to appoint a

---

[27]Luther Lee and E. Smith, *The Debates of the General Conference of the ME. Church, May, 1844, To Which Is Added, a Review of the Proceedings of Said Conference,* (New York: Orange Scott for the Wesleyan Methodist Connection of America, 1845); Mathews, *Slavery and Methodism,* 246-70.

[28]*True Wesleyan,* July 13, 1844.

committee on secret societies. A disturbance accompanied the discussion, but the committee was appointed. In time the group recommended a rule that all members of secret societies be excluded from membership. Scott and Horton argued against such a rule; Smith supported it. Smith vigorously denounced Scott and his arguments. Lee later observed that a debate on admitting the devil into membership could not have stirred more animation. Lee demanded that Smith come to order; Smith defied him. Lee tried again, "You will come to order if there's power enough in this house to bring you to order." The delegates rose to their feet affirming, "The chair shall be sustained."[29] Smith complied.

The issue of secret societies had geographical dimensions. Generally it was the West versus the East. Cyrus Prindle submitted a resolution that the Connection be divided into two general conferences that would reflect the east-west opinions. Scott, Horton, and Prindle were particularly concerned about the negative effects of a strong stand against secret societies, because to insist on rules against such societies could only impede the future growth of their infant church. For the West, however, purity could not be subsumed to expediency, and Prindle's resolution mustered only three votes. Eventually the delegates passed the following rule, after a bitter struggle:

Question. Have we any directions to give concerning oath-bound societies?

Answer. We will on no account tolerate our ministers and members in joining secret oath-bound societies, or holding fellowship with them, as in the judgment of the Wesleyan Methodist Connection it is inconsistent with our duties to God and Christianity to hold such connections.

The stage was thus set for future problems, since the founders, most of them Masons, argued that only the organizing convention in Utica had power to pass such restrictive rules.[30]

In other matters, the General Conference adopted the *True Wesleyan* as its official organ, and, after substantial debate, especially by Scott and Horton who favored leaving its offices in Boston, ordered its removal to New York City. Lee was elected editor of the publication and also of the *Juvenile Wesleyan.* Not everyone, however, was enamored with Lee's appointment; a hostile reporter wrote in another church paper that "they have jumped over O. Scott's head, and made Luther Lee editor, whose caustic and bitter pen will involve the Connection in quarrels with their neighbors."[31]

In each of the annual conferences, significant growth had been reported, most of it coming in the recent months. President Lee admonished the delegates to remain solid in their purpose, reminding them: "The eyes of the slave and the

---

[29]*True Wesleyan,* October 12, 1844; Lee, *Autobiography,* 272.

[30]See George Pegler, *Autobiography of the Life and Times of Reverend George Pegler* (Syracuse, N.Y.: Wesleyan Methodist Publishing House, 1875), 420-22, for a description of Smith; See also, *True Wesleyan,* November 30, 1844.

[31]From the *Olive Branch,* in the *True Wesleyan,* November 2, 1844.

slave's friends are upon us. Our union is their only hope."³² On October 10, the session adjourned, and wearily Lee and his wife set out for Syracuse to prepare to move to New York.³³

In New York, the Lees located near the Wesleyan Book Room. The next four years passed quickly for Lee. His work on the *True Wesleyan* consumed most of his time. He regularly reported the progress of such social issues as temperance, female moral reform, female working conditions, educational reforms, and in the realm of politics, the Liberty Party and its candidates. In national issues, the annexation of Texas filled several columns. Of course, Lee took a strong stand in opposition to proslavery policies.³⁴

During his tenure as editor, Lee and his colleagues never forgot the useful purpose that camp meetings served, not only in evangelism but also in the cause of antislavery, temperance, and other reforms of the era. A June 1846 issue of the paper advertised such a camp, which was to serve as the "annual feast of tabernacles" for the New York Conference. "All who believe the Gospel is opposed to slavery and intemperance, as well as to other sins, come and hear it preached in that beautiful grove," at Verplank's Point, fifty miles up the Hudson from New York City.³⁵

The second General Conference convened on October 4, 1848 at King Street Chapel in New York City. Lee was not reelected as president. He was, however, reelected as editor of the *True Wesleyan*. He vowed, however, that it would be the last time he would serve.

Lee kept up a steady flow of articles in the *True Wesleyan* concerning his hatred of the Fugitive Slave Law passed in the autumn of 1850; he was especially effective in his discourse, since he, by that time, had firsthand experience with slave owners. He continued to edit the paper and made regular forays in the cause of enlarging the denomination, and, of course, to speak on behalf of reforms.

Early in the spring of 1852, Lee wearied of journalism and the editorship of the *True Wesleyan*. It was time for him to move on to other challenges. He resigned the editorship and accepted the pastorate at his old church in Syracuse. The issues throughout April were replete with accolades that various conferences and individuals sent in, recognizing the superior manner in which Lee had acquitted himself. He chose to make the break prior to the annual New York Conference.³⁶

---

³²*True Wesleyan*, October 19, 1844.
³³*True Wesleyan*, October 12, 1844; Lee, *Autobiography*, 273.
³⁴See *True Wesleyan*, "Who Is Birney?" July 6, 1844; "Horton Will Vote for Birney," July 20, 1844; "Debate on Texas," March 16, 1844; "Oregon and War," May 2, 1846; and "A Few Reasons Why Christians Should Not Smoke," October 11, 1845, for a sampling of Lee's attitude on general reform.
³⁵Under "Editorial Ramblings," Lee frequently wrote of leaving the "city of dust, smoke, and noise" to travel to a camp meeting, where he frequently was an evangelist. *True Wesleyan*, August 25, 1849.
³⁶"The Editor's Farewell," *True Wesleyan*, April 24, 1852.

By the end of 1885, Lee concluded his labors as a Wesleyan Methodist pastor in Syracuse, and later that year entered a new phase in his life as a professor at the fledging college the Wesleyans had founded near Jackson, Michigan. While he continued to advance the cause of several social reforms throughout his lifetime, his remaining focus would essentially be that of education at what became Adrian College. In 1867 he returned to the MEC where he pastored, superannuated and ended his earthly labors in 1889.

Lee is remembered by religious historians for his efforts to end the institution of slavery, to advance the cause of women preachers, to lead in female moral reforms, to arouse the nation to the evils of liquor and all that it entailed, and as a college professor to promulgate the doctrine of holiness in the Wesleyan tradition.

Chapter 5

Radical Holiness Becomes a World Christian Movement: The Influence of Isabella Sarah Leonard in Great Britain, Australia and Singapore, 1881-1892

David Bundy

Miss Isabella Leonard

Isabella S. Leonard (1840-1911) looks across a century at us through a single printed photograph. She is at once sympathetic, determined, intense, disciplined, intelligent, strong and lonely.[1] She appears as Ella K. Crossley described her, "nothing if not direct."[2] She was a woman, single, with many women friends, respected as a colleague by powerful leaders of the global Holiness Movements.

---

[1] Lucy Prescott Vane, "Miss Isabella Leonard," *Way of Holiness* 3, 1 (April 1911), 4.
[2] E. K. Crossley, *He Heard from God: The Story of Frank Crossley* (London: Salvationist Publishing and Supplies, 1959), 62.

She sought to live out her "calling" at a time when ministry options in the church were marginally available to women. Following guidance she claimed from the Holy Spirit, she traversed the globe with the dual missions of leading people into the experience of entire sanctification and enabling the ministry of women.

In seeking her goals, Leonard was one of the quiet forces that transformed the Radical Holiness Movements from feisty proponents of their local faith and social visions to participants on the world stage. Her involvement on four continents accelerated, supported and/or created Radical Holiness groups and institutions. During the period 1881-1892 she made significant contributions to the global development of the Radical Holiness Movements in the context of Victorian/Edwardian Britain and Colonial Australia.

Leonard and the more famous male Radical Holiness evangelists were participants in the American and Victorian/Edwardian optimism of the post-1870 period that continued up to World War I. Holiness was gaining adherents worldwide, using new technologies including publishing and transportation. Like most Radical Holiness believers before 1901, her preaching and social action were fueled by a post-millennial eschatology. She negotiated the structures of power and privilege to present her Holiness vision, as part of the wave of democratization in religion. Using network theory, with attention to issues of power raised by Michel Foucault and nuanced by others,[3] her relationships, publications, and writings, this essay examines her contributions to the Radical Holiness Movements during what must have seemed for her a blessed decade.

The sources for the study are five books for which she was editor and sometimes contributor, a pamphlet,[4] a number of articles in the Holiness press, and a large number of references in church documents, mission publications, newspapers, government documents, and transportation records, which are scattered in publications from the USA, Great Britain, India, Singapore and Australia. To complicate matters, the one extensive obituary contains errors of name, fact and date.[5] More helpful is a testimony by Leonard written the year before her death and published posthumously.[6]

---

[3]Michel Foucault, *Histoire de la sexualité* (Paris: Gallimard, 1976-1984), idem, *Sécurité, territoire, population: cours au Collège de France, 1977-1978* (Paris: Seuil, Gallimard, 2004).

[4]Isabella S. Leonard, *Letter to an Inquirer Seeking Heart Purity* (n.p.: n.p., n.d.). There is no internal evidence to assist with approximate dating of the publication.

[5]Vane, "Miss Isabella Leonard," 4-5. Lucy Prescott Vane (1827-1929) and Leonard were lifelong friends, fellow organizers in the early Woman's Foreign Mission Society, and Holiness advocates.

[6]I. S. Leonard, "Forty-three years in Canaan," *Way of Holiness* 1, 12 (March 1910), 139; Isabella Leonard, "A Witness to the Cleansing Power," *Way of Holiness* 10, 12 (March 1919), 5; *Way of Holiness* 11, 1 (April 1919), 5. Note that the sources remain fragmentary, with most of the documentation coming from a little more than a decade of her frenetically busy life.

From Doctor's Daughter to Evangelist in England

The early life of Isabella Leonard was a life of privilege in pre-Civil War southern Indiana. Her father, Sommerville E. Leonard, was a published scholar, medical doctor and abolitionist.[7] He was part of the cultivated leadership of New Albany, Indiana, where he was founding chair of the board of Indiana Asbury Female College.[8] The family home radiated privileged class, comfort and stability. Her home and the Methodist Episcopal church of her youth provided a warm piety that was urbanely Holiness. The Sunday prayer meetings held in the Leonard home reinforced that piety.

Isabella Leonard was graduated from Indiana Asbury Female College in 1858, and, like many other young educated women, Isabella Leonard took advantage of the new opportunities for women. She became first an evangelist (1858-1867), primarily for children, and toward the end of that period, after much study and spiritual stress, experienced entire sanctification during a service in a Methodist Episcopal church on January 11th, 1867.[9]

Leonard served as Preceptoress at Hamline University (1867-1868) and at Illinois Female College (1868-1869; now MacMurray College). Later in 1869 she joined the Woman's Foreign Mission Society (WFMS) of the Methodist Episcopal Church and was a founder of the Western Regional WFMS organized on 4 April 1870 in St. Louis, under the leadership of "our beloved Mrs. W. Willing with Isabella S. Leonard, assistant corresponding secretary."[10] She was also involved in the founding of the national periodical publication of the WFMS, *Heathen Woman's Friend*, and served on the editorial board for several years.[11] It was during this period that she came into contact with Isabella Thoburn and James Thoburn, Methodist Episcopal missionaries to India and with Bishop William Taylor. The WFMS involvement lasted throughout her lifetime, although the intensity of that relationship varied greatly.

---

[7]S. E. Leonard, "Art. II: A Case of pregnancy attended by a remarkable discharge from the uterus, followed by a safe delivery," *Western Journal of Medicine and Surgery* 3 (1841), 87-91; Pamela R. Peters, *The Underground Railroad in Floyd County, Indiana* (New Albany, IN: Author, 1999), 162, 163.

[8]*Local Laws of the State of Indiana, passed at the Thirty-fourth Session of the General Assembly* (Indianapolis: John D. Defrees, 1850), 59-61. S. E. Leonard, "Indiana Asbury Female College," *The Daily Ledger* 2 (25 August 1851), 2. *Occasion of the Opening of Indiana Asbury Female College on February 27th 1852* (New Albany: Morman & Matthews, 1852).

[9]Vane, "Miss Isabella Leonard," 4. See the description of the experience in Isabella Leonard, "A Witness to the Cleansing Power," *Way of Holiness* 11, 1 (April 1919), 5. See also: Leonard, "Forty-three years in Canaan," 139: "To-morrow, January 11th 1910 will be the forty-third Anniversary of my entering the blessed experience of entire sanctification."

[10]Anonymous, "Historical Note: A Side Light on our History," *Heathen Woman's Friend* 25 (1893), 272-273.

[11]Isabella (Bella) S. Leonard was one of the original editorial committee. See, for example: *Heathen Woman's Friend* 1, 13 (Jun 1870), 207; *Heathen Woman's Friend* 2, 2 (Aug 1870), 24; *Heathen Woman's Friend* 2, 8 (Feb 1871), 96.

According to the obituary by Lucy Prescott Vane, "On March 21st, 1873, Miss Leonard received a definite call to evangelistic work. 'This one thing I do'— was her motto. After her call she had eight years unbroken work in America."[12] Her evangelistic work, was primarily in the towns, cities and camp meetings of the USA Mid-West. There are numerous enthusiastic news items published in local newspapers. Her preaching at the Silver Lake Camp Meeting, near New Albany, Indiana, attracted national attention: "Isabella Leonard was one of the most impassioned leaders in the exercises, and helped bring many to the anxious seat."[13]

Leonard was not an inexperienced evangelist or writer when she stepped onto the world stage at the Ecumenical Methodist Conference, held in London, 1881. She arrived with letters of recommendation from William Taylor and from several other American Methodist Episcopal luminaries. Taylor wrote: "The success of Miss Leonard in conjunction with our pastors, in soul-saving work for Jesus, and the entire sanctification of believers, has been very marked through a long series of years."[14] Her name and the names of other women were not recorded in the published proceedings, nor were the women recognized as delegates. The American Methodist Episcopal women were there to observe and to protect their interests, with the assistance of sympathetic male colleagues who did serve as delegates.[15]

After the London Conference, Leonard remained in England until 17 December 1883, working as an evangelist. Much of what is known of her schedule is found in a diary and letters of Harriett Mosely who experienced sanctification under Leonard's ministry, and who became her protégé and traveling companion. Thus we know that on Sunday, 16 December, before accompanying the ailing Mosely to Australia and the prescribed drier climate, Leonard "took a service in a large Wesleyan church in Plymouth."[16]

Australia, 1884-1886/1887

The evaluations of Leonard's evangelistic work by Wesleyan Methodist pastors in England were certainly positive for she arrived in Australia on 14 February

---

[12]Vane, "Miss Isabella Leonard," 4.

[13]*Los Angeles Herald* (28 November 1890), 3.

[14]As cited, without documentation, in Evans, *Evangelism and Revivals in Australia, 1880-1914*, First Volume. (n.p.: n.p., 2007), 62.

[15]*Proceedings of the Oecumenical Methodist Conference, held in City Road Chapel, London, September 1881*, introduction by Rev. William Arthur, M.A. (Cincinnati: Walden and Stowe; New York: Phillips and Hunt, 1882).

[16]Isabella S. Leonard, *The Power of Grace: Or, Memorials of Harriett Mosely* (London: Richard K. Dickinson [1886], second printing [1888]), 23-29, *et passim*. Quote page 48. The introduction was signed by Isabella Leonard, 28 January 1886 in Sydney, NSW, Australia.

1884[17] bearing letters from British pastors recommending her to their Australian colleagues.[18] At a New South Wales District Meeting in March 1884, Leonard was introduced to the pastors, and letters of reference from the USA and Britain were read. In circuit after circuit, pastors received her offers "to conduct meetings with special reference to the promotion of holiness, in connection with the ministers and people of the Methodist Church."[19] Respected pastors became her supporters, sponsors and co-workers in the meetings. These included James A. Carruthers, James A. Nolan, J. Oram, William G. Taylor, John Watsford and S. Wilkinson. When Harriett Mosely became too ill to travel with Leonard, it was arranged for her to live in the parsonage of the Central Methodist Mission in Sydney with the W. G. Taylor family.[20]

Leonard introduced herself again, but to the entire Methodist public, in an open letter to the "Ministers and Members of the Wesleyan Church of New South Wales." The letter signed on 15 April 1884 was published in the *Weekly Advocate* of 10 May 1884 and sought to rally the Wesleyan Methodist Church, clergy and laity, to the cause of "Scriptural holiness." She affirmed that her voyage to Australia was "so contrary to my desires," "so signally of God's calling." She urged the Wesleyan Methodist Church to "unite with me to ask and claim of God a gracious awakening upon the subject of Christian holiness for Methodism of New South Wales." She attributed to "the suggestion of the Holy Spirit" that "a Prayer League be formed of such as will at least press this matter before God's throne." She implored each reader to join with her and "send your name, as a member of the Prayer League…and we shall together be strengthened by this union in prayer and faith."[21] This Prayer League probably insured the quick success of the Holiness periodical *Glad Tidings* in June 1885. There was no competing structure.

---

[17]"Extracolonial Passengers. Arrivals in South Australia," *South Australian Register* (Saturday 16 February 1884), 2, reported the arrival of Misses Leonard and Mosely on the steamer *Port Phillip*, from London, as did the report "Shipping, Port Adelaide. Arrived," *Adelaide Observer* (Saturday 16 February 1884), 4. Leonard and Mosely arrived February 14th on the *Port Phillip*.

[18]Evans, *Evangelism and Revivals in Australia, 1880-1914*, 62. Daryl L. Lightfoot and Sue Pacey stated that prior arrangements had been made by John Watsford, head of the Australian Wesleyan Methodist delegation to the London conference, for Leonard to make an evangelistic tour to Australia. No evidence of this has yet, to my knowledge, been published. Daryl L. Lightfoot and Sue Pacey, "Ministering Women of the Methodist Episcopal Church of America in New South Wales (Part 1) Miss Isabella Leonard in New South Wales 1884-1886 and Miss Sophia Blackmore," *Historical Bulletin. World Methodist Historical Society* 38, 1 (2011), 11.

[19]*Weekly Advocate* (15 March 1884), 404, cited in Evans, *Evangelism and Revivals in Australia, 1880-1914*, 60-61.

[20]W. G. Taylor, Letter to Leonard, 16 February 1886, published in Isabella S. Leonard, *The Power of Grace*, 144.

[21]*Weekly Advocate* (10 May 1884), 50. The text is cited in its entirety in Evans, *Evangelism and Revivals in Australia, 1880-1914*, 64-65.

The timing of the arrival of Leonard and Mosely could scarcely have been more fortuitous. There was a lot of interest in the doctrine of entire sanctification among the Methodists, the result of the work of evangelists from inside and outside Australia, from William Taylor to John Inskip, W. B. Osborne and John Watsford, for almost two decades. There was also a passion to evangelize, which had not always gone well. A Wesleyan Methodist from Mittagong reported that evangelistic marches through the streets were greeted by "a running hail of rotten eggs." He observed, "however romantic rotten eggs and brickbats may appear in the history of early Methodism, we did not find them conducive to piety in the least degree."[22] The desire to communicate with the expanding population and to improve the spiritual life of the church was conducive to a partnership with Isabella Leonard.

Throughout 1884 and most of 1885, Leonard, sometimes accompanied by Mosely, preached in the Wesleyan Methodist Churches. Services were sometimes announced in the newspapers;[23] published reviews were always positive.[24] Camp meetings, usually in the form of a series of full days of meetings, were conducted. The first that has been identified was at St. Leonard's Wesleyan Methodist in Sydney.[25] The *Sydney Morning Herald* published an informative brief advertisement for a quite intense, but apparently typical, week in April 1884:

> A six-days' MISSION, for the Promotion of Holiness will be commenced to-morrow, and continued every evening till Friday next. Services will be at 11 a.m., 3 p.m., and 7 p.m. Miss Leonard, of the M. E. Church, will conduct the mission. Bible readings will be held on Monday and Wednesday at 3:30 p.m. A camp-meeting will take place on the St. Leonard's Reserve on Good Friday.... Several ministers and others are expected to assist in these services. All classes are invited. Voluntary contributions will be received at the close of the services towards expenses of the mission.[26]

---

[22] *Weekly Advocate* (3 May 1884), 45, cited in Evans, *Evangelism and Revivals in Australia, 1880-1914*, 62. Isabella Leonard had her own struggles, but the Miss Leonard noted as the winner of an assault case in Cooma in August 1884, was apparently not "our" Miss Leonard: "Evening News Cablegrams," *The Manaro Mercury, and Cooma and Bombala Advertiser (NSW)* (Saturday 23 August 1884), 3: "At Cooma Police Court yesterday, the case of *Miss Leonard* v. Reilly for assault was settled by defendant paying professional and court costs and witnesses' expenses, Mr. Craig for complainant."

[23] For example, the announcement of services in West Kangaloon: "Wesleyan," *The Bowral Free Press* (Saturday 29 March 1884), 3.

[24] All of the published reports of Leonard's work during 1884-1886 in the *Weekly Advocate* (Wesleyan Methodist) have been collected and transcribed by Robert Evans, *Evangelism and Revivals in Australia, 1880-1914*, 62-74.

[25] *Christian Colonist* (Friday 4 April 1884), 3: "A Miss Leonard, credited from the American Methodist Episcopal Church, is announced to conduct a mission in Sydney, 'for the promotion of holiness.'"

[26] "St. Leonard's Wesleyan Church," *The Sydney Morning Herald* (Saturday 5 April 1884), 2.

The *Christian Colonist* reported in May that Leonard had conducted "a Holiness Mission at Mittagong, Bowral and Kangaboo, New South Wales."[27] In September 1884, similar services were conducted by the "lady evangelist" in the Wesleyan Methodist Church of Illawara: "There were very fair audiences in each instance, and Miss Leonard spoke earnestly and feelingly. Services will be conducted through the week by the same lady…"[28] December 1884 found Leonard in Gunning, NSW:

> It was publically announced at the Wesleyan Church that Miss Leonard (of whom we have heard so much of late) will commence a series of evangelistic services in Gunning next week. From what we have heard from other places where Miss Leonard has recently laboured, we may confidently expect much good to follow the above services. The first will take place next Sabbath.[29]

Leonard's work, while focused on the Wesleyan Methodists, had an important ecumenical component. In addition to cultivating the Bible Christians, Primitive Methodists and the Free Methodists, Leonard worked with the Salvation Army.[30] During a visit of Colonel Ballington Booth and Major Howard from London in September 1884, her role was highlighted in the Maitland press: "…a large and enthusiastic meeting was held in the Barracks in the evening.… Miss Leonard, a lady from America, adorned the meeting; appealing to them if they were working for God as the Salvation Army were doing. She gave some of her experiences when speaking to women of their souls."[31] She was the primary spirituality speaker; the men regaled the crowd with impressive statistics about the Salvation Army; theirs was a different use of power.

As Leonard was preaching throughout New South Wales, changes were happening in Sydney. The Wesleyan Methodist Conference had nearly voted to close York Street Wesleyan Methodist Church. Against his preferences, William G. Taylor (1845-1934) was assigned to the congregation. It was in severe decline. Deciding radical changes were needed, he renamed the church the Central Methodist Mission and began (April 1884) to evangelize in Sydney. For example, an advertisement in the *Sydney Morning Herald* of 5 May 1884 announced sermons inside and an open air service, as well as joint services, and solidarity with the Gospel Temperance Mission of Richard T. Booth.[32]

Taylor's methods paralleled those of the Salvation Army, which worked in Sydney beginning in 1883. He used street preaching, brass bands and even "shocking pink" posters and handbills to advertise services. A singer of some

---

[27]"News of the Churches," *Christian Colonist* (Friday 16 May 1884), 3.

[28]"The Scrap Album," *Illawara Mercury* (Tuesday 23 September 1884), 2.

[29]*Goulburn Evening Penny Post* (Thursday 25 December 1884), 5.

[30]Leonard (and Mosely) regularly worked with the Salvation Army. See Leonard, *The Power of Grace*, 60, 70, 120, 130.

[31]"The Salvation Army. Visit of Colonel Booth and Major Howard," *The Maitland Mercury and Hunter River General Advertiser (NSW)* (Saturday 20 September 1884), 13.

[32]"Advertising," *Sydney Morning Herald* (Saturday 10 May 1884), 2.

ability, he also made imaginative use of choral and solo music in his services and after-meetings. He stressed the place of prayer...."[33]

It is unclear exactly when Taylor and Leonard made contact or when Mosely moved into his home. Certainly Leonard's preaching, reported on 9 November 1885 at a camp meeting organized by Taylor, was not her first involvement with his effort to renew his moribund congregation. It was decided during the camp meeting to have meetings at the Mission for the "promotion of holiness."[34] Two days later, the first Holiness Convention took place at the York Street church. According to the report published in the Wesleyan Methodist *Weekly Advocate*, Isabella Leonard was the primary preacher and answered questions from the audience on entire sanctification. Both questions and answers were published in a two-page supplement to the *Weekly Advocate*. Another holiness meeting was scheduled for later in the week.[35] A three-day convention was scheduled for early December. Once again, Leonard was a speaker.

Between the November and December events, the Tasmania District of the Wesleyan Methodist Church read a letter from J. A. Nolan "respecting Miss Leonard, a lady evangelist, who is being instrumental in doing much good in the promotion of holiness, and is working in conjunction with the Methodist Church." It was decided to recommend inviting her to conduct meetings, "as opportunity may permit."[36]

In January 1886 a day-long Holiness convention took place at the Central Methodist Mission. At that event, in the evening both George Müller of Bristol and Isabella Leonard preached, advocating Holiness: "a large number responded" and "some fifty publically avowed themselves as inquirers and many of them stepped into blessed enjoyment of this grace."[37] Mosely died on 7 December 1885. On 28 January 1886 Leonard signed the introduction to Mosley's published diary. In a letter to Leonard, Taylor wrote, "To me personally she was helpful in my search after this great blessing. Her arguments were forceful, but her life

---

[33]Don Wright, "Taylor, William George (1845–1934)," *Australian Dictionary of Biography*, National Centre of Biography, Australian National University, http://adb.anu.edu.au/biography/taylor-william-george-8766/text15365, published first in hard copy 1990, accessed online 10 February 2016.

[34]*Weekly Advocate* (14 November 1885), 271, cited in and transcribed by Robert Evans, *Evangelism and Revivals in Australia, 1880-1914*, 70.

[35]*Weekly Advocate* (21 November 1885), Supplement, cited in and transcribed (without the questions or answers) by Robert Evans, *Evangelism and Revivals in Australia, 1880-1914*, 71.

[36]"Wesleyan District Meeting, Hobart," *Daily Telegraph* (Tuesday 17 November 1885), 3.

[37]*Weekly Advocate* (30 January 1886), 355, cited in Evans, *Evangelism and Revivals in Australia, 1880-1914*, 72.

was the argument that ever carried most weight."³⁸ In the introduction, Leonard stated, "The entire profits, if any ... will be given to Missionary Work in India and Bishop Taylor's Work in Africa, in both of which Miss M[osely], was so deeply interested."³⁹ The publication sold well enough to merit a second printing in 1888.

The stage was set for the organization of the United Methodist Holiness Association (sometimes called the Methodist Holiness Association) in mid-1886, which sought to bring together persons from the different Methodist churches (Wesleyan Methodist, Primitive Methodist, Bible Christian, and United Free Methodist). The Australian Methodist political climate was favorable to this endeavor because the various Methodist groups had been discussing union for a long time.⁴⁰ The program of the Association was to maintain a "Union for daily prayer," hold a monthly meeting for the promotion of holiness in Sydney, provide speakers for churches wanting holiness evangelists, and publish holiness literature. The periodical publication of the Association, *Glad Tidings* (1886-1944) had great success. Thanks, it would appear, to Leonard's network and the interest raised by her preaching, the initial circulation was about 10,000 copies, moving to 15,000 within the year, far exceeding expectations.⁴¹ The program of the Association was that of Isabella Leonard.

Isabella Leonard, now "the celebrated evangelist," continued to preach in New South Wales, Queensland and perhaps Tasmania, even attracting Anglicans to her services.⁴² Then it was reported that she was on her way to India.

> The novelty of a lady preacher was witnessed recently in the Wesleyan Church, Hay. Miss Leonard... a lady evangelist, conducted three services on Sunday, Monday and Tuesday evenings.... Large congregations on Sunday listened to the earnest but calm address of the lady preacher. At her invitation a large number came out from their seats and knelt around the Communion rail. Miss Leonard believes and teaches that it is possible for a Christian to live free from sin. This, we understand, is one of the distinctive doctrines of the Methodist Church, and also of the

---

³⁸W. G. Taylor, Letter to Isabella S. Leonard, 16 February 1886, published in Leonard, *The Power of Grace*, 144-145, quote 145. It is unfortunate, that in his autobiography both Leonard and Mosely were written out of the history. See William George Taylor, *The Life-story of an Australian Evangelist, with an account of the origin and growth of the Sydney Central Mission* (London: Epworth Press, 1920).

³⁹Leonard, *The Power of Grace*, 9.

⁴⁰For a summary of this discussion, see: Ian Breward, "Methodist Reunion in Australia," in *Methodism in Australia, A History*, Glen O'Brien and Hilary M. Carey, eds. (Burlington, VT: Ashgate, 2015), 119-131. Breward did not mention the Methodist Holiness Association.

⁴¹Evans, *Evangelism and Revivals in Australia, 1880-1914*, 73. There appears to be no complete file of *Glad Tidings* in existence, and it is not available from the period of Leonard's involvement.

⁴²"Home News by Cable, London, Thursday," *Armidale Express and New England General Advertiser* (Tuesday 26 October 1886), 5.

Salvation Army. Miss Leonard subsequently left for Melbourne, where she will conduct a mission and then proceed to India.[43]

Leonard left Melbourne for India with a protégé, Sophia Blackmore. This relationship and the personal connections of Leonard that were brought to bear in Blackmore's case had an important impact on Singapore. Assisted by William Oldham and her Methodist Episcopal WFMS friend, Mary Clarke Nind,[44] Leonard secured Blackmore's appointment as a WFMS missionary to Singapore.[45] It remains unclear exactly how long Leonard was in India at this juncture. There is also the tantalizing comment that she originally planned to leave India "early in 1888," but was now undecided.[46]

Great Britain, 1888-1892

From India, Leonard traveled to Great Britain, specifically Manchester. According to Ella K. Crossley, Leonard was invited to preach at tent meetings on the Manchester estate of Francis (Frank) William Crossley (1839-1897).[47] During the summer of 1889, after such a meeting, which also featured William and Catherine Booth, Francis Crossley experienced entire sanctification. Shortly thereafter, he had a discussion with Leonard about the practical implications of that religious commitment.[48] The result: Crossleys sold "Fairlie," their luxurious

---

[43]*Gundagai Times and Tumut, Adelong and Murrumbidgee District Advertiser* (Friday 10 December 1886), 2; See also Anonymous, "News," *Heathen Woman's Friend* 18 (January 1887), 182: "Leonard...sailed for India last month in company of Rev. and Mrs. C. P. Hard."

[44]See the volume written "By her Children," *Mary Clarke Nind and her Work* (Chicago: Published for the Woman's Foreign Missionary Society, 1906), 29-34 (regarding Isabella Leonard), 199 (regarding Sophia Blackmore). Leonard convinced Nind to lead the Mid-Western section of the WFMS.

[45]Theodore R. Doraisamy, *Sophia Blackmore in Singapore* (Singapore: General Conference Women's Society of Christian Service, Methodist Church of Singapore, 1987); Lightfoot and Pacey, "Ministering Women of the Methodist Episcopal Church of America in New South Wales," 11-15.

[46]"From Missionary Letters," *Heathen Woman's Friend* 19, (8 February 1888), 217-218.

[47]J. Rendel Harris, *The Life of Francis William Crossley* (London: James Nisbet & Co., 1900); it is unclear how the connection with the Crossleys was made, but it was probably through the Salvation Army, of which Crossley, a friend of the Booth family, was a major supporter. Crossley first developed an efficient rubber processing machine and then purchased the British and American patents for the internal combustion gasoline engine, producing improved versions. In addition to supporting the Salvation Army, he subsidized Holiness publishing, built healthy housing for his employees and supported Holiness missions and evangelism around the world. He built a Richard Crossley Hall at Northfield for Dwight L. Moody (1885) and attended Keswick (and other) Conventions on occasion.

[48]Harris, *Life of Francis William Crossley*, 127; Crossley, *He Heard from God*, 62.

estate, and founded Star Hall, a multidimensional ministry center in Ancoats, a major industrial slum in central Manchester.

Emily Kerr Crossley, wife of Francis, described Star Hall and its ministry, noting that "the separation of rich and poor had often troubled us." Star Hall provided ministry facilities and an apartment for the Crossleys and "a dwelling house for the yet unfound workers…[and]on August the 4th, 1889, work was begun." One of the first residents of Star Hall was Isabella Leonard.[49]

She made it clear that their goal, like that of the Salvation Army was to transform lives and living using the experience of sanctification.[50] The Autumn Holiness Conventions were important events.[51] The sermons of the first two were edited by Isabella S. Leonard.[52] Among the speakers at the first convention were I. S. Leonard, G. D. Watson, and Francis Sanford.[53] At the second conference in 1890 speakers included I. S. Leonard, G. D. Watson, Mr. and Mrs. James Rendel Harris, and William McDonald.[54]

Leonard also worked with Richard Reader Harris, QC, a former civil and mining engineer in Britain and Bolivia, who became a prominent lawyer in London. His conversion to Holiness Christianity brought a concern for the poor, both for their social and spiritual needs. Beginning in 1885 he established a "Mission Hall" in Speke Hall in London, which was modeled after the work of the Salvation Army and after William Boardman's and Mary Baxter's Bethshan. Harris purchased a building (1887), and attracted a congregation of more than 1,400. In 1889 he experienced entire sanctification at Star Hall and immediately

---

[49] She was still there in 1891, when she was recorded in the British census. "Star Hall," 1891 England Census, Lancashire, Manchester, Ancoats, District 47, 5. It reported 10 single women listed as "domestics" including Isabella Leonard also described as an "evangelist-preacher." Also living there: Francis William Crossley, "head", Emily Crossley, "wife", Francis Crossley, "son" and Tessie Ann Kerr, "Visitor," "School Teacher" from Scotland.

[50] Mrs. Crossley [Emily Kerr Crossley], "Star Hall," *Tongues of Fire* 1, 6 (June 1891), 3 (quotes); *Tongues of Fire* 1, 7 (July 1891), 3; *Tongues of Fire* 1, 8 (August 1891), 3. Note that Crossley spoke at the Speke Hall's 4th "Anniversary Meeting," *Tongues of Fire* 1, 6 (June 1891), 4-5.

[51] See also the summary of an article by J. G. Gladwin in the *Bombay Guardian* in *Tongues of Fire* 1, 5 (May 1891), 3. Gladwin attended the November 1890 convention. According to Gladwin, an "occasional paper," *The Star*, listed 22 scheduled weekly meetings in Star Hall or in the streets of Ancoats, Manchester. No copies of this paper have been found.

[52] Isabella S. Leonard, ed. *Addresses on Holiness delivered at Star Hall Convention, Manchester, November 18th to 25th, 1890* (London: S. W. Partridge, 1891).

[53] On Francis Dwight Sanford see "The Late Rev. F. D. Sanford," *King's Highway. A Journal of Scriptural Holiness* 24 (1895), 32-33. This was compiled from information by his widow, Mary E. Sanford, and from a newspaper account in Worcester, MA, USA.

[54] Isabella S. Leonard, ed. *Addresses on Holiness delivered at the Star Hall Convention, Manchester, October 18th to 25th, 1891* (London: S. W. Partridge, 1891). See "Manchester Convention," *Tongues of Fire* 1, 11 (November 1891), 4.

invited G. D. Watson and Francis Sanford to preach at Speke Hall.[55] Sanford had been in London earlier (1885) at the Healing Conference organized by William Boardman and Asa Mahan.[56] The conference provoked extensive discussion about holiness and healing in the British press. That reputation, and the recommendations of Boardman and Mahan[57] may have been the basis for the invitation to Star Hall. It is reasonably certain, however, that none of the male American evangelists would have been invited to Star Hall without the approval of Isabella Leonard.

Harris renamed the "Mission Halls" as the "Pentecostal Missions" (1890),[58] and continued to establish other "Pentecostal Missions." He worked with persons from all denominations and supported Holiness Conventions in non-Anglican locations. The ecumenical approach brought accusations that he, like the Salvation Army, was intending to establish a new denomination. Harris, who described his ministry as "nonsectarian," made the decision to stay in the Anglican Church. He insisted that his were missions, not churches. Converts were urged to remain in the church but to worship in the Pentecostal Mission halls.[59] The goal was similar to John Wesley's: call nominal Christians back to "Scriptural Holiness," not into a new "sect."

However, because of the criticism, the "Pentecostal Mission" was combined with the "Pentecostal Mission Prayer Union" and in February 1891 was renamed the "Pentecostal League"[60] and, eventually, the "Pentecostal League of Prayer."[61] Among the many who joined the Prayer Union and Pentecostal League of Prayer were all of the residents and workers at Star Hall, including Isabella Leonard and the Crossleys.[62] In January 1891, Reader Harris began to publish his periodical

---

[55]"Fishers of Men. Notes on an Address by F. D. Sanford," *Tongues of Fire* 1, 2 (February 1891), 5.

[56][W. E. Boardman and Mary Boardman], *Record of the International Conference on Divine Healing and True Holiness ... 1885* (London: J. Snow and Co., 1885). This was soon followed by the reprinting of an article by Sanford's good friend A. B. Simpson, "The Signs of the Times," *Tongues of Fire* 1, 3 (March 1891), 7.

[57]Asa Mahan, "Baptism of the Holy Ghost,' *Tongues of Fire* 2, 9 (September 1892), 5.

[58]Mrs. Reader Harris, "Our New Name. The Pentecostal Mission," *Tongues of Fire* 1, 1 (January 1891), 3; Rutherford Davison, "Why a 'Pentecostal Mission,'" *Tongues of Fire* 1, 2 (February 1891), 2.

[59]Richard Reader Harris, "The Unsectarian Holiness Movement," *Tongues of Fire* 1, 2 (February 1891), 2.

[60]Richard Reader Harris, "The Pentecostal League," *Tongues of Fire* 1, 3 (March 1891), 4.

[61]Note the parallels with Leonard's projects in Australia. See the announcement: "The Pentecostal League: Prayer Union of the Pentecostal Mission," *Tongues of Fire* 2, 1 (January 1892), 11 [often inserted in later issues] and Reader Harris, "The Pentecostal League," *Tongues of Fire* 2, 10 (October 1892), 1-2. On the organization, see Ian M. Randall, "The Pentecostal League of Prayer: a Transdenominational British Wesleyan-Holiness Movement," *Wesleyan Theological Journal* 33, 1 (1998), 185-200.

[62][Richard Reader Harris], "Manchester and Bristol Holiness Convention," *Tongues of Fire* 2, 22 (October 1892), 6: "... Mr. and Mrs. Crossley and others working with them, are members of the Pentecostal League."

Tongues of Fire and other Holiness literature. As in Australia, the organization served as a speaker's bureau to supply Holiness mission teams and Holiness preachers. Despite his Anglican loyalties, he became an ardent premillennialist and a British-Israel advocate. Isabella Leonard worked closely with Reader Harris in Holiness Conventions and with the Pentecostal League of Prayer through its transitions.

Isabella Leonard was very active throughout England during this period, but also managed a trip to the USA.[63] With Crossley and/or with his support, she conducted Holiness missions in many cities. For example, she was frequently in Bristol ministering or participating in meetings.[64] Beginning in 1891, these were sometimes mentioned in *Tongues of Fire*, including Conventions at Bristol[65] and Colwyn Bay in northern Wales.[66] These Conventions in late 1891 also included, in addition to Francis W. Crossley and Isabella Leonard, the other Americans (Watson, McDonald, Sanford and Gill) brought to England by Crossley. The early 1892 Conventions featured Crossley and Isabella Leonard.

In addition to publishing addresses from the two Star Hall Holiness Conventions, Leonard edited two volumes by G. D. Watson to make them more readable for British audiences. In doing so she smoothed the rough often wooden language of Watson, removing repetition, correcting bad grammar and adopting English spellings. She shortened each text significantly. Most importantly she removed the Methodist identity and polemic from the volumes so they could be dispassionately read in Britain outside Methodist circles. These were the first publications of Watson in England and established his reputation there. It is unclear what Watson thought of her efforts but he profited from them.[67] The date of Leonard's departure from England is not presently known. As more

---

[63]"Miss Isabella Leonard has also returned to the States, but is expected to be in England again in time for the Star Hall Convention, which begins, (D.V.) October 18th." *Tongues of Fire* 1, 7 (July 1891), 1.

[64]For example, see the reports: "Trying His Strength," *Bristol Mercury* (8 January 1891), 8; "United Women's Missionary Meeting," *Bristol Mercury* (7 February 1891), 3; "Bazaar," *Western Daily Press* (Saturday 24 October 1891), 3.

[65]The Convention was advertised: "Advertisements & Notices," *Bristol Mercury* (Saturday 17 October 1891), 4. The principal speakers were to be W. McDonald, G. D. Watson, Joshua Gill, and Miss Isabella Leonard. Reports were published: A Bristolian, "Nine Days' Holiness Convention in Bristol," *Tongues of Fire* 1, 12 (December 1891), 3, 7; Robert H. Fallon, "Bristol," *Tongues of Fire* 2, 1 (January 1892), 8; Anonymous, "Bristol: The Recent Holiness Meeting," *Tongues of Fire* 2, 2 (February 1892), 9-10. A presentation of Isabella Leonard was published: "Alive to God: Notes of an Address at the Bristol Praise Meeting," *Tongues of Fire* 1, 1 (January 1892), 5. Note that Isabella Leonard had already been in Bristol several times working with independent urban missions and other ministries.

[66]Thos. Lloyd, "Colwyn Bay, North Wales," *Tongues of Fire* 1, 1 (January 1892), 10. [ISL and Crossleys]

[67]George Douglas Watson, *A Holiness Manual...*. Second edition, revised and edited by Isabella S. Leonard (London S.W. Partridge & Co., 1891) and *idem, White Robes; or, Garments of Salvation*, revised and edited by Isabella S. Leonard (London: S. W. Partridge, 1891).

transportation records are searched, the answer may be found. Lucy Prescott Vane summarized (1911) Leonard's life of travel:

> Miss Leonard crossed the Atlantic nine times doing evangelistic work. She spent the greater part of her eight years abroad in England in the various bodies of Methodism, at Star Hall, and at other places. She went four times to India and four times to Australia, spending a longer or shorter time in each country as God led her. Five years ago she returned for the last time.[68]

During the period 1901-1907, she was frequently in Los Angeles, and a regular preacher and Holiness Meeting leader at the Peniel Hall.[69] She was listed as an endorser of the call to the General Holiness Assembly, 1901, but was not listed among those who attended.[70] Leonard also maintained her relationships with the WFMS,[71] and in 1909 was mentioned as an influential member of its Highland Park Auxiliary (Los Angeles).[72] She died in Phoenix, cared for by her protégé Lucy Prescott Vane, on 22 January 1911.[73]

Conclusion

Isabella Leonard became part of the evolving Radical Holiness network in the USA early in her evangelistic career, 1873-1881. As a camp meeting evangelist, she established relationships with such luminaries as William Taylor, G. D. Watson, Charles H. Stalker and David B. Updegraff, working as their colleague. During her first visit to Britain, she worked primarily, but not exclusively, in Wesleyan Methodist churches. Returning to England in 1888, she became an important

---

[68]Vane, "Miss Isabella Leonard," 4.

[69]See, for example, "Peniel Hall," *Los Angeles Herald* (7 July 1901), 5; "Peniel Hall," *Los Angeles Herald* (10 August 1902), 7; "Peniel Hall," *Los Angeles Herald* (16 August 1902), 7; *Los Angeles Herald* (6 September 1902), 7; "Peniel Hall," *Los Angeles Herald* (30 August 1903), 7; *Los Angeles Herald* (29 June 1907), 6.

[70]S. B. Shaw, *Echoes of the General Holiness Assembly held in Chicago, May 3-13, 1901* (Chicago: S. B. Shaw, n.d.), 13.

[71]For example, "List of New Life Members of the Society," *Woman's Missionary Friend. The Quarterly. Pacific Branch* (November 1898), 188, reported an event at University Church, Los Angeles where "Miss Isabella Leonard and Mrs. Lucy O. Voire, formerly beloved collaborators in the Western Branch of the Women's Foreign Missionary Society were present and spoke to the edification of all." A year later, "Ministers in Conference," *Los Angeles Herald* #356 (21 September 1899), 8, reported that the WFMS "...held its anniversary at 2:30 oclock, when short and interesting addresses were made by Bishop Ninde and Miss Isabella Leonard, formerly an evangelist in India, on 'Foreign Missionary Work.'"

[72]"Briefs," *Women's Missionary Friend* 51 (November 1909), 409: "Highland Park... Lucy Prescott Vane and Isabella Leonard are both members of this Auxiliary, which may account somewhat for its vigor."

[73]Vane, "Miss Isabella Leonard," 4. See also the anonymous note, *Heathen Woman's Friend* 43, 5 (May 1911), 186.

part of the Radical Holiness Movement where as a woman she had far more opportunities for service than among the Wesleyan Methodists. She connected the British Radical Holiness Movement to that in the USA, and influenced both the Crossleys and Richard Reader Harris. She maintained her relationships with the Salvation Army in Britain and in Australia. Late in life she worked with the Peniel Mission in Los Angeles and continued to work with the local WFMS chapters of the Methodist Episcopal Church.

In Australia, she became nationally renowned as a Holiness evangelist. Working broadly with the Methodist churches and the Salvation Army, she was present at the beginning of the Central Methodist Mission (April 1884), developed a "Prayer League," Holiness Conventions, and was the prime mover of the United Methodist Holiness Association. Probably because of the radical nature of the Holiness revival and the Central Methodist Mission, all within the loyal Methodist contexts, the connections between the Australian and North American Radical Holiness Movements evolved differently in Australia than in Great Britain, the United States, or Canada.

Leonard was focused on the importance of the experiences of conversion and sanctification; she was little involved in doctrinal experimentation. Theologically she appears to have used lightly Daniel Steele and was appreciatively critical of G. D. Watson and other North American Radical Holiness theologians. She worked with people of significantly different theological persuasions in Britain, Australia and in the USA. In Britain, she worked with Crossley, Govan and Reader Harris, all of whom attempted to transcend denominational barriers and conflict with the existing churches.

Leonard's use of power was typical of women finding their way toward public cultural involvement in the late nineteenth century. It was "soft-power," through networks, public discourse and religious publishing.[74] There was no access to juridical power except through sympathetic men. There was no quarrel with technological development. She was comfortable with Crossley, his wealth and his preoccupations with technology. Like her Radical Holiness colleagues, she was not against modernity, but committed to the transformation of individuals in order to transform society. She convinced Crossley that there should be a redistribution of resources to the improvement of the lives of the poor.

Thus, Isabella Sarah Leonard contributed significantly to the global development of the Radical Holiness Movements, and her contributions were clearly as important as those of some of her better known male colleagues. The Holiness Movements of four countries were definitively shaped during this period: Great Britain, Australia, the United States, and Singapore; and those in India were enriched by her efforts.

---

[74]See a discussion of the term "soft-power" in Joseph S. Nye, Jr. *Soft Power: The Means to Success in World Politics* (New York: World Affairs, 2004).

Chapter 6

Radical Holiness Evangelism: Vivian Dake and the Pentecost Bands

Howard A. Snyder

Wanted! ten thousand to labor in every land. Wanted! those who will work without salary. Wanted! those who will take the fare by the way and shout, "Glory to God!" Amen!. . . . Let all the faint-hearted pack their satchels and leave quickly to make room for the Gideons, the Shamgars, the Daniels, the Davids and the Deborahs, the Marys, the Priscillas, and the Dorcases, who are coming. Amen! All hail! With fingers in your ears, eyes on the mark, feet on the thorny path, hands filled with pitchers and lamps, hearts aflame, on to victory! — Vivian A. Dake, October, 1891[1]

Introduction

The rise and the influence of the Pentecost Bands within the Free Methodist Church (FMC) in the 1880s and 1890s is the story of a dynamic evangelistic, church-planting, and missionary movement that in the end could not be contained within denominational boundaries. Yet that is only part of the story. For it is clear that the Pentecost Band movement tapped into and channeled a significant amount of spiritual and social energy that was dissipated or diffused after 1894, but which actually spread in several directions and still has some impact today.

The Pentecost Bands arose at a time of rapid social and religious change, much of it fueled by massive immigration from Europe, urbanization, and rapid industrialization and economic expansion. This was also a time of rapid church growth, particularly in the cities, and of the rise of new religious movements, including Christian Science in the East and Mormonism further west. The Salvation Army began work in the United States in 1880, and "in ten years it had marched across the continent and was working in practically every large city in the country."[2]

---

[1]Ida Dake Parsons, *Kindling Watch-Fires: Being a Brief Sketch of the Life of Rev. Vivian A. Dake* (Chicago: Free Methodist Publishing House, 1915), 77.

[2]William Warren Sweet, *The Story of Religion in America* (New York: Harper and

Although Free Methodists did have a number of city churches and started rescue missions or other urban ministries in Pittsburgh, Chicago, and other cities, the Pentecost Bands and the FMC were centered mostly in small-town and rural America, particularly in the Midwest. The story of the Bands is mostly the story of earnest young Free Methodists (many of them new converts) following the expanding network of railway lines to towns where evangelistic meetings could be held and churches established.

The Free Methodist Church, 1880-1900

The FMC, founded in 1860, had approximately 13,000 members in 1880 and nearly 29,000 in 1900.[3] The period 1886-1894, when the Pentecost Bands were most active in the denomination, was especially a period of growth. During this period, the FMC considered itself a "radical" holiness body. Though maintaining some irenic contact with the broader Holiness Movement, its leaders and writers often warned against too low a standard of holiness: an experience that did not go deep enough, was not sufficiently world-denying, and compromised particularly with the amusements and ostentations of the age.[4] The term "radical" had a positive connotation, as suggested by the article "Radical Holiness," reprinted approvingly from *The Christian Witness* in *The Free Methodist* in October, 1894. Pointing out that "radical" means "root," and that "Sin has a root in man," the author observes: "We are sometimes charged with being radical on the subject of holiness. . . . We firmly believe that we would be radically wrong not to be radical on this subject."[5] Authors called for "a thorough work" and warned against "popular holiness." Vivian Dake was a radical in this sense, but also in the sense that he argued for aggressive, innovative measures in evangelism and missions.

Vivian A. Dake (1854-1892)

Vivian Adelbert Dake was born on February 9, 1854, at Oregon, Illinois. His father, Jonathan Woodcock Dake, had been a charter member of the FMC in 1860. The family later moved further west to Iowa, and it was here that Vivian Dake's ministry began.[6]

Brothers, 1930, 1939), 526.

[3]*Minutes of the Annual Conferences of the Free Methodist Church* (Chicago: Free Methodist Publishing House, 1901), 252; Wilson T. Hogue, *History of the Free Methodist Church of North America,* 2 vols. (Chicago: Free Methodist Publishing House, 1915), 2:182, 189.

[4]Some sense of Free Methodism's position within the late nineteenth-century Holiness Movement can be gained from Charles B. Jernigan's *Pioneer Days of the Holiness Movement in the Southwest* (Bethany, OK: Arnett Publishing Company, 1964).

[5]"Radical Holiness," *The Free Methodist* (October 3, 1894), 6. See also J. B. Chapman, "Radical Holiness," *God's Revivalist and Bible Advocate,* 42:29 (July 17, 1930), 1.

[6]Parsons, 18. The chief biographical sources on Dake are this book by his widow and Thomas H. Nelson, *Life and Labors of Rev. Vivian A. Dake, Organizer and Leader of Pen-*

Vivian was a bright child, and musically inclined. He was clearly converted at age nine, wandered from God, but was "wonderfully reclaimed" shortly after entering Chili Seminary (North Chili, New York; now Roberts Wesleyan College) at the age of eighteen. After graduating from Chili Seminary he completed three terms at Rochester University, but he soon left to enter the ministry.[7] He wrote, "I would rather have the gift of devil-dislodging faith than all the learning that can be acquired at earth's schools."[8]

Dake married Lenna Bailey in 1876, but she died a few months later. In 1878 he married Ida May Campbell who survived him by a number of years and wrote his biography. Meanwhile he began pastoral and evangelistic ministry in Iowa where he served a series of circuits from 1876 to 1882 and saw considerable evangelistic fruit. He wrote after one revival, "At two-thirty in the morning I took seven more into the church, all young people, most of whom had been saved since the doors were opened in the evening."[9]

Dake seems to have been unfailingly zealous and self-assured in his ministry. At age twenty-five he wrote, "I pledge myself to spend [my life] in blowing the gospel trumpet with no uncertain sound."[10] He was always concerned with involving believers in ministry. His wife wrote, "He seems from the very first to have taken a stand with the primitive church fathers in getting everybody at work and thus multiplying their talents and usefulness."[11]

Dake transferred to the Minnesota and Northern Iowa Conference in 1882 where within a year he was chairman of the conference's three districts. He soon wore himself out, and T. B. Arnold, denominational publishing agent and a close friend of Dake, persuaded him to take an extended vacation in the fall of 1884. Visiting the Michigan Conference, he agreed to accept the Spring Arbor charge. Shortly thereafter, in response to prayer, he experienced healing and "began immediately to be more active."[12]

The following year, 1885, having transferred to the Michigan Conference, Dake was appointed conference evangelist. In July he began organizing groups of young people into Pentecost Bands to assist in the work. He soon moved to Chicago and used the denominational publishing house as his mailing address and unofficial headquarters while itinerating in evangelistic work. For the next five years Dake was occupied with evangelism and overseeing the rapidly-expanding work of the Bands.

The primary legacy of Vivian Dake's life was the Pentecost Band work and the indelible impression he made on scores of Free Methodist young people.

---

tecost Bands (Chicago: T. B. Arnold, 1894).
    [7]Parsons, 20.
    [8]Nelson, 21.
    [9]Parsons, 31.
    [10]Parsons, 25.
    [11]Parsons, 26.
    [12]Parsons, 35.

Founding and Growth of the Pentecost Bands, 1885-1892

In organizing the Pentecost Bands, Vivian Dake was employing a small-group method that was part of the common heritage of Methodist and Holiness peoples. The name Pentecost Band "was suggested to him because it appeared to be a return to primitive Pentecost methods, for in the revival at Pentecost converts as well as preachers engaged in spreading the gospel."[13]

The origins of the Pentecost Bands trace back to July of 1882 when Vivian and Ida Dake, with others, began a revival at Mankato, Minnesota. Thomas Nelson relates,

> Soon after this meeting began, [Dake] organized the first Pentecost Band. It was not the result of a sudden impulse on his part, for this matter had been on his heart and prayed over for months. While at Ottumwa, Iowa, some time before, the Lord made His will known to him, giving, as he felt, even the name by which the Band should be called.... This was in August, 1882. Mr. D. was unanimously chosen as leader. This first Pentecost Band was ere long dissolved, but again sprang into being and took permanent form in Parma, Mich., in the year 1885.[14]

The Parma Pentecost Band, designated Band No. 1, opened work in Parma, Michigan (near Spring Arbor) on July 25, 1885, beginning with a street meeting and an evening service. Dake led the opening service and preached, then left the work in the charge of this band of four young women. Nelson notes, "As the workers prophesied for the first time in public, the Spirit applied the truth spoken and God set His seal on the work at once, pouring out His Spirit in convicting and converting power."[15] Soon a second band of young women was holding meetings in nearby Hanover. Later the first band of men was formed. Thus Dake was quickly establishing the pattern of the bands: small groups of young men or young women; a high degree of mobility, with bands moving fairly quickly from one site to another, often being replaced by another band; and members of one band, as soon as they had gained a little experience, becoming the leaders of new bands. The whole system was set up for mobility, flexibility, and rapid expansion.[16]

Evidently Free Methodist founder B. T. Roberts was well aware of Dake's strategy, for he wrote on July 31, 1885, "Organize your bands. Push out. Be as aggressive as the Salvation Army, but more holy, more serious and have no nonsense about it."[17]

---

[13]Parsons, 36. Thus for Dake the term "Pentecost" connoted evangelism and revival more than it did specifically a "Pentecostal" baptism in the Spirit.

[14]Nelson, 73.

[15]Nelson, 102. See the manuscript journal, "North Parma Pentecost Band" (Marston Historical Center, Free Methodist Headquarters, Indianapolis, IN) which begins with a sort of constitution for the Bands and includes the initial minutes of the official board of the Parma Free Methodist circuit.

[16]Nelson, 87.

[17]Nelson, 80.

In creating the Bands, Dake seems to have opened a reservoir of youthful energy that was waiting to be tapped. This was especially so in the case of women. Within seven years over thirty bands were functioning, with women outnumbering men by nearly two to one. The total number of band workers appears to have been about 125 in 1892.[18]

The primary work of the bands was evangelism and church planting, both in North America and overseas. Typically a band would ride the railroad into a Midwestern town, rent a vacant store or hall or set up a tent, and hold meetings for several weeks. Door-to-door visitation, tract distribution (especially at railway stations), and street meetings and marches attracted crowds to the evening services. There, demonstrative worship, singing, and fresh personal testimonies and exhortations increased the interest. Often two or even three of the band members would preach or exhort in the same service. Opposition and occasional arrests added an air of excitement. When dramatic conversions occurred, as they often did, the meetings gained even more notoriety. Frequently the result of a revival series was the organization of a small Free Methodist congregation and the erection of a church building.[19]

The bands were almost entirely self-supporting, living from such offerings or gifts of food or clothing as their work might generate. Workers often lived very sacrificially, especially in the opening stages of a revival endeavor. Anecdotes about Band members often recall their going without food, or subsisting for days on donations of potatoes or vegetables while holding meetings and visiting house to house.

An article on the Pentecost Bands in the 1891 *Encyclopedia of Missions,* apparently written by Dake, gives a good overview of Band work. The article delineated Band work as follows:

> A band is composed of four workers, of whom one is a leader and another an assistant leader. They enter into a field where work is needed, hold street-meetings, visit from house to house, hold public services in church, tent, or hall, and throw everything else aside in desperate efforts to "pluck brands out of the burning." They are earnest, enthusiastic, and noisy. Their methods may be called shortcuts to win souls.[20]

---

[18]Nelson lists Band No. 34 as active in 1892 (p. 309), although it is not clear that all thirty-four bands were in operation at the same time. The first issue of *The Pentecost Herald* (April, 1894) lists thirty-three active bands. Of thirty-three bands I have been able to identify, twenty were female, ten were male, and three were mixed, involving married couples. Of 208 names of band members I have identified as active in the 1880s and 1890s, 128 are female and 80 are male, a ratio of about 62% to 38%.

[19]Often, it appears, there were more converts than the number that became FMC members. Converts were not always willing to take the narrow way as defined by the Free Methodists.

[20]Edwin Munsell Bliss, ed., *The Encyclopedia of Missions,* 2 vols. (New York: Funk & Wagnalls, 1891), 2:214-15. By this date the Bands had organized eight new societies in Michigan and twenty-five in Illinois.

Change and Controversy, 1892-1895

From early on Vivian Dake had had a global missionary vision. In 1882, shortly after the Free Methodist General Missionary Board was formed, Dake told the board he felt called to Africa; however "the church took no action to send him."[21] In 1891, Dake departed for Africa. On board a steamship bound for Liberia, he met Methodist missionary Bishop William Taylor, whose foreign mission work was becoming well known, as were his appeals for U.S. churches to send missionaries and his advocacy of "self-supporting" mission work. Dake had several conversations with him.[22]

When Dake died on the trip to Africa in 1892, relations between the Pentecost Bands and the FMC, which had already become problematic, became even more complicated. The Bands were inevitably controversial simply because of their semi-autonomy. As a youth movement they displayed a dynamism and zeal that sometimes clashed with denominational leaders seeking to consolidate and organize on a firmer basis. In addition there were specific organizational and doctrinal issues.

Dake left Thomas Nelson, one of the Band divisional leaders, temporarily in charge of the work when he left for Africa, and so Nelson succeeded Dake as head of the Bands after the founder's death.[23] Both he and his wife (Flora Birdsall Nelson) had been active in the Bands for several years. His accession to leadership seems to have caused some tension within the Bands as well as complicating relations with the denomination. E. E. Shelhamer was, with Nelson, one of several divisional leaders at the time of Dake's death, and some Band workers thought he should be Dake's successor. Shelhamer argued for shared leadership among the divisional leaders, however, feeling that no one was qualified to fill Dake's shoes. Nelson was opposed to this and assumed control of the Bands. This appears to have been a key factor leading to E. E. and Minnie Baldwin Shelhamer leaving the Band work in 1895.[24]

Within the FMC, controversy concerning the Bands clustered around three related issues: the semi-autonomy of the Bands and their linkages with other "fringe" movements, support of missionary work, and the Bands' particular understanding of "radical" holiness:[25]

---

[21]Byron S. Lamson, *Venture! The Frontiers of Free Methodism* (Winona Lake, IN: Light and Life Press, 1960), 129-30.

[22]E. Davies, *The Bishop of Africa; or the Life of William Taylor, D. D.* (Reading, MA: Holiness Book Concern, 1885), 57-63, gives a summary of Taylor's principles; see William Taylor, *Story of My Life* (New York: Hunt and Eaton, 1895), 613-18. Dake also made a brief trip to Germany in 1889, and went to Norway on his way to Africa to visit Pentecost Band missionaries sent there three years previously.

[23]Nelson, 52.

[24]Information supplied this writer by Esther Shelhamer James, April, 1990, based on conversations with her father, E. E. Shelhamer.

[25]Hogue, 2:190-96.

1. Autonomy and linkage with independent ventures. Though Vivian Dake was an ordained elder in good standing in the Michigan and later Illinois Conferences of the FMC from 1885 until his death, the Pentecost Bands had no official linkage with the denomination except through him. Often Dake was given encouragement by Free Methodist leaders, and Band work was always carried out in cooperation with conference, district, or local leaders. But the movement was under no direct denominational control. It was Dake, and later Nelson, in consultation with colleagues and workers, who made the key decisions. This created a certain uneasiness as the size and breadth of Pentecost Band work increased. In response, Dake argued that his loyalty to the church was not in question, and that the churches organized and turned over to the denomination proved he had no intention of creating a separate church.[26] In an open letter to the denomination shortly before leaving for Africa he wrote, "the church . . . shall have the classes and church buildings. I have no ambition but for souls, no desire but to glorify God, and no aim but to gain heaven."[27]

The issue was complicated, however, by Dake's free association with many people within and beyond Free Methodism who shared his vision and his brand of radical holiness. Dake began conducting annual Harvest Home camp meetings each July, over the anniversary date of the Bands, which became in effect interdenominational and almost national rallies. Up to three thousand people attended the 1891 Harvest Home gathering.[28] C. S. Hanley, editor of *The Firebrand,* wrote in his paper, "There were representatives of nearly all denominations at this meeting. They came from far and near, but the bulk of those attending were from the FMC, as this work is a child of Free Methodism."[29]

Clearly something was going on here that was broader than the FMC itself. Dake was informally in association with several key figures who headed independent ministries within and beyond the FMC. Chief among these were C. S. Hanley, an ordained Free Methodist and editor of *The Firebrand;* C. W. Sherman of the Vanguard work in St. Louis and at this time a Free Methodist; S. B. Shaw, publisher and editor of the *Michigan Holiness Record;* and Robert Lee Harris, a Free Methodist until 1889 who later founded the New Testament Church of Christ (NTCC).[30]

---

[26]Dake said his policy was "to go upon no circuit unless the pastor and official board desire us to come. We have been at work largely upon new ground." Nelson, 470.

[27]Nelson, 469.

[28]See the descriptions of the 1890 and 1891 Harvest Home camp meetings in Parsons, 40-42 and 48-52.

[29]Quoted in Parsons, 49, and in Nelson, 299-300.

[30]Solomon B. Shaw, who for some years was a Free Methodist, wrote (or compiled) and published several influential books including *The Great Revival in Wales, Also an Account of the Great Revival in Ireland in 1859* (1905), which is credited with helping to spark the Azusa Street Revival. See Vinson Synan, *The Holiness-Pentecostal Movement in the United States* (Grand Rapids: Eerdmans, 1971), 97; Richard M. Riss, *A Survey of 20th-Century Revival Movements in the United States* (Peabody, MA: Hendrickson Publishers, 1988), 50.

In his dissertation on Mary Lee Harris Cagle, Robert Stanley Ingersol calls this informal association of independent or semi-independent leaders the "Free Methodist Radical Alliance." A key figure initially was Robert Lee Harris (Mary Lee Cagle's first husband), a Free Methodist from Texas who was intent on missionary work in Africa according to the independent self-support approach advocated by William Taylor. Ingersol writes, "A central feature of the radical alliance was its members' activities 'on the independent line,' outside normal denominational oversight, though the radicals maintained nominal commitments to their annual conferences."[31]

Ingersol adds, "The term 'radical Free Methodist' is derived from the left-wing orientation of the party and more particularly from the distinction its members drew between 'radical' and 'popular' holiness, the latter regarded as an antinomian corruption of the former; thus E. E. Shelhammer [sic], onetime Pentecost Band member . . . and later Free Methodist revivalist, was author of a booklet entitled *Radical Versus Popular Holiness Contrasted.*"[32]

The term "radical Free Methodist" could be somewhat misleading here, however, as Free Methodists generally during this period considered themselves "radical" and used that term positively, as we have seen. But Ingersol rightly points out that "the radicals [in his sense] differed from mainstream Free Methodists by a matter of degrees."[33] He describes this coalition as "avidly evangelistic," rigid in standards of dress and behavior, committed to independent "faith work" in both home and foreign missions, suspicious of institutional authority, and desiring the restoration of the New Testament Church.[34]

Ingersol thoroughly documents a number of significant linkages between the Pentecost Band movement, these other figures, and the beginnings of the NTCC. A key link was *The Vanguard* publication which served for a time as the official organ of the Pentecost Bands and also as the missions organ of the NTCC. The Mission Training work in St. Louis was part of the Vanguard ministry and was under the direction of Bessie Abrams Sherman; Dake viewed it as part of the Pentecost Band work and assigned Band workers to help there.[35] Two of several key Pentecost Band figures in this network were Bessie and Susie Sherman, daughters of C. W. Sherman. Bessie was a Pentecost Band leader who went to India under the Bands in 1899.[36] Susie Sherman worked with the Vanguard ministry, was a

---

[31]Robert Stanley Ingersol, "Burden of Dissent: Mary Lee Cagle and the Southern Holiness Movement." Ph.D. Dissertation, Duke University, 1989, 79.

[32]Ingersol, 79. See E. E. Shelhamer, *Popular and Radical Holiness Contrasted,* 2nd ed., rev. (Atlanta, The Repairer, 1906). The first edition was entitled *Bible Standard of Regeneration and Holiness.*

[33]Ingersol, 80.

[34]Ingersol, 80-81.

[35]Bliss, 2:214.

[36]Ingersol, 125; manuscript journal of Pentecost Band No. 2 in India, August 23, 1899 - August 13, 1905, a copy of which is in the Marston Historical Center, Free Methodist Headquarters, Indianapolis, Indiana.

Pentecost Band member and a charter member of the NTCC, and later a Vanguard missionary in Africa and died there in 1895.[37]

Ingersol documents several of these interconnections in some detail and argues that much of the character of the NTCC, one of the antecedent bodies of the Church of the Nazarene, was shaped by this "radical Free Methodist" impulse, mediated through the Pentecost Bands. He sees this influence particularly in terms of the affirmation of leadership gifts of women.[38]

2. Support of foreign missionary work. A second area of controversy concerned the sending of missionaries under Pentecost Band auspices to other lands and soliciting support for them within Free Methodism. This was precisely the period when denominationally-sponsored Free Methodist missions were being developed, and Dake appeared to be in competition with the denominational program. Dake himself said, "At first I did not see missionary work connected with the band work. But as time went on, conviction began to settle on individual laborers, with reference to work in foreign lands. As they had stood by us on the home field we felt it our duty to stand by them in the foreign field."[39] By 1891 Dake had sent Pentecost Bands to Africa, Norway, and Germany and was preparing to send them to India, Australia, and England.[40] He wrote, "The home-work is for the purpose of training workers and raising money for the foreign work."[41]

Dake's view of foreign missions does tend to align him with the "Free Methodist radical alliance" that Ingersol describes. According to Nelson, Dake

> . . . argued that Boards of necessity were slow and cumbersome and . . . there was a more expeditious mode of accomplishing the work. He interpreted the action of Paul and Barnabas, as recorded in the thirteenth chapter of Acts to be on this plan. He said when they felt the call of God to do foreign missionary work, they did not go to Jerusalem to see the leaders, nor did they even write to an executive committee, but simply stated their convictions to those there assembled, who acknowledged the call of the Holy Ghost, ordained them and sent them out. Then they went trusting God for everything. This he thought to be the apostolic mode.[42]

Dake's approach thus clashed philosophically to some degree with that of the denomination, and raised as well the always-sensitive issue of promotion and fund-raising.

---

[37]Ingersol, 125, 127, 132-33, 135, 158; Lamson, 257; Wilson T. Hogue, *G. Harry Agnew, A Pioneer Missionary* (Chicago: Free Methodist Publishing House, 1905), 190-97.

[38]On the NTCC see, in addition to Ingersol, Timothy L. Smith, *Called Unto Holiness: The Story of the Nazarenes: The Formative Years* (Kansas City, MO: Nazarene Publishing House, 1962), especially 153-59, 168-71; Jernigan, *Pioneer Days . . .* , 89, 116-17; and Floyd T. Cunningham, ed., *Our Watchword and Song: The Centennial History of the Church of the Nazarene* (Kansas City, MO: Beacon Hill Press of Kansas City, 2009), 113-25.

[39]Nelson, 469.
[40]Bliss, 2:214.
[41]Bliss, 2:214-15.
[42]Nelson, 53.

3. Understanding of Holiness. The third issue, the specific understanding of holiness, also involved the "radical alliance." Dake and others like him stressed "the death route" in experiencing entire sanctification. Necessary to obtain holiness, he said, are "First, light; second, conviction; third, confession; fourth, crucifixion; fifth, saving or appropriating faith."[43] Like many other Free Methodists, he criticized "popular holiness" that put such emphasis on faith that it neglected the necessity of crucifixion—facing up to the depths of sin and a total dying to self.

It was in part this focus, probably at times carried to an extreme, which increased the perception that the Pentecost Band movement was moving toward fanaticism. Prominent among the issues identified as fanatic was a particular interpretation of "Social Purity" which held that sexual union in marriage should be for procreation only ("marital purity"). This was an emphasis of a number of people in Free Methodism and in the holiness "radical alliance" of this period, particularly H. A. ("Auntie") Coon, a holiness worker who was often employed by the Pentecost Bands.[44]

This constellation of issues spelled increasing controversy for the Pentecost Bands just at the time that Dake died and leadership fell into the hands of the less charismatic and perhaps less stable and more authoritarian Thomas Nelson. Both the 1890 and 1894 quadrennial Free Methodist General Conferences were urged to provide some regulation for the Bands. The 1890 General Conference adopted four guidelines:

> 1. Chairmen of Districts, and Evangelists appointed by the General or Annual Conference, may organize Bands for evangelistic work; but no person shall become a member of such a Band without the recommendation of the Society to which he belongs.
>
> 2. The rules and regulations of such Bands shall be subject to the approval of the Annual Conference to which the Leader belongs, or within the bounds of which he holds his membership.
>
> 3. No Evangelist or Band shall appoint or hold meetings where they will interfere with the regular work of any preacher duly appointed to a circuit, or station, or district.
>
> 4. Those who labor successfully in a Band for one year may be licensed by the Quarterly Conference from year to year as Band workers.[45]

The annual conferences affected by Band work subsequently adopted somewhat more restrictive "Band Rules" providing, among other things, that bands be known as "Free Methodist Bands," that they operate under the authority and

---

[43]Parsons, 176.

[44]On Auntie Coon, see E. E. Shelhamer, ed., *Life and Labors of Auntie Coon* (Atlanta: Repairer Office, 1905). The "marital purity" line was picked up for a while by *Vanguard* and *Firebrand* writers. *The Vanguard* carried a regular "Social Purity" column reporting on the so-called "national purity crusade."

[45]Hogue, *History of the Free Methodist Church,* 2:194-95.

supervision of the conference, and that they promote the *Free Methodist* paper.⁴⁶ Dake was left without appointment in 1891 by the Illinois Conference because he would not give assurance that he would operate strictly within the rules, feeling that they would restrict the commission God had given him.⁴⁷

When Vivian Dake suddenly died a few months later, the question of the Bands' relationship to the denomination devolved primarily upon Thomas Nelson, also a member of the Illinois Conference. The 1893 session of the conference carefully examined the question of Pentecost Band work in passing on Nelson's character and was sufficiently satisfied with Nelson's promise to confine his labors within the bounds of the conference "as much as possible" that they granted his request to be given the relation of conference evangelist and ordained him elder.⁴⁸ Apparently the conference did not insist on further restrictions on the Band work nor that they be called "Free Methodist Bands."

The following year, the Illinois Conference adopted several resolutions concerning the Bands which were conciliatory in tone. It asked the General Conference meeting later that year to recognize the Bands "as an evangelistic movement which . . . should be tenderly cared for" and appoint Nelson as general leader for a term of four years (i.e., until the subsequent General Conference).⁴⁹ This action was taken out of recognition that the Bands were a denomination-wide movement and needed more general coordination. Significantly, had the proposed action come to pass, the Pentecost Bands would have been established as an auxiliary, or a missions/evangelism sodality, within the denomination. This conference action was in part a response to an acknowledgement by the Bands at their 1894 Harvest Home of some "unwise and independent methods" on their part.⁵⁰

A cooperative arrangement between the denomination and the Bands seemed to be in the making. Nelson recommended to the General Missionary Board two young women from the Pentecost training school in St. Louis as suitable candidates for mission work in India, and Sivert and Lillian Ulness, originally sent to Norway under the Bands, applied to and were accepted by the mission board.⁵¹

The action proposed by the Illinois Conference was considered but not adopted, however, by the 1894 General Conference. The conference approved an irenic but rather general statement reaffirming the regulations of 1890, but took no further action.⁵² This was to throw the issue back to the annual conferences; yet, as the Illinois Conference had recognized, the Bands were now a denomination-

---

⁴⁶See, for example, the rules adopted by the Illinois Conference, *Minutes,* 1891, 54.

⁴⁷Report of Ministerial Relations Committee, Illinois Conference, *Minutes,* 1891, 54-55.

⁴⁸*Minutes,* 1893, 98-99.

⁴⁹*Minutes,* 1894, 76-77. The committee report noted that "there are some eighty or ninety workers composing the Pentecost Bands, and less than fifteen of these workers have a membership within the bounds of this conference, but are distributed throughout the conferences and States." *Minutes,* 1894, 77.

⁵⁰*Minutes,* 1894, 76.

⁵¹"Proceedings of the Annual Meetings," *Minutes,* 1894, 188.

⁵²Hogue, *History of the Free Methodist Church,* 2:197-99.

wide movement and could not adequately be dealt with at the conference level. In a sense, this General Conference decision was the critical action, for here the denomination missed the chance to recognize the Bands as a movement and make provision for the movement within its structure.

The result was that the Bands would soon become an independent organization. Hogue says only that the General Conference action "was unacceptable to Mr. Nelson" and his followers, and that the Bands therefore "decided to withdraw" from the denomination.[53] The fact appears to be that the church missed its opportunity to provide an official and workable denomination-wide linkage for a denomination-wide movement.[54] From this perspective the loss of the Pentecost Bands to the denomination was less a matter of hostility and opposition than a failure of foresight and structure. On the other hand, hostility to the Bands in some sectors of the church probably undermined the constructive steps proposed by the Illinois Conference.

Independence and Diffusion, 1895-1958

In April of 1894, the Pentecost Bands began their own newspaper, *The Pentecost Herald* because *The Vanguard* had declared its independence from the FMC. The paper was at first published at Uniontown, Pennsylvania, with Thomas Nelson listed as editor. The first issue contains an explanation of the rationale for the new paper:

> We have been associated with the Vanguard for a number of years, and in representing our evangelistic work through its columns, we have endeavored to help bless the world. It being personal property over which we had no control, and its managers having formed new church relations, and adopted a course we cannot sanction, we sever our relations to it with the kindest feelings, and send out this little messenger with fervent prayer that it may prove worthy of its name, in proclaiming liberty to the captives.[55]

In the same issue, Mary Weems Chapman, office editor and business manager, encapsulates much of the Bands theology at this time with the Moody-esque comment, "This world is like a wrecked vessel. A few more revolutions and time will be no more. Our one business is to get as many precious souls off the wreck as possible before it goes down. We have no time to spend fighting each other's methods, we must haste to the rescue of lost souls."[56]

---

[53]Hogue, *History of the Free Methodist Church,* 2:199.

[54]On the importance of such linkages in renewal movements, see Howard A. Snyder, *Signs of the Spirit: How God Reshapes the Church* (Grand Rapids: Zondervan, 1989), 277-78.

[55]*The Pentecost Herald,* 1:1 (April, 1894), 2.

[56]Ibid. Mary Weems Chapman was an early member of the NTCC and a Pentecost Band and Vanguard missionary to Liberia. See Ingersol, 93, 160, 191; Bliss, 2:214; Hogue, *History of the Free Methodist Church,* 2:253.

Ten months later the Pentecost Bands formally announced their withdrawal from the FMC in a statement headed "Withdrawn" in the *Pentecost Herald*. The reasons given highlighted the issues:

> In consideration of the growing opposition on the part of the FMC generally, to the teachings, the mode of operation, and distinctive nature of the Pentecost Bands; and in consideration of the fact that we cannot fulfill our promise made last Fall to harmonize with the Church without forfeiting the divine favor by changing our views on the conditions of receiving the experience of holiness, by disorganizing the Bands and abandoning what we feel to be a heaven-born evangelism, we have decided to quietly withdraw from the Free Methodist Church.[57]

From this point on, then, the Pentecost Bands were an independent organization and began establishing their own churches.

After the General Conference of 1894 and the withdrawal of the Pentecost Bands from the denomination in early 1895, some of the new churches founded by the Bands were faced with the question of loyalty and identity. Most of the new converts and congregations elected to remain with the FMC rather than continue with the Bands. Harmon Baldwin became a leader in the Pittsburgh Conference where he continued to use the evangelistic band approach; the Shelhamers moved south, opening up Free Methodist work in Georgia and Florida. Other Band workers, both men and women, became pastors in the FMC. With time the Pentecost Bands became primarily a foreign missions society with a gradually declining home base of congregations in the Midwest. The name was changed to Missionary Bands of the World, Incorporated, in 1925.[58]

The energy that had been evident in and generated by the Pentecost Bands became diffused in several directions:

1. A major part of the energy continued on in the Pentecost Bands and Missionary Bands of the World, though in a diminished sense. The Bands continued to attract and deploy missionaries and to maintain their adherence to radical holiness as they understood it, but much of the original dynamism was gone.

2. A significant part of the energy of the movement remained within the denomination. Former Band workers served the church as pastors, evangelists, church planters, foreign missionaries, or as local church workers.

---

[57]"Withdrawn," *The Pentecost Herald*, 1:11 (February, 1895), 2. *The Pentecost Herald* published a list of Band workers in each issue. Ninety-four were listed in the first issue, in 1894; 85 in issue 1:10 (a month before withdrawal); 91 in 1:11, the issue with the withdrawal statement; and 72 the next month. The withdrawal statement was signed by fifty-eight Band members, indicating that around sixty or seventy percent of the workers opted to stay with the Bands and leave the denomination while a number of others stayed in the FMC.

[58]Ira F. McLeister and Roy S. Nicholson. *Conscience and Commitment: The History of the Wesleyan Methodist Church of America* (Marion, IN: Wesley Press, 1976), 242-43.

3. Some part of the Bands impulse went with E. E. and Minnie Baldwin Shelhamer when they started their new ministries in Atlanta, employing some of the methods of Vivian Dake, working both within and beyond the denominational context.[59]

4. A part of the Bands impulse was diffused more broadly into the church as the Vanguard and *Firebrand* ministries also severed ties with the FMC during this same period. As the so-called "radical alliance" broke up, some part of the Pentecost Band impulse was channeled into the NTCC, and thus indirectly into the Church of the Nazarene.

The Pentecost Bands/Missionary Bands of the World reportedly had sixteen congregations in the U.S. in 1906, eleven in 1926, six in 1936, and eleven in 1954. Membership declined from 487 in 1906 to 241 in 1926 and 236 in 1954.

The Bands made at least two unsuccessful attempts to unite with other bodies. In the 1930s, the Bands and the Church of God (Holiness), a small restorationist holiness group in Missouri and Kansas with which C. W. Sherman had united about 1897,[60] took steps toward merger but opposition developed within the Bands.[61] Apparently this period of association resulted in some Band workers transferring to the Church of God (Holiness).[62]

A second attempt occurred in the 1950s when the Bands sent a letter to one of the Free Methodist bishops inquiring whether the Free Methodists would be interested in reuniting. When the Bands received no response, they entered into negotiations with the Wesleyan Methodist Church. The Free Methodist bishop later remembered the letter and contacted the Bands, but by then, in 1958, union with the Wesleyan Methodists was nearly finalized.[63] In 1958, responsibility for the Bands' remaining overseas work was assumed by the Wesleyan Methodist Church.[64]

---

[59]See Bertha B. Smith and Julia A. Shelhamer, *A Remarkable Woman: The Life of Mrs. Minnie B. Shelhamer* (Atlanta: The Repairer, [n.d.]), and E. E. Shelhamer's autobiography, *The Ups and Downs of a Pioneer Preacher* (Atlanta: Repairer Publishing Company, 1915), republished with some revisions as *Sixty Years of Thorns and Roses* (Cincinnati: God's Bible School and Missionary Training Home, n.d.; reprinted in 1969).

[60]Ingersol, 159. On the Church of God (Holiness), see Smith, *Called Unto Holiness,* 29-30; Charles Edwin Jones, *Perfectionist Persuasion: The Holiness Movement and American Methodism* (Metuchen, NJ: Scarecrow Press, 1974), 58.

[61]Maude Kahl, *His Guiding Hand* (Overland Park, KS: Herald and Banner Press, 1970), 140, 185.

[62]Kahl, 185, 198.

[63]Personal correspondence with two of Dake's grandchildren, December 10, 1979.

[64]Jones, *Perfectionist Persuasion,* 209-213; "Missionary Bands of the World, Inc.," typed sheet, part of L. R. Marston's file in his research for *From Age to Age A Living Witness.* Marston Historical Center, Free Methodist Headquarters, Indianapolis, Indiana. See Elmer T. Clark, *The Small Sects in America,* rev. ed. (Nashville: Abingdon Press, 1965), 77.

Some Missiological Issues

Questions of Structure. From 1885 to 1895, the Pentecost Bands functioned informally as a mission sodality within the FMC. The Bands were loosely, but fairly effectively, structured through the leadership of Vivian Dake, who traveled from place to place, visiting Bands and preaching in meetings. A key to the structure and vitality of the movement was the annual Harvest Home camp meetings, which were spiritual high points and also times of organization and planning. Another organizational feature was the end-of-year Ingatherings, held regionally or divisionally. There were Band rules, and Bands usually had their own mottos, such as "Only for Souls" or "Holiness to the Lord." One member of each Band kept a secretary book or journal.[65]

Structurally the Bands were quite similar to early Methodism, and Dake's position within the denomination much like that of Wesley within the Church of England, though of course on a much smaller scale numerically (if not geographically).

Dake had given careful thought to Band organization for some time before the venture was launched in 1885. He had worked out an ingeniously simple and flexible band structure capable of rapid expansion. Normally each band consisted of four persons (all men or all women, if unmarried, or a married couple and one or two single workers) but the composition of a band might change suddenly as new workers were added, bands were reorganized, or a worker died. An assistant leader was in effect an apprentice who might become the leader of the same or a new band.

The FMC found it difficult to be tolerant of or work out an effective arrangement with the Pentecost Bands. This was due partly to the denomination's small size and its own struggles as a relatively new movement. Still, Byron Lamson, writing around 1960, considered it highly unfortunate for Free Methodism that the zeal and aggressive evangelizing impulse of the Bands were lost to the denomination. From his perspective as General Missionary Secretary for many years Lamson wrote:

> The rate of church growth suffered a drastic moderation from this time. To the present day, Free Methodism does not have the early evangelistic drive, the sense of mission, the sacrificial concern for saving the lost world that characterized the founders of the movement and that was incarnate in Vivian Dake. In correcting errors and regulating the fiery zeal of youthful Band workers, the church itself seemed to somehow lose its "first love" for the lost world.[66]

The Ministry of All Believers. The Pentecost Bands were in effect a "lay" evangelizing, church-planting order, a sodality structure within a denomination

---

[65]The best sources on Pentecost Band organization are the article "Pentecost Bands" in Bliss, 2:214-15, and the handwritten "North Parma Pentecost Band" journal or notebook, 1885, cited above.

[66]Lamson, 135.

which in some ways was itself still structured somewhat like a sodality; a form of *ecclesiola* within the *ecclesia*.[67]

Clearly the Pentecost Bands provided expanded ministry opportunities beyond what was available in the denominational structure and in most local churches for many young Christians, most of whom had no formal training or ordination.

For the most part, Free Methodists did not consciously stress the ministry of all believers or the gifts of the Spirit. The FMC largely took over the ecclesiastical structure of the Methodist Church, including the clergy dominance that had developed by that time. Significantly, the FMC did provide for equal ministerial and lay representation in denominational decision-making bodies, largely in reaction to the way B. T. Roberts and other pastors had been treated by the dominant clergy in the Genesee Conference of the Methodist Episcopal Church.

Reports in Free Methodist annual conferences repeatedly complained about the lack of adequate support for pastors. One senses the heavy burdens and hard work that were the lot of most Free Methodist preachers during this time. There was virtually no call, however, for an expanded understanding of ministry. One notes concerns and complaints about the decline of the class meeting; it seems clear that the class meeting structure was not vital at this time and that class leaders had nothing like the pastoral role that they had in early Methodism. In this sense, the Pentecost Bands may be viewed as an attempt to correct an ecclesiological and structural weakness within the denomination.

Evangelism and Church Growth. The Pentecost Bands added a significant number of new congregations to the denomination. It would appear that the Bands were responsible for starting over one hundred new congregations within a ten-year span, not all of which survived. It seems clear that the Pentecost Bands were a more significant factor in the growth of the denomination prior to 1900 than is generally recognized.

Overall, the Pentecost Bands provide a fascinating picture of a new movement arising within a relatively young and small denomination, and an interesting perspective on issues of holiness theology, practice, and mission in the late nineteenth century.

---

[67]T. Joe Culumber, "The Pentecost Bands: A Mission Sodality in Early Free Methodism" (Doctor of Ministry Research Paper, Fuller Theological Seminary, 1977, 55 pp.); Snyder, chapter two.

Chapter 7

"Planning and Prevailing for the Children": E. E. Shelhamer and Julia Arnold Shelhamer on Children and Parenting

Gari-Anne Patzwald

"Lord, if these children can't be looked up to at school as extraordinarily bright, if they can't be extraordinarily pretty or have extra nice clothes, here's one thing they can be—they can be extra-ordinarily spiritual. Help them to determine to be above average in living close to God." With these words, popular holiness evangelist E. E. Shelhamer expressed his wishes for his children and, by extension, for all children.[1]

E. E. Shelhamer and his evangelist wife Julia Arnold Shelhamer were particularly interested in ministry to children whom they viewed as carriers of original sin who needed to be saved from inborn evil tendencies that were fed by secular society. They employed a variety of methods in this ministry, including lectures, revival services, books and tracts, and radio broadcasts, to encourage children to find the means to live perfect Christian lives and serve God, and to provide parents with guidance for raising good, Christian children. The Shelhamers also worked to make their own family an exemplary model of the perfect Christian family.

Elmer Ellsworth Shelhamer was born in rural Western Pennsylvania in 1869, one of seven children. While attending Wheaton College in Illinois, he was converted under the ministry of evangelist Vivian Dake and joined Dake's Pentecost Bands. In 1892, he met a dynamic young Bands worker, Minnie Baldwin, and they were married the following year. The couple left the Bands and established a mission in Atlanta under the auspices of the Free Methodist Church,

---

[1] Quoted in Esther Shelhamer James, "My Wonderful Father," in Julia A. Shelhamer, *A Spartan Evangel: Life Story of E. E Shelhamer as told by himself and his wife* (Winona Lake, IN: Light and Life Press, 1951), 172. The title of this essay is a chapter heading in E. E. Shelhamer and Julia A. Shelhamer. *How to Train and Save Your Children* (Fort Wayne, IN: Old Time Religion Tabernacle, n.d.).

a mission that would eventually result in E. E. Shelhamer's being credited with establishing the Free Methodist Church in Florida and Georgia.²

Minnie Shelhamer died in childbirth in 1902, and the following year, E. E. married Julia Arnold whose parents, evangelists Adelia Nichols Arnold and I. R. B. Arnold, had five daughters who had, as young children, become involved in their family's ministry, which, for several years, was conducted on a barge known as "the Floating Chapel" on the Mississippi and Ohio Rivers. Eventually, Adelia Arnold separated from her husband and established a ministry to African Americans in Atlanta. It was there that Julia met E. E. Shelhamer.

Julia may have been influenced in her interest in ministry to children by her mother, who conducted children's meetings, and by her uncle, T. B. Arnold, a Free Methodist minister, publisher, and editor who was so moved by the plight of orphaned children on the streets of Chicago that he began to take them into his home. He formed the Chicago Industrial Home for Children in 1888. In 1891, the home moved to Woodstock, Illinois and became known as the Woodstock Children's Home.³

The Shelhamers subscribed to the doctrine of marital purity, which dictated that sexual relations were solely for the purpose of conceiving children and that children who were "products of lust," were "about half-damned when they are born and many of them entirely damned when but fifteen years of age.⁴" Consequently, salvation began before conception, and, if children were not properly conceived, it was particularly important to make efforts to save them as soon as possible after they were born.

---

²On the establishment of Free Methodism in Georgia and Florida, see Wilson T. Hogue, *History of the Free Methodist Church of North America. Vol. 2.* (Chicago: Free Methodist Publishing House, 1915), 120-2.

³Jane Arnold Masters, "Rev. T. B. Arnold Chronology," *Woodstock Friend,* Fall/Winter 1999, 3-5. On the Woodstock home, see http://www.hearthstonewoodstock.org/About/allhistory.htm. (Accessed May 20, 2015). T. B. Arnold's possible influence on Julia is suggested by her identification of herself as "the niece of T. B. Arnold" in her biography of her husband, *A Spartan Evangel.* Julia's sister, Jennie Jolley also evidenced an interest in children. She and her husband, E. O. Jolley donated funds to establish the Jolley Home for needy children in Conyers, Georgia in the 1930s. In the 1940s, probably in an attempt to take advantage of the Shelhamers' fame as evangelists, the Home's property was designated Shelhamer Memorial Acres, and contributions were solicited in that name. The home now operates as Elks Aidmore Children's Center.

⁴E. E. Shelhamer, *How to Train,* 5. In addition to the Shelhamers' own advice on parenting, *How to Train and Save Your Children* contains excerpts from John Wesley's writings on childrearing and advice from Free Methodist founder B. T. Roberts. With regard to many social issues, such as marital purity, E. E. cited surprisingly few references to scripture to support his views. This obviously did not trouble him. When an attendee at one of his meetings challenged E. E.'s opposition to the use of tobacco "since the Bible does not mention tobacco," rather than citing scripture that others might have in the same situation, E. E. replied that the Bible does not mention tobacco, "simply because it is too filthy," and "the Bible is a book of principles covering every unclean thing without necessarily mentioning it in so many words." (Shelhamer, *Spartan Evangel,* 50).

The Shelhamers believed that even very young children could be converted. As E. E. wrote, "We ought by all means to insist upon our children's being saved just as early as possible. I have known of little ones three, four, and five years of age who were gloriously blest, and when they are saved that young they will likely never depart from God, provided the parents deal gently and wisely with them." As evidence, the Shelhamers noted that their daughter Evangeline had joined the church at the age of three.[5]

The Shelhamers admonished parents to keep the salvation of their children "uppermost" in their minds, and to pray for them constantly. They stressed the importance of being willing to spend whatever was necessary to live close to "a good church" so that children can "go regularly to a spiritual Sunday School, or attend old-time revival meetings."[6]

Like many holiness preachers and writers, the Shelhamers seemed to believe that evil was more attractive than good, and that the smallest diversion from the paths of righteousness put one on a slippery slope to total depravity. They warned parents about several things that put their children in danger. These included: using "wine to season mince pies," and "whisky and sugar for colds, and patent medicine containing alcohol when sick"; letting young girls go "half dressed"; allowing boys "to play with neighbor boys, [and] to remain on the streets after dark," where they might learn "coarse jokes and love-songs"; and permitting secular music in the home because there was "always danger that when marches, waltzes and quicksteps are used, even for practice . . . one rarely discontinues their use after once having started." Children might not even be safe at church where serialized stories in Sunday School papers and magazines might give children "a desire for fiction, instead of a taste for deep, logical, mind-stretching literature."[7]

While she recognized that the Bible indicated that corporal punishment might be appropriate in some instances, Julia believed that it should be avoided partly because "a man does not know his own strength when punishing a little one, even in love; and when angry, he has no conception of the unnecessary pain and possible injury he may inflict." Julia thought that instead a parent should strive to set a good example for her or his child because "a child is the embodiment of the faults and virtues" of the parent.[8]

The Shelhamers were concerned that motherhood, "although a blessing for most women . . . often discourages all effort to work for God," and therefore might interfere with the setting of a good example. To combat this, the Shelhamers were ready with ten suggestions for mothers to work for Jesus. Among these were: call on friends and enlist their aid in evangelization; get acquainted with the unsaved

---

[5]Ibid 24-5. On Evangeline's early conversion, see the *Kingswood Voice,* March 1930. Evangeline began to appear with her parents at evangelistic meetings at the age of eighteen months.

[6]E. Shelhamer and J. Shelhamer, *How to Train, 24.*

[7]Ibid., 28-30. In 1916, in an effort to keep alcohol and spices out of such things as mince pies, Julia sold alcohol-free flavorings through advertisements in the Shelhamers' Atlanta ministry's monthly newspaper, *The Repairer.*

[8]Julia Shelhamer in Ibid., 6-7.

in the community and hold "cottage meetings" for them; visit jails and hospitals one day and asylums and almshouses another, doing "all you can for the inmates of these places; of course, keep a good supply of tracts and other literature on hand to distribute at these various places"; rent a small "school house, hall, or vacant church" and begin services; and get children together and have a service or tell Bible stories.

The Shelhamers realized that it just might not be possible for a mother "to get out much." In that case, she could loan good books to friends, neighbors, and "the poor degraded people of your city whom you may meet by inquiring of associated charities, the policemen or the Salvation Army." Finally, the mother could write letters, because, "a good encouraging letter or one filled with warning or advice may accomplish great good." They concluded, "If a woman is conscientious and systematic regarding the use of her time, something like the foregoing plan may be carried out without neglecting either her home or family and in the same length of time that most women spend for mere pleasure seeking." However, the Shelhamers were forced to admit that one might need to hire someone to tend to the children in order to have afternoons free for evangelistic activities.[9]

With regard to having time for both family and soul winning, E. E. considered the possibility that adoption was a mistake for Christian workers who have no children because "parental affection is lacking and to set in to cultivate it, one does so at the expense of spiritual development and a passion for souls." The fact that Julia's sister, Lucia, and her clergyman husband Dudley W. Rose had two adopted children who were described by relatives as "difficult" may have affected the Shelhamers' views on adoption.[10]

While her husband preached at worship services for adults, Julia often attended Sunday School classes where she attempted to convert children. One of her great successes occurred at Albuquerque, New Mexico, in February of 1946, when she preached to children on Sunday morning and forty children answered her altar call with thirty-three professing conversion. That evening, she held a children's meeting at which ten children came to the altar and "2 fine boys prayed through gloriously."[11]

As part of their revival meetings, E. E. often met separately with boys and Julia with girls to promote their agenda to encourage pure thought and clean living. Julia, who had started her evangelistic career at a young age, also led the young people in outreach activities. Holiness bibliographer Charles Edwin Jones remembers that in conjunction with a revival at a Church of God (Holiness) Church in Kansas City, Missouri in the early 1940s, his sister was part of a youth group

---

[9] E. E. Shelhamer and Julia Shelhamer, *How to Help or Hinder a Revival.* 3d ed. Reprint ed. (Salem, OH: Allegheny Publications, 1992), 39-44.

[10] E. E. Shelhamer, *The Ups and Downs of a Pioneer Preacher* (Atlanta: Repairer, 1915), 264; Stephen James, e-mail to author, December 30, 2015.

[11] Julia Arnold Shelhamer, diary, 1946. Shelhamer Family Papers, B. L. Fisher Library, Asbury Theological Seminary.

that accompanied Julia on a sojourn to a neighborhood tavern to hand out tracts.[12]

Publications were always key to the Shelhamers' ministry, and they produced two books of advice and warning for distribution to adolescent readers and their parents—*Heart Talks to Girls* by Mrs. Julia A. Shelhamer and *Heart Talks to Boys* by E. E. Shelhamer.[13] The emphasis in both books is on the relationship between thoughts and actions.

In her book, Julia describes four ways that the body can be harmed by impure thoughts: they lead to some form of outward sin; they affect one's appearance—gait, carriage, general features, and "look of the eye"; they draw blood from organs that need it and abnormally develop other organs; and, in what appears to be an appeal to the sin of vanity, "they injure the complexion." In relation to the last, Julia notes that the impure thoughts take "roses from the face and the lustre from the eye, until the little girl thinks she must use rouge and powder in their place." She blames the misdirection of blood for injury to the mind that depends on "the rich, new blood that is supplied by the heart" and which, without it, lapses into a "semi-dormant state." This state is evident in the fondness that many young women have for fiction, particularly a love story "that helps feed the flame of lust which is already blazing in the heart."[14]

In his book, E. E. states emphatically (in bold letters) that "All sin begins with a thought," and that "when we come to the judgment, no doubt we will find that God has placed a higher premium upon holy thought [again in bold letters] than upon holy deeds. . . .because an act is not acceptable to God unless the inner intention is for His glory."[15]

Since both books include messages to parents that emphasize the importance of providing information on subjects related to sex, they do not shy away from sensitive issues. For example, both strongly condemn the practice of masturbation, which E. E. labels, "The Greatest Sin of the World," in a chapter title, and a subject to which he returns repeatedly throughout the book. In *Heart Talks to Girls*, Julia includes only a brief discussion of the matter and refers readers to the chapter on masturbation in *Heart Talks to Boys*. Both books contain horror stories of what happens to people who engage in the practice. In *Heart Talks to Boys*, it is the "overseer" of a mental institution who blames it for the conditions of two-thirds of the institution's male patients; in *Heart Talks to Girls*, it is a young man from a good Methodist family who loses his ability to speak in public due to "self-abuse."[16]

---

[12]Charles Edwin Jones, letter to the author, March 21, 2015.

[13]Both books are available in several editions or printings. For the purpose of this paper, *Heart Talks to Girls* is an edition published by Repairer Publishing Company, Atlanta, Georgia. *Heart Talks to Boys* is an edition published by The Student of Prophecy, Barbados, T.W.I. As with most Shelhamer publications, neither work is dated, and there is no indication they were copyrighted.

[14]J. Shelhamer, *Heart Talks to Girls*, 9-10.

[15]E. Shelhamer, *Heart Talks to Boys*, 10.

[16]J. Shelhamer, *Heart Talks to Girls*, 14; E. Shelhamer, *Heart Talks to Boys*, 42. On the belief that there is a link between masturbation and mental illness, see E. H. Hare, "Mas-

While Julia imposed the responsibility for moral living on girls, because "boys are more easily led astray," E. E. admonished boys to become protectors of women. In fact, E. E. suggested that "in each community Boys organize a PURITY BAND, the object of which will be The Protection of Girls, The Circulation of Clean Literature, and the Living of Pure Lives."[17]

Julia also produced a book of edifying stories that teach such values as honesty, temperance, truthfulness, and Sabbath keeping, and which describe the rewards for doing right and the punishments for doing wrong. There are also stories of children as young as two years old being instrumental in the conversion of others. The stories are sentimental and reflect the Victorian Era in which Julia was raised. Typical of them is the story of "Brave Ben," a young man who is anxious to find employment so that his "poor mother" will be "able to live." Responding to a "Help Wanted" sign in a hotel window, Ben is offered a job that occasionally involves serving liquor to travelers. Knowing that God and his mother would disapprove of his taking the job, and fearing that it could lead to his own taking to strong drink, he turns it down. A prosperous traveler overhears Ben's reasons for refusing the job and offers him employment as his clerk because he is looking for a clerk whom he can trust, "a boy who is faithful to God, faithful to his mother, and faithful to his own conscience."[18]

E. E., who had done hard physical labor as a youth in order to earn money to buy his own clothes, firmly believed in the value of hard work. He wrote, "Parents make no greater mistake than to let their children grow up unaccustomed to hard labor and self-denial. The more a child is humored the more he becomes self-willed and less liable to submit to God or man. The less he is familiar with hardships the less easily he can adapt himself to them, or sympathize with others under similar circumstances."[19]

The Shelhamers believed that salvation was "much more important" for children than education.[20] Reflecting the anti-intellectualism of the radical Holiness Movement, they were strongly opposed to public education, possibly at least partially due to the experiences they had had as children in public school, E. E. having been teased because his family could not afford to buy him new clothes more often than every two years and his clothes were often ill-fitting and ragged, and Julia because, as a child of traveling evangelists, her education was erratic and she found that "the secular school failed to give [her] the type of training she needed for the work that God had chosen for her."[21]

---

turbatory Insanity: The History of an Idea," *British Journal of Psychiatry* 108 (January 1962): 1-25.

[17] J. Shelhamer, *Heart Talks to Girls*, 21; E. Shelhamer, *Heart Talks to Boys*, 3. The author has no evidence that Purity Bands were ever successfully formed.

[18] Julia A. Shelhamer, *Thrilling Stories for Young and Old* (Cincinnati: God's Bible School and College, n.d.), 47-49.

[19] E. E. Shelhamer, *Experiences in Travel and Soul Saving*. Reprint ed. (Salem, OH: Allegheny Publications, 1992), 5.

[20] E. Shelhamer, *How to Train*, 5.

[21] Glen Williamson, *Julia: Giantess of Generosity* (Winona Lake, IN: Light and Life

As E. E. wrote, "The education of our youth is becoming a great problem to conscientious parents. The fact is, in most of our public schools the morals are so corrupt that they poison the mind of a child before he is ten years of age." E. E. further asserted that "many of our religious schools seem little better" because "these so-called holiness schools are not pronounced against the first approaches of fashion, foolishness, and flirting."[22]

Julia did not hesitate to confront young women whom she felt were not living up to her standards. In *Heart Talks to Girls*, she tells of approaching a fashionably attired young woman on a railroad platform in Asheville, North Carolina to tell her that her sleeveless dress was causing impure thoughts in two young men whom Julia had overheard talking about the young woman.[23]

Unfortunately, Julia's attempts at reform were not always without their problems. In her diary for September 25, 1945, Julia wrote, "Today I spoke to a 16 yr old girl across St. because of her nakedness (shorts). It caused a big uproar. I suffered much." Reflecting on the incident the following day, she wrote, "Maybe I better not reprove any more. I must be polite. Lord help us."[24]

While Julia tended to use the stick of the dire consequences of impure thinking and bad behavior in *Heart Talks to Girls*, later in life, she was not averse to using the carrot of bribery to reach her goals with children. In 1975, she wrote a note on the back of an envelope that read, "This one hundred dollars is to be divided among the girls in your school whose skirts are long enough and wide enough so that standing or sitting their knees are covered at all times." Continuing in the same vein, she placed an advertisement in the December 15, 1980 issue of the *Wesleyan Advocate* that read: "I would like to offer $3.00 cash to any boy or girl, 12 years of age and under, who is able to successfully repeat Exodus 20:3-17 from memory to his or her Sunday School teacher or pastor. As it is, I have

---

Press, 1969), 39. Eventually on her own initiative, Julia enrolled at Evansville Seminary in Evansville, Wisconsin.

[22]E. E. Shelhamer, *Sermons that Search the Soul* (Kansas City: Nazarene Publishing House, 1926), 198. According to E. E. and Julia's youngest daughter, Esther Shelhamer-James, the Shelhamer children's education was as erratic as their mother's had been. Their son Everett "would go to whatever school was in the town her parents were staying in, sometimes 2 weeks, sometimes a month or two." Evangeline attended high school in Centralia, Washington, for one year and attended college at Kingswood College in Kentucky.(A Harrisburg, Pennsylvania newspaper lists an Evangeline Shelhamer as a student at Camp Curtin Junior High School in 1919, and since E. E. and Julia Shelhamer were ministering in Pennsylvania at this time, this student may well be their daughter. [*Harrisburg Telegraph*, November 26, December 3 and 6, 1919]). After Esther was born, her parents traveled less and she attended school in California where "she was always 2 years ahead of her age group," and where she probably completed seventh grade. She attended Frankfort Pilgrim Holiness School in Frankfort, Indiana for one semester before going to God's Bible School to complete her education. (David James to Stephen James, e-mail, March 28, 2016, forwarded to the author). Everett also attended Kingswood College and God's Bible School. *The Hub* (Little Valley, NY), January 24, 1946.

[23]Julia A. Shelhamer, *Heart Talks to Girls*(Atlanta: Repairer Publishing Co.), 22-23.

[24]Julia Shelhamer, diary, 1942-1946, Shelhamer Family Papers.

$102.00 on hand for this purpose." She received letters from pastors in seven states reporting on students who had succeeded in the task, as well as letters from several recipients thanking her for their rewards.[25]

The Shelhamers saw children as potential evangelists. As Julia wrote in their book *How to Train and Save Your Children,* "Teach your children to win souls by giving them tracts and books to distribute, and by taking them with you on your rounds of gospel work. . . . If you keep your children busy for God, Satan will not have such an advantage over them. Husband and I took our baby Evangeline to the death cell of the Atlanta jail. The little one sang a song for the condemned criminal...."[26]

As the daughter of I.R.B. Arnold, who was a pioneer in the use of media for religious instruction through the use of stereopticon views, it is not surprising that Julia would take to the airwaves in the 1930s and 1940s when she and her family were living in Cincinnati at God's Bible School, which had its own radio station. Many of her radio talks were directed to children, teaching them such virtues as respect for their parents.[27] Julia was also responsible for children's programs at the School's annual Mount of Blessing Camp Meeting for several years in the 1930s.

E. E. believed that ministers had a special responsibility to direct their children into religious vocations. He wrote, "It would seem that ministers, who in reality are Levites, should raise children only for their tribe—the ministry. Why? While the family was growing up, the parents were more or less handicapped in the work of soul winning. Hence, in order to recompense this loss, some, if not all, of their children should take up the same line of work and accomplish what the parent failed to accomplish." Consequently, Julia noted that E. E.'s "greatest ambition was that [their children] should win souls for Christ. Therefore from babyhood up, he trained them in this line of work."[28]

The Shelhamers believed that parents could act as agents of their children's salvation by "entering into a secret covenant between themselves and their God." To that end, according to E. E., they "entered into a specific covenant . . . to pray and fast at least one meal each Tuesday for the salvation of our children. God told us as a result, He would save them all and call all into ministry." Although E. E. boasted that God had "done that very thing," their attempts to nurture full-time dedicated Christian workers to carry on the traditions of the Shelhamer and Arnold families met with somewhat mixed results.[29]

---

[25] Julia Shelhamer, Shelhamer Family Papers. There is no indication to whom she planned to send the offer of rewards for proper skirt lengths or if the offer was ever actually made.

[26] E. Shelhamer and J. Shelhamer, *How to Train,* 32.

[27] Scripts of some of her broadcasts for 1933 are available in the Shelhamer Family Papers at Asbury Theological Seminary.

[28] *Spartan Evangel,* 166.

[29] E. Shelhamer, *How to Train,* 23; E. E. Shelhamer, *Searching Sermons for Saints and Sinners* (Cincinnati: God's Bible School, n.d.), 7. According to Wallace Thornton, an expert on the radical Holiness Movement, the belief that ministers have a special responsibility to produce children who will carry on their ministries is not common in the Movement

Julia wrote: "We have found that young people attend church much better if there are those of their age who assist in the meetings, so our children are given their parts to perform in our evangelistic work, even to praying at the altar with seekers. Esther sang her little solos and Everette preached his little sermons. All testified; and Evangeline, our oldest, became so proficient in soul-winning that at an early age she accompanied her father on many of his evangelistic trips. Even Baby Juliette attracted a certain class of people to the services."[30]

The Shelhamers were both saddened by the loss of their daughter Juliette who died in 1915, just short of her second birthday. Julia wrote later that Juliette was a

Shelhamer Family, 1928. Front row: Julia Arnold Shelhamer, E. E. Shelhamer; back row: Evangeline Shelhamer Surbrook, Walter Surbrook, Everette Shelhamer, Esther Shelhamer (Photo courtesy of the B. L. Fisher Library, Asbury Theological Seminary)

model child, using words like "angelic" and "modest" to describe her. According to Julia, Juliette's "favorite song was 'Around the Throne of God in Heaven'. . . [which] she sang beautifully, holding long on the last note and clapping her little hands to keep time."[31]

E. E. obviously felt considerable guilt for having been so busy with his work that he had not spent more time with Juliette. He wrote,

> I remember our sweet, blue-eyed, golden-haired girl, who when she occasionally slipped into the study where I was battling with a stack of mail or working on a new book, would whisper or speak in an undertone to her mother and say, "Papa." Though I generally smiled and gave a kiss, I feel a sense of sadness now that I did not take more time to let her climb up into my arms and "yove" (love) me. But I

---

and may have been unique to the Shelhamers. (Personal interview by the author, Indianapolis, IN, June 17, 2015). In his book, *Radical Righteousness: Personal Ethics and the Development of the Holiness Movement* (Salem, OH: Schmul Publishing Company, 1998), Thornton suggests that E. E. Shelhamer was on the radical fringe of the already radical Holiness Movement (114-116). Others suggested that E. E. Shelhamer's views were unusual or unique, including S. W. Stone who, in his memorial tribute to E. E., wrote, "In his writings, he was a man by himself, original in his own findings, and wrote about many important things that others did not seem to write about." *Free Methodist*, February 21, 1947.

[30] J. Shelhamer, *Spartan Evangel*, 166.
[31] Julia A. Shelhamer, *Thrilling Stories*, 1.

was too busy. . . . Had I but known that the little blossom would have been with us so short a time, I would gladly have given her some of the time I have spent in tears, kneeling at the little grave. The experience taught him that "being too much absorbed, even in good things, is not best for the soul, mind, or body."[32]

In 1930, the pair was devastated again when their daughter Evangeline Shelhamer Surbrook, a talented and promising evangelist, died suddenly in childbirth at the age of twenty-five. The loss was particularly difficult for Julia who struggled to understand why God would take such a promising worker so young. She frequently dreamed about her lost daughter and expressed feelings that Evangeline was still with her. Julia mourned Evangeline's death for the remainder of her life and often spoke of her lost daughter in her sermons and teaching.[33]

E. E. and Julia encouraged their only son Everett to become an evangelist. During the 1930s he accompanied his father on foreign mission trips and conducted services, either as primary evangelist or with others. In 1936, he married Frances Baker, with whom he conducted evangelistic meetings under the auspices of the Free Methodist Church in the 1930s and 1940s. He was a talented musician, who, according to family members, "was a spectacular pianist who would often compose hymns off the cuff" while he was conducting services. Children's programs were featured parts of Everett's and Frances's ministry.[34]

During World War II, Everett supported the war effort by working in a wire factory in Fort Wayne, Indiana. After a brief sojourn into farming, he donated land for the construction of a Pilgrim Holiness Church in Churubusco, Indiana, which he pastored for several years. In 1955, he moved to Huntington, Indiana, where he was employed at the Schact Rubber Company until his retirement at the age of seventy.

After relocating to Huntington, Everett wrote short edifying pieces that he placed as advertisements in a local newspaper. These articles often reflected his concerns about the potential atheistic influences of communism. He was also an active labor union member and an avid tennis player.[35]

The Shelhamers encouraged their youngest daughter Esther to engage in ministry, which she did apparently somewhat reluctantly when, as she noted in a 2005 interview, her father "shoved me forward" to perform at his revival meetings.[36] However, Esther did have a call to carry on the Shelhamer/Arnold mission, with special emphasis on ministry to people of color that had been a

---

[32]E. Shelhamer, *Sermons that Search*, 220-1.

[33]See Julia Shelhamer, diaries, September 17, 1932; March 3, 1945; and July 17, 1947; Shelhamer Family Papers, for example.

[34]Stephen James to the author, e-mail, July 26, 2015. See announcements of revivals held by Everett and Frances Shelhamer in the *Free Methodist* for March 7, March 21, July 4, and October 17, 1941.

[35]Everett's first name was originally spelled "Everette." As an evangelist, he was sometimes billed as "E. E. Shelhamer, Jr.", although his father's first name was Elmer. Information on Everett's life after E. E.'s death was provided by his nephew, Stephen James (e-mail to the author, July 27, 2015). Everett died in Huntington in 2003.

[36]Esther Shelhamer James, interview with Don Joy, 2005.

calling of both of her Nichols great grandparents, who had sheltered escaped slaves on the Underground Railroad, her grandmother Adelia Arnold, and her parents.

After completing her high school education at God's Bible School, Esther served for two years in the dispensary of a Free Methodist mission in Burundi, which she reluctantly left when called back to the United States by her parents. She planned to return at a later date, but the plan had to be abandoned due to travel restrictions imposed by the United States government during World War II.

In 1942, Esther married fellow God's Bible School student Gilbert James, who shared her desire to do mission work. The Free Methodist Church sent the couple to Shreveport, Louisiana where they were instrumental in the development of an African American Free Methodist ministry. Four years later, Gilbert was reassigned to the denomination's Department of Interracial Evangelism. After earning his doctorate from Northwestern University, he joined the faculty of Asbury Theological Seminary in Wilmore, Kentucky where he was responsible for the development of a pioneering urban ministry program. Esther, who had studied piano while a student at God's Bible School, was an accomplished accompanist for music programs in Wilmore. She also worked in the seminary library, helping to select Methodist-related titles for the collection. Like other members of her family, she is an active distributor of tracts.[37]

After E. E. Shelhamer's death in 1947, Julia moved to Washington, D. C. to establish the Shelhamer Memorial Mission in memory of her husband. Supported by a small income from an annuity, as well as some funds from the Free Methodist Church and donations from her many contacts, she began a ministry to African Americans with a special emphasis on children.

Shortly after her arrival in Washington, Julia and her sister Helen Arnold "went out to [the] lowest Negro dist. to locate a preaching place," and held two "wayside" services for African American children.[38] They were able to make a down payment on a brick house in an area known as "Hell's Half-Acre" where it was estimated that there were five thousand African Americans within a two-block radius. Here they established their mission. Their first convert was a young African American boy.

Although the Shelhamer Memorial Mission served people of all ages, it was most successful among its target audience—young people. At one point, Helen Arnold had over one hundred infants on her cradle roll. Julia wrote, "We are giving young people a chance to develop their talents by making gospel calls, praying with derelicts who come begging for bread, conducting street meetings, singing solos, preaching, and exhorting." The Mission donated Gospels to a local

---

[37]Esther Shelhamer James, interview by Don Joy. When Esther attended the Joint Meeting of the Society of Pentecostal Studies and the Wesleyan Theological Society in Lexington, Kentucky, in 2003, she arrived with a handful of tracts to distribute when the opportunity arose. As of 2016, she is living with her son in Cary, North Carolina, and still enclosing tracts in her personal letters.

[38]Julia Shelhamer, diary, 17 September 1947, Shelhamer Family Papers.

school and to the Metropolitan Boys Club, and they held a three-week children's revival.[39]

Julia saw a need for the children to experience time away from their urban environment. Consequently, she raised funds that enabled her to establish "Camp Shelhamer," a retreat in Virginia at which city children could spend a few days in the summer thanks to sponsorships solicited by Julia through her extensive list of supporters.

A lasting legacy from the Washington mission was in the person of Gene Alston, a boy who lived down the street from the Mission. Gene was mentored by Julia, and he became one of many African American young people whose college educations were paid for with funds that Julia raised. Gene attended Greenville College and later, somewhat reluctantly, became the first African American student to attend Asbury Theological Seminary. Eventually earning a doctorate from St. Louis University, he had a successful career as a Free Methodist pastor, principal of a Christian school in Shreveport, Louisiana, and public school teacher.

Julia left the Mission in 1959 and relocated to Winona Lake, Indiana, but she continued to use her extensive list of contacts to raise money for the Mission until it closed in 1965, a victim of urban renewal. Reunions of Mission participants were held into the 1990s.

Julia moved again, this time to Wilmore, Kentucky, to be near Esther. There she continued her ministry to African Americans, speaking in African American churches and conducting religious services and educational programs for African American adults and children in nearby Keene, Kentucky. She also arranged with a teacher in the Wilmore public school to pay children to visit her in her home and read the Bible to her. She felt that this would help them in their studies and give her "a chance to endeavor to lead them to Christ."[40]

As her health declined, she enlisted the help of others, particularly Esther, to maintain an active ministry of fundraising and distributing tracts by mail. Julia died in 1981 at the age of 101. It was only fitting that a small fund of memorial donations was given to support the Shreveport school that had been associated with the interracial ministry of Esther and Gilbert James.

Julia Shelhamer wrote that children, "draw us nearer to Christ in our efforts to be more childlike toward Him." They also "teach us to have the same attitude toward the junior part of the world that Jesus had" when He admonished his disciples to "suffer the little children to come unto me, and forbid them not, for such is the kingdom of heaven."[41] In their ministries, E.E. and Julia Shelhamer demonstrated their commitment to helping others to appreciate the roles that they and their children can play in the work of the kingdom.

---

[39]Williamson, *Julia,* 93.

[40]Julia Shelhamer to Friend in Jesus, undated form letter, Shelhamer Family Papers, Asbury Theological Seminary.

[41]Julia A. Shelhamer, *A Whisper to Women* (Cincinnati: God's Revivalist Office, n.d.), 95.

Chapter 8

Single Vision, Separate Spheres: Iva Durham Vennard and the Methodist Episcopal Church[1]

Priscilla Pope-Levison

Iva May Durham Vennard
Courtesy of MidAmerica Nazarene University

The term "separate spheres" has been championed by many historians in the last several decades as a primary means by which to understand, analyze, and describe women's lives in American culture. "Separate spheres" is a term that has multiple

---

[1]Support for this paper came from a Lilly Theological Research Grant administered by the Association of Theological Schools which funded a research trip to the archives at B. L. Fisher Library, Asbury Theological Seminary. The archivist, Dr. William Kostlevy, was generous with his time, his knowledge of the holiness movement, and the archives' resources. Editorial support was provided by colleagues Nancy Hewitt, John R. Levison, and Russell E. Richey.

meanings. When used as a metaphor, "separate spheres" can refer interchangeably to, as Linda K. Kerber proposes, "an ideology *imposed* on women, a culture *created by* women, a set of boundaries *expected to be observed* by women."² Along with its metaphorical function, "separate spheres" is descriptive in its literal sense of a physical space apart from men's space that women claim as their own. In this connection, Kerber cites Estelle Freedman's article on the separatist strategy of "female institution building" among middle-class predominantly white women in the years 1870-1930. Through this strategy, women developed organizations separate from men's in the public sphere.³ According to Freedman, this strategy "helped mobilize women and gained political leverage in the larger society" while, at the same time, it maintained "the positive attraction of the female world of close, personal relationships and domestic institutional structures."⁴

Rosemary Skinner Keller reached the same conclusions in an earlier study of women's organizations in the Methodist Episcopal Church (MEC). In her article, "Creating a Sphere for Women," she views the formation of a separate sphere for women's religious activities as essential to their developing a powerful organization of their own, training themselves for broader positions of leadership, and for strengthening sisterhood among the women of the church.⁵ In the final sentence, she writes, "In looking back, we can conclude that by developing an autonomous organization which opened up expanded purpose, sisterhood, and leadership for women, the founders possessed the enlightened vision and practical know-how to begin a movement which one day would enable women and men together to eliminate a separate sphere for women in church and society."⁶

This essay focuses on the life of a woman evangelist, Iva May Durham Vennard,⁷ who experienced neither sisterhood nor leadership opportunities through the separatist strategy of "female institution building" in women's organizations in her denomination. Even though her life spans the same years as

---

²Linda K. Kerber, "Separate Spheres, Female Worlds, Woman's Place: The Rhetoric of Women's History," *Journal of American History* (1988): 17.

³Ibid, 31-2.

⁴Estelle Freedman, "Separation as Strategy: Female Institution Building and American Feminism," *Feminist Studies* (1979): 513-7.

⁵Rosemary Skinner Keller, "Creating a Sphere For Women," in *Women in New Worlds*, eds. Hilah H. Thomas and Rosemary Skinner Keller (Nashville: Abingdon, 1981), 247.

⁶Ibid, 259-60.

⁷Iva May Durham married Thomas Vennard in 1904. In this essay, she is referred to as either Iva May Durham/Iva May, or Iva Durham Vennard, depending on which years of her life are being discussed. For general references, she is referred to as Iva Durham Vennard. Most of the information on her life is found in a biography (*Alabaster and Spikenard: The Life of Iva Durham Vennard, D.D., Founder of Chicago Evangelistic Institute*, [Chicago: Chicago Evangelistic Institute, 1947]) written by Mary Ella Bowie, a student and long-time faculty member at Chicago Evangelistic Institute, and a close personal friend of Iva May's. In the introduction, it states that Bowie had "a partiality for her subject that would make her slow to see faults, and slower to record them." (John Paul, "Introduction," *Alabaster and Spikenard*, 17.) Despite this disclaimer, Bowie's biography provides the most complete account of Vennard's seventy-four years.

do the studies by Freedman and Keller, and even though she was a member of the same denomination that Keller describes, Vennard had to move her evangelistic ministry into a space apart from the separate spheres of female institutions that some MEC women had built for themselves.

Vennard's ostracism confirms the reality that some historians have observed that not all women were accepted by other women into their separate sphere. Based upon her research into the lives of working-class women and slave women, Nancy Hewitt contends that community can exclude as well as include and that women's history, as is men's, is one of "diversity, discontinuity, and conflict."[8] Sara Evans, in *Born for Liberty*, supplements Hewitt's argument with other examples of women, such as Native American and immigrant women, who did not experience the nourishment of "female community in the separate sphere of home, religion, and female association."[9]

However, while Vennard's experience of exclusion corroborates the examples proffered by Hewitt and Evans, it differs in one important aspect. Vennard shared the same class, race, and social standing as the women in the women's organizations of the MEC. She was not "other than" in any of these categories. In contrast, in Hewitt's and Evans's studies, the women who find themselves outside the separate spheres that white middle-class women created differ in an essential characteristic, either class or race.

Considering that Vennard was of the same economic, social, racial, and educational background as were the women in the Woman's Home Missionary Society (WHMS) of the MEC, it appears that the one aspect that mitigated against her acceptance into the separate sphere for women, or, for that matter, the separate sphere for men, was her unwavering commitment to evangelism. She was a woman evangelist. As such, she found herself caught in the conflict between women's creating a sphere for women and men's preserving a sphere for themselves.

On the one hand, as a deaconess evangelist, Iva May faced formidable female opponents within the separate sphere of the WHMS; her zeal for evangelism became an embarrassment to them. On the other hand, as founder and superintendent of a deaconess training school committed to evangelism, Iva May confronted male opponents in the St. Louis Annual Conference who charged her with training women preachers under the guise of deaconess work. As she came to discover through heartbreaking opposition from organizations headed by women as well as men, women evangelists within the MEC fell between the separate spheres.

---

[8]Nancy A. Hewitt, "Beyond the Search for Sisterhood: American Women's History in the 1980s," *Social History* 10 (1985): 316. See also page 300.

[9]Sara M. Evans, *Born for Liberty: A History of Women in America* (New York: Free Press, 1989), 96.

Her Early Years

Iva May Durham was born in 1871 near Normal, Illinois. She was converted in 1883 at age twelve and joined the MEC shortly thereafter. Six years later she claimed sanctification after attending first a holiness camp meeting in Decatur and then a revival preached by the "chief expositor-evangelist" of the holiness movement, Joseph H. Smith.[10]

After being graduated from the Illinois State Normal University in 1890, Iva May taught school for a year and worked as a high school principal for two years. She briefly attended Wellesley College. She became acquainted with Dr. Charles De Garmo, professor of modern languages and reading at Illinois State, who was appointed president of Swarthmore College in 1891. De Garmo offered her a scholarship to Swarthmore for her senior year as well as an extended stay in Europe with his family. However, she returned to the camp meeting that summer and encountered Joseph Smith, who expressed disappointment with her with these words, "When I knew you a few years ago, I thought you were one young woman who was going to be spiritual; and more than that--a spiritual leader. But I see you seem to have gone mostly 'to top.'"[11]

Smith's remarks "awoke once more the old gnawing restlessness and dissatisfaction of soul," and Iva May realized that she had neglected to consult God about her plans. As she prayed through her distress about her ambition, her intellectual life, and her desire to be in close communion with God, she resolved to decline the scholarship. When she told De Garmo, "...with his voice full of kindness, he replied, 'I would so much rather you would be a noble woman than a great scholar.'"[12]

Her decision had been a difficult one and Iva May, in search of direction, reached for her Bible and opened it to Isaiah 60:1, which she claimed as her life verse, "Arise, shine; for thy light is come, and the glory of the Lord is risen upon thee."[13] Opportunities immediately came her way to participate in revival meetings, first as a singer, then as a preacher. One request came from a Christian couple in Lodge, Illinois, where "there was no pastor and no regular church service. This one Christian man rented an abandoned saloon building, and someone loaned an organ. Miss Durham had to be the entire evangelistic party. She led the singing, played the organ, preached, and conducted the altar service. But the room was filled night after night." Her biography recalls Iva May's feelings about that revival, "It was a far cry from Wellesley and the New England Conservatory, but my heart was at rest through it all."[14]

---

[10]Delbert R. Rose, *Vital Holiness: A Theology of Christian Experience, Interpreting the Historic Wesleyan Message*, 3rd. ed. (Minneapolis: Bethany Fellowship, 1975), 8. Joseph H. Smith (1855-1946) was a Methodist minister, a leading figure of the National Holiness Association, and a mentor, confidante, friend, and colleague of Vennard's.

[11]Bowie, *Alabaster*, 46.

[12]Ibid, 48.

[13]Ibid.

[14]Ibid, 52.

At first, Iva May was quite hesitant about being an evangelist since evangelism involved preaching, and "she just did *not* approve of women preachers. It was all right to speak, to lecture, to give messages, but to come out in the open as a *woman preacher*--that did not appeal to her at all." She prayed for guidance with the hope that God "would excuse me from preaching, and let me be perhaps a singer or a social worker."[15] Eventually she accepted her calling as an evangelist and in her later years declared, "Evangelism has been the chief accent of my ministry."[16]

Separate Spheres: A Deaconess Evangelist

Iva May Durham entered the Deaconess Home in Buffalo, New York in 1895. She was undoubtedly influenced by a speech she had heard that summer by Lucy Rider Meyer, founder of the Chicago Training School, and by a visit from deaconess friends of the family. One of the friends was Libbie Smith, Superintendent of the Deaconess Home. Not surprisingly, the Superintendent assigned her new deaconess to conference evangelism. At the invitation of churches, Iva May led revival meetings throughout the Genesee Conference. Three years later she was appointed Deaconess-at-large by the General Secretary, Jane Bancroft Robinson, a position that required Iva May to travel throughout the country representing the Deaconess Bureau of the WHMS. This institutional promotional work interfered with her evangelistic ministry, but when she protested to the General Secretary, Bancroft Robinson's reply was, according to Bowie, that "evangelism was not the method of the W. H. M. S."[17] It was through her travels, however, that Iva May became acquainted with several bishops, particularly James M. Thoburn and James N. FitzGerald, who were to become her ecclesiastical patrons in her battles with the separate spheres within the MEC.

In a final attempt to reconcile the programmatic focus of deaconess work with her evangelistic ministry, Iva May sent a proposal to Bancroft Robinson in which she outlined her idea, what Bowie coined her "illumination," for the establishment of a Department of Evangelism within the Deaconess Bureau. Iva May offered "to take the position of deaconess-at-large again if she might be permitted to 'organize an evangelistic department with a course of study for evangelists at the Washington headquarters as a beginning.' She herself would give a month in the fall and another in the spring to teaching these classes."[18] The General Secretary refused her request. Vennard's biography records several reasons for Bancroft Robinson's negative response: "that the Secretary of the W.H.M.S. did not want evangelism emphasized; that such a course would not fit the training school schedule; that too many of the students would want to do evangelistic

---

[15]Ibid, 54-5.
[16]Iva Durham Vennard, "The Evangelism for This Day: An Address," (Chicago: Chicago Evangelistic Institute, 1933), 1.
[17]Bowie, *Alabaster*, 85.
[18]Ibid, 89.

work because it was more sensational; and that they would be unwilling to accept positions in institutions, and to be under appointment of the deaconess officers."[19]

By all accounts, evangelism fell outside Bancroft Robinson's vision for the Bureau of Deaconess Work of the WHMS. In the penultimate chapter of her book, *Deaconesses in Europe and Their Lessons for America*, she outlined the field of deaconess work that she envisioned for America based on her two-year field research of deaconess institutions in Europe. According to Bancroft Robinson, deaconess work encompassed three areas: nursing, teaching, and assisting a pastor. None of these areas related to evangelism, not even that of a pastor's assistant. As she explained, such a deaconess would need skills in nursing, education, and perhaps even in financial planning, but not in evangelism.

> When the minister makes pastoral calls, and, entering working-men's homes, finds sickness and scanty resources, he has no deaconess to call to his aid with her cheerful words of encouragement and her loving sympathy, that are better than money and medicine. It is not charity alone that is wanted in such cases; it is the knowledge of how to use proper means to make the sick one comfortable, how to lessen the burden on the family that a small additional call for work and care has so sadly taxed; how to enlighten the ignorance that is so common without wounding the susceptibilities that are so human.[20]

That Bancroft Robinson's vision held sway within the Bureau for Deaconess Work is evident from her annual reports to the WHMS in which she meticulously outlined every sphere of deaconess work and each institution's financial and statistical merits. In the annual report for 1899-1900, the lone reference to evangelism is to Iva May Durham, who is listed as "Deaconess Evangelist." Information on her work appears in a column of statistics at the end of a several page report by Bancroft Robinson and her sister, Henrietta A. Bancroft, Field Secretary of Deaconess Work. These statistics report the number of miles Iva May had traveled, the number of addresses she had given, the money she had raised, and so on. At the bottom of the statistics, a two-line editorial note reads, "Miss Durham's service and influence are not to be measured by material standards, as her work as Deaconess-at-Large has aimed at spiritual rather than material results. She has, however, procured substantial money aid for the Society, as future events will disclose".[21]

This cryptic editorial note sheds further light on the conflict between Iva May Durham and the WHMS. First of all, the wording of the note gives evidence that the Bureau of Deaconess Work recognized a distinction between the material and spiritual realms. Further, within this division there is a hierarchy; the material realm has priority over the spiritual realm. The material realm fills every one of the Secretary's reports with an overwhelming collection of financial, personnel, property, and institutional statistics; whereas the spiritual realm, represented by Iva May's ministry, received no mention in the narrative report, and her

---

[19]Ibid, 90.

[20]Jane Bancroft, *Deaconesses in Europe and Their Lessons for America* (New York: Hunt & Eaton, 1889), 245-6.

accomplishments had to be justified by a final reference to her material results, the "substantial money aid for the Society" that she raised.

Second, in the face of the preference for the material realm, the note appears to be an apologetic by the WHMS for Iva May's ministry. In other words, Iva May's contribution to the WHMS had to be judged by other standards, not the usual standard of material statistics, as that was not her main work. Nevertheless, she still contributed to the material realm by raising substantial money. That an editorial note had to be added to interpret Iva May's statistics underscores that evangelism did not fit within the "female institution building" of the WHMS.

Bancroft Robinson did not see a role for evangelism in deaconess work; yet hers was not the only opinion. Her long-time nemesis, Lucy Rider Meyer, who was also a prominent figure in MEC deaconess work, was of the opinion that the work of visitor/evangelist deaconesses was important, so important in fact, that these deaconesses should be well trained before embarking on their work. "It is not a light matter to undertake in any degree to be the spiritual guide and help of an immortal soul; and those who are to make this their constant work should be as well prepared as possible, by qualities both natural and acquired."[21]

The deaconess school founded by Lucy Rider Meyer, the Chicago Training School, trained visitor/evangelist deaconesses from its inception. Deaconesses were required to study a range of topics, including the Bible, church discipline, and church history, and visitor/evangelist deaconesses selected from elective courses offered in Individual Evangelism, World Wide Evangelism, and The Psychology of Evangelism.[22] In the afternoon, deaconesses embarked on practical field work, which, for the deaconess visitor, might entail visiting house to house, holding prayer meetings, teaching children's Sunday School classes, and assisting a pastor in related tasks.[23]

---

[21]Lucy Rider Meyer, *Deaconesses, Biblical, Early Church, European, American, with the Story of the Chicago Training School, For City, Home and Foreign Missions, and the Chicago Deaconess Home*. 2nd ed. (Chicago: Message Publishing Company, 1889), 68-9. The disagreement between Bancroft Robinson and Meyer initially erupted over the question of where, or to what organization, should deaconess work belong. Meyer contended that deaconess work belonged to the church, Bancroft Robinson countered that it belonged to the WHMS. For substantial discussions of this feud, see Mary Agnes Theresa Dougherty, "The Methodist Deaconess: 1885-1919: A Study in Religious Feminism," Ph.D. diss., University of California, Davis, 1979, 55-67; Isabelle Horton, *High Adventure: Life of Lucy Rider Meyer* (New York: Methodist Book Concern, 1928), 190-7; and Woman's Home Missionary Society, *The Early History of Deaconess Work and Training Schools for Women in American Methodism, 1882-1885, with Supplement Answering Certain Objections*. 2nd ed. (Detroit: Speaker-Hines Press, 1912?).

[22]The Chicago Training School also trained nurse deaconesses. Lucy Rider Meyer, "The Mother in the Church," *Methodist Review* 83 (September, 1901), 730. The list of courses, drawn from a 1910 catalogue, comes from an appendix in Isabelle Horton's history of the early years of the Chicago Training School, *The Builders: A Story of Faith and Works* (Chicago: Deaconess Advocate Co., 1910), 205.

[23]Meyer, *Deaconesses*, 71.

Along with visitation evangelism, the training school also advertised preparation for deaconess evangelists, "Women who will become Pastors' Assistants, or Gospel Evangelists as speakers and singers."[24] Deaconess evangelists participated in revivals and, on occasion, occupied unfilled pulpits.[25]

Given the differing attitudes toward deaconess evangelists, the question arises whether Iva May Durham would have found a wider opportunity for evangelism outside the WHMS and Bancroft Robinson's control, perhaps under the patronage of Lucy Rider Meyer. An article on evangelism in Meyer's Chicago Training School's publication, *The Message*, written the year after the school began, provides a provisional answer. The article defined evangelism as "bringing the gospel into contact with unsaved souls." It went on to explain that "the church of God is responsible not for conversion but only for contact."[26] In her dissertation on Methodist deaconesses, Mary Agnes Dougherty contends that their priority was social service first with evangelism as a desirable by-product. She remarks, "The deaconess movement's place among the earliest exponents of the social gospel hinged on its advocacy of social service over evangelization."[27]

This sentiment contrasts markedly with that of Iva May who never wavered from her belief that "the supreme task is soul winning."[28] Iva May expressed her own opinion on the relationship of evangelism and social service in an article entitled, "Studies in Missionary Problems and Methods," written while she was touring foreign mission fields. Outlining four lines of mission work--industrial, medical, educational, and evangelistic--she left no doubt where her priorities lay. "The first three phases of missionary work are but feeders, they are the avenues of approach and the means of preparation. To use the old figure, they are the bait on the hook, but we have not landed the fish until the individual has been *brought into saving touch with the Lord Jesus*."[29] We may infer, then, that the priority Iva May accorded evangelism would also have exceeded Meyer's vision for deaconess work, although the Chicago Training School would have offered, nonetheless, a more hospitable arena for developing evangelistic ministries.

---

[24]Horton, *Builders*, 193. Depending on the type of evangelism the deaconess did, she was referred to either as a "visitor" or as an "evangelist." The two terms seemed to denote different methods of evangelism. A visitor concentrated on one-on-one evangelism; an evangelist would have had a more public ministry, including revival work and preaching. For instance, an 1893 graduate of the Chicago Training School, Vanluah Jacques, ministered as a deaconess visitor to prisoners and then as a deaconess evangelist in an evangelistic center on an Ohio riverboat. Dougherty compiles separate statistics on deaconesses who were primarily visitors and deaconesses who were primarily evangelists. (Dougherty, "The Methodist Deaconess," 97, 102.)

[25]Ibid, 130.

[26]*The Message*, (November, 1889), 7, cited in Dougherty, "The Methodist Deaconess," 122.

[27]Dougherty, "The Methodist Deaconess," 122.

[28]*Heart and Life* 10 (October, 1920), 6-7.

[29]Ibid.

Separate Spheres: A Training School Founder and Superintendent

In the midst of her travail with the Bureau for Deaconess Work, Iva May met Bishop Thoburn in 1901 at Camp Sychar in Mt. Vernon, Ohio. As they discussed deaconess work, she shared with him her "illumination" for a deaconess training school in evangelism. Bowie records that Thoburn's response was, "This is an answer to the prayers of my sister Isabella in India. She has been asking God to save the Deaconess Order, and to make it a soul-winning agency."[30] He urged her to found the school herself and promised to write a letter to the Methodist bishops outlining her "illumination." In October of that year, Iva May received a letter from Bishop FitzGerald, Secretary of the Board of Bishops, which contained the bishops' authorization and the suggestion of St. Louis as the location.

In 1902, Vennard founded Epworth Evangelistic Institute (EEI) in St. Louis, advertising it as "A school of practice for Deaconesses, Evangelists and Missionaries."[31] Epworth's curriculum resembled Meyer's Chicago Training School, with instruction in Bible, theology, evangelism, and sociology. The academic component was coupled with practical work in evangelism, city mission, and settlement work.[32] What distinguished EEI from other deaconess institutions was, as its name suggested, that it gave priority to training deaconesses in evangelism.[33] Epworth was designed "to give the impulse of direct soul-winning to every department of Christian service."[34]

From her earliest days in St. Louis, Iva May was the target of vehement local opposition from several clergymen and laymen. Iva May's biography records that their complaints targeted several issues.[35] One issue was Iva May's expansion of women's roles at Epworth. Her opponents objected to instruction in theology and Bible by Epworth's faculty, which consisted of Iva May and several other women; they believed that teaching these subjects was the responsibility of preachers, all of whom by definition were male. They objected to training deaconesses in theology in the first place; deaconesses allegedly had no need of theology because they attended to the material sphere. These objections prompted them to accuse

---

[30]Bowie, *Alabaster*, 91.

[31]See the full-page advertisement in *Minutes of the Thirty-Ninth Session of the St. Louis Annual Conference, Held in Clinton, MO, March 20th to 25th, 1907* (Clinton, MO: Republican Printing Co., 1907), back page.

[32]Epworth Settlement, which was founded by the Institute, ran a Night School, Boys' Club, Kindergarten, Sunday School, and evangelistic services.

[33]Among the seventeen schools listed in *The Methodist Year Book 1909*, Epworth was the only deaconess institution to include the word "evangelistic" in its name. Epworth was also the only one to advertise that it trained evangelists. (Stephen V. R. Ford, ed., *The Methodist Year Book 1909* [Cincinnati: Jennings & Graham, 1909], 213.) The only other institution to mention evangelism was the Chicago Training School. (Ibid., 211.)

[34]*Minutes of the Thirty-Ninth Session of the St. Louis Annual Conference*, back page.

[35]See chapters 12, 13, 15, 17-19 in Bowie, *Alabaster*.

Iva May of "training women preachers under the guise of deaconess work."[36] Another issue was theological; they objected to Iva May's teaching on holiness as being too narrow. The last issue concerned Iva May's priority on evangelism. Her opponents labeled evangelism as old-fashioned and insisted that it had been superseded by religious education. However, their most revealing objection was personal; they believed that Iva May was a "dangerous and powerful woman."[37]

The opposition, led by the district superintendent, came to a crisis point in the fall of 1909 when Iva May returned from maternity leave to find sweeping changes at Epworth, including a revised school charter; an altered course of study without evangelistic courses; and a new faculty roster, with clergymen replacing Epworth faculty as teachers of Bible and theology. The district superintendent defended his alterations by appealing to the preservation of separate spheres. According to the district superintendent, men and women, preachers and deaconesses, have been accorded separate spheres.

> Methodist preachers do not want deaconesses who study theology. We can attend to that ourselves. We want women as helpers who will work with the children, care for the sick, and visit the poor. If our deaconesses are trained in theology they will become critical of the preachers, and that will be the end of the deaconess movement.[38]

Vennard had heard this rationale of the separate spheres before when she was a deaconess evangelist in the WHMS. In 1900, at the WHMS's annual meeting, Iva May would have heard a report by the Reverend Dr. A. H. Ames, Superintendent of the Lucy Webb Hayes National Training-School for deaconesses in Washington, D.C., in which he made the following statement:

> Preachers and deaconesses represent the two ministries of the Christian Church: the ministry of the Word and the ministry of work; the expounding and enforcing the message which God has ordained for the quickening and perfecting of souls, and the making that Word real in the removal or mitigation of sorrow, poverty, and pain.[39]

---

[36]Ibid, 124.

[37]This epithet was the result of a mistaken idea that she had considerable influence with the church hierarchy. Ibid, 136.

[38]Ibid, 145.

[39]A. H. Ames, "Lucy Webb Hayes National Training-School," *Nineteenth Annual Report*, 137. The Woman's Board of Home Missions of the MEC, South, anticipated this argument and included a statement in their annual meeting minutes entitled, "What a Deaconess Is, and What She Is Not." The first line under the category, "What A Deaconess Is Not," reads, "1. She is *not a preacher*." Mary Helm, "What a Deaconess Is, and What She Is Not," *Fourth Annual Meeting of the Woman's Board of Home Missions, M. E. Church, South, Held in Centenary Church, Richmond, Virginia, April 18-23, 1902* (Nashville: Publishing House of the Methodist Episcopal Church, South, 1902), 119.

To preserve these separate spheres, Ames contended, "The education of a deaconess must be conformed to our idea of the proper scope and sphere of her mission. True education is that which fits one best for the duties which are to be performed."[40]

Although Ames represented many MEC clergy, not all MEC clergymen agreed with him. Bishop Thoburn, who had been largely responsible for the official recognition of the office of deaconess at the 1888 General Conference, disagreed with Ames's restriction of deaconess work to the "mitigation of sorrow, poverty, and pain." As he stated in a lecture on deaconess work:

> ... the deaconess is not set apart for any one special form of work, but rather for any work which the Church can find for her. The varieties of work which need to be done are almost endless. I notice a persistent inclination on the part of the public generally to regard the work of the deaconess as simply and solely the duty of visiting the poor and nursing the sick; *but this is limiting her sphere in the most arbitrary way*. ... this is but a small part of the work which is to be done. A deaconess may be set aside for any form of work to which she is adapted.[41]

"Any form of work" for a deaconess, in Thoburn's opinion, could include preaching. He reasoned, first of all, that God had anointed Christian women to prophesy at Pentecost, and that women in the early church did prophesy. Further, the word "prophesy" he argued, was used interchangeably in the Bible with the word "preaching."[42] His simple deduction was that "women are anointed for this kind of service."[43] Elsewhere he elaborated on this sentiment,

> The vexed question of the right or propriety of women exercising the prophetic gift calls for only a brief word here. The prophet Joel certainly predicted that the daughters should prophesy; the daughters of Philip the evangelist did prophesy; and from the discussion of the question in the First Epistle to the Corinthians it is made abundantly evident that women were accustomed to exercise this gift ... The question is happily settling itself, and it seems highly probable that before many years it will cease to be a subject of serious controversy.[44]

Thoburn believed that deaconesses were a tremendous force for winning souls to Christ. In his lecture at Calvary Methodist Episcopal Church in New York City in 1892, he said that one day an evangelistic troop of five hundred Methodist deaconesses working in New York City "will bring more souls to Christ and add more members to our Church in this city of New York in one year than all the Churches in the city today have added during the past ten years."[45]

---

[40] Ames, "Lucy Webb Hayes National Training-School," 137.

[41] J. M. Thoburn, *The Deaconess and Her Vocation* (New York: Hunt & Eaton, 1893), 22.

[42] J.M. Thoburn, *The Church of Pentecost* (Cincinnati: Jennings & Pye, 1901), 124. See also pages 129 and 164-5.

[43] Bowie, *Alabaster*, 91.

[44] Thoburn, *The Church of Pentecost*, 164-5.

[45] Thoburn, *The Deaconess and Her Vocation*, 123.

Under Thoburn's patronage, Vennard initially found a way around the separate spheres and made her "illumination" come true at EEI. However, despite powerful advocates in Bishops Thoburn and FitzGerald, Vennard felt compelled by the mounting opposition in St. Louis to offer her resignation. In 1910 she resigned as Superintendent of the Institute. The school was renamed Epworth Deaconess Institute, and Isabelle Horton became its superintendent.

Vennard, however, was not defeated; she began again, in another city, with other supporters. Though she herself remained a lifelong member of the MEC, she moved her evangelistic ministry and training school into the embrace of the holiness movement when the Christian Witness Company invited her to start anew in Chicago.

In the fall of 1910, Chicago Evangelistic Institute (CEI), an inter-denominational, coeducational holiness training school, opened its doors with Vennard as its principal.[46] Finally, freed from the separate spheres of deaconesses and preachers, female and male, in the MEC, Vennard brought together the two essential ingredients to fulfill her "illumination" for a training school—evangelism and holiness. In the cause of holiness evangelism, CEI trained men and women who participated in both the ministry of the Word and the ministry of work. Issue after issue of *Heart and Life*, the publication of CEI, included reports of alumnae, such as Lela G. McConnell, pastor and founder of Kentucky Mountain Holiness Association, and D. Willia Caffray, evangelist and the first woman licensed in the twentieth century as a local preacher by the Methodist Church.[47]

---

[46]Vennard's evangelistic ministry did find an amenable sphere within the holiness movement in which women enjoyed greater freedom than did their counterparts in mainline denominations. (See Lucille Sider Dayton and Donald W. Dayton," 'Your Daughters Shall Prophesy': Feminism in the Holiness Movement," *Methodist History* 14 [1976]: 67-92, and Susie C. Stanley," 'Tell Me the Old, Old Story': An Analysis of Autobiographies by Holiness Women," *Wesleyan Theological Journal* 29 [Fall, 1994]: 7-22.) The antecedents of this phenomenon can be traced back to Phoebe Palmer (1807-1874), who underscored the importance of public testimony to one's sanctification experience. For Palmer, "testimony was not only essential to the promulgation of Christian holiness, but even more essential to the personal retention of that grace. One had to give public testimony in order to be 'clear in his experience.' Indeed if personal testimony lagged, it was one of the most certain signs of a lack of religious life ..." (Melvin E. Dieter, *The Holiness Revival of the Nineteenth Century*, 2nd ed., Studies in Evangelicalism, No. 1 [Lanham, MD: Scarecrow Press, 1996], 31.) As a result of Palmer's teaching and example as well as that of other holiness leaders, many holiness women found freedom for their evangelistic ministries in the holiness movement.

[47]For information on Lela McConnell's ministry, see her books, *The Pauline Ministry in the Kentucky Mountains, or, A Brief Account of the Kentucky Mt. Holiness Association*, 8th ed. (Berne, IN: Light and Hope Publications, 1940) and *Faith Victorious in the Kentucky Mountains: The Story of Twenty-two Years of Spirit-filled Ministry* (Berne, IN: Economy Printing Concern, 1950). On D. Willia Caffray, see "Biographical Material," dictated by D. Willia Caffray in 1967, D. Willia Caffray Papers, B. L. Fisher Library, Asbury Theological Seminary.

In spite of her accomplishments, history has not favored Vennard, and she has been largely forgotten. Among her remarkable achievements: she founded and presided over two educational institutions for a total of forty-five years[48]; she preached at churches and camp meetings throughout the world; she was a board member and treasurer of the National Holiness Missionary Society, an organization that she helped to create; she served on the Executive Board of the American Association of Women Preachers; she was the editor of *Inasmuch* at EEI and *Heart and Life* at CEI; she wrote three books, including a book on Revelation, a book on holiness entitled, *Heart Purity*, and a book of sermons entitled, *Upper Room Messages*; and she received a local preacher's license from the MEC in 1920. Vennard's significance as mentor and educator of a generation of evangelists, preachers, teachers, missionaries, and musicians cannot easily be measured since the names and faces and ministries of her legacy, the majority of whom were women, have been lost to history.

Beyond Separate Spheres: An Evangelist's Legacy

Through the life of Iva May Durham Vennard, a woman evangelist, we see the complexity embedded in the term "separate spheres." Neither of the separate spheres in the MEC, as Vennard experienced them, was monolithic. Although the consensus within each sphere was powerful enough to warrant her judicious decision to move her evangelistic ministry and training school under the auspices of the holiness movement, there were dissenters from the majority in each sphere.

On the one hand, the opposition she faced from male clergy and laity for encroaching on their sphere is not surprising. For those who had established and perpetuated separate spheres in the MEC and who had at the 1880 General Conference rescinded local preacher's licenses issued to women, thereby denying them ordination and banning them from most leadership roles, even having the patronage of powerful bishops did not make a woman evangelist who trained other women to be evangelists acceptable. Yet within the male sphere there was disagreement over the role of deaconesses as well as the overarching question of women's ministry. These complexities within the separate spheres must be underscored lest generalizations of unanimity be perpetuated.

Within the female sphere, there were complexities as well. As we have seen, Jane Bancroft Robinson and Lucy Rider Meyer disagreed about deaconess evangelists. Perhaps had Vennard, like Meyer, operated outside the WHMS within only a loose organizational affiliation, she might have been able to create space within the separate sphere for her evangelistic ministry as other deaconess evangelists had. But the separate sphere, as Vennard experienced it, within an organization whose strategy was "female institution building," did not sanction a woman evangelist whose ministry was primarily of the Word, not the work.

---

[48] CEI relocated to University Park, Iowa in 1951 and was renamed Vennard College in 1959. The College closed in 2008.

The life of Iva May Durham Vennard raises the question, "For which women and for which ministries were spaces created in woman's separate spheres?" Discussions of separate spheres must address the complexities that Vennard faced and look more closely at which women were accepted into the separate spheres and which existed beyond them.

Chapter 9

Dr. Tenney, the Free Methodist Church, and the Twentieth Century Wesley Revival

William Kostlevy

Mary Alice Tenney
Photo courtesy of Ruby Dare
Library, Greenville College

Introduction

Mary Alice Tenney, "Dr. Tenney" to her students at Greenville College and "Mae Alice Tenney" to family and closest friends, has not received the attention warranted by her remarkable career as an educator and interpreter of John Wesley and early Methodism. Her most important scholarly work *Blueprint for a Christian World: an Analysis of the Wesleyan Way* (1953) is seldom cited. Drawing on the early Wesley revival writings of George Croft Cell, Maximin Piette and Umphrey Lee, Tenney's work anticipates the bold and often overstated claims of Wesley's theological depth and sophistication. Although in fairness to the founder of Methodism, the acuity of Wesley's intellect does seem considerably enhanced when read side by side with popular late nineteenth and early twentieth century Holiness literature; but then Wesley, unlike the real founder of the Church of the Nazarene, Bud Robinson, never dedicated a book to something as useful as a Jersey cow.

Mary Alice Tenney was raised in an Iowa Congregational home with a deep respect for the ethical rigors of radical Free Methodism. Her father, a successful farmer and businessman, served on the Greenville College Board of Trustees. Like many Free Methodists, her family had deep roots in the radical spiritual heritage of Charles G. Finney and Oberlin College. She was educated at Drake University, Greenville (Illinois) College (1914), the University of Southern California (M.A., 1919), the University of Minnesota, and the University of Wisconsin (Ph.D., 1939). She served on the faculties of Los Angeles Pacific College (1915–1917), the University of Illinois, and Greenville College (1921–1955), where she was chair of the Division of Language, Literature and Fine Arts (1930–1955). She was a role model for two generations of young Free Methodist women who admired her independence of spirit, love of learning and passion to expand the outlooks of her students. In 1948, her grateful students funded a sabbatical in England that resulted in her book *Blueprint for a Christian World* (1953), which she abridged and revised for lay audiences as *Living in Two Worlds* (1958), and an important series of biographically based devotional talks given to the Women's Missionary Society of the Free Methodist Church during the Free Methodist centennial of 1960 and published as *Adventures in Christian Love* (1964).

Although it is largely unknown today, Tenney was an important catalyst for the recovery of the evangelical social vision. Following E. Stanley Jones and her own family's roots in the ethically activist perfectionism of Charles G. Finney, Tenney insisted that the essence of a vital Christianity was a life of radical discipleship lived in conformity with the ethical teachings of Jesus. Fittingly, she was suspicious of what she believed to be the excessive emotionalism and lack of ethical vigor in much Holiness teaching.

Interpreting Wesley

Today Tenney's insistence that Wesleyans seek renewal through a recovery of Wesley and the spirituality of early Methodism seems remarkably commonplace, but this was hardly the situation in the 1930s and 1940s. While assuming direct continuity with Wesley, few had actually read widely or deeply in the writings of the founder of Methodism. As a body, Free Methodists tended to view themselves as the true heirs of Wesley. Fittingly the Free Methodist Church (FMC) course of study required that ministers, including lay preachers, read Wesley's *Plain Account of Christian Perfection*, some of Wesley's sermons, and editions of his writings supporting Christian perfection highly edited by Holiness Movement leaders J. A. Wood and William McDonald.

While Wesley was continually included in the required readings for the FMC course of study, he was read less by groups that emerged directly out of the nineteenth century Holiness Movement, such as the Church of the Nazarene and the Pilgrim Holiness Church. In its earliest *Manuals*, the course of study of the Church of the Nazarene did not include any Wesley writings. Beginning in 1907 selected Wesley sermons were included for the first time, later to be supplemented with Wood's Holiness oriented *Perfect Love*. In 1928 Wesley was dropped from the reading list, but eventually restored in 1952. The Pilgrim Holiness Church did require that course of study students read *A Plain Account of Christian Perfection* but did not require students to read any of Wesley's sermons. The Methodist Episcopal Church and the Methodist Episcopal Church, South did keep editions of Wesley's sermons in print and for a time in the nineteenth century sold the fourteen volume edition of Wesley readings edited by Thomas Jackson.[1]

Tenney's interest in Wesley was a product of a revival of interest in Wesley that was, in part, inspired by the international situation of the 1930s when many found comfort in the pervasive popular view that while Wesley's ideas were unexceptional, his social significance was extraordinary. Having brought discipline to the unruly early proletariat, Wesley had saved England from the unfortunate fate of a revolution similar to the French Revolution. For many in the deeply divided depression decade of the 1930s, the threat of Communism suggested that unless a similar evangelical revival occurred another revolution would usher in an age of Communist totalitarianism. For others, especially young secularized radicals and Communist academics with little interest in saving bourgeois democracy, Methodism presented a specter of a different kind--the threat of counter revolution. In part because so many of them had been raised in dissenting Protestant or, like the distinguished Marxist historian E. P. Thompson, Methodist homes, the evangelical threat took on a highly personal character. Depending on the time periods of their research and areas of expertise, these scholars, however, did privilege radical religious groups with special agency. While some had a few words of praise

---

[1] I am drawing on material from William Kostlevy, "Wesley in the Holiness Movement," in *Historical Dictionary of the Holiness Movement* (Lanham, MD: Scarecrow Press, 2009), 312-313. See also Floyd Cunningham, ed. *Our Watchword and Song: The Centennial History of the Church of the Nazarene* (Kansas City: Beacon Hill Press, 2009), 492-498 and Mark Quanstrom, *A Century of Holiness Theology: The Doctrine of Entire Sanctification in the Church of the Nazarene, 1905-2004* (Kansas City: Beacon Hill Press, 2004), 203-209.

for Wesleyan splinter groups, most shared the assumptions of Thompson whose sarcastic chapter "The Transforming Power of the Cross," in *The Making of the English Working Class* attempted to answer the question of how Methodism accomplished the remarkable, if diabolical, feat of being both the religion of the oppressed and the oppressor.[2]

If they paid attention at all to the growing Holiness and Pentecostal denominations of the depression era, to say nothing of the continued vitality of Holiness strains in the Methodist Church, scholars saw these as expressions of the rapidly declining and largely rural movement of the dispossessed. All missed the first signs of a remarkable renaissance of Wesleyan studies that would transform not only the Holiness people themselves but turn Methodist and Wesleyan studies into a virtual growth industry as well. Among the most important was the decision of the Nazarene Publishing House in cooperation with Zondervan to reissue the Jackson edition of Wesley's works in the 1950s.[3]

Tenney and the Free Methodist Interpretation of Wesley

While not wanting to overstate Tenney's role in the Wesley renaissance, her leadership in the FMC and mentorship of Free Methodist youth, especially women, makes her a not inconsequential figure in the mid century revival of Wesley studies. Today remembered mostly as a classroom teacher and advocate of radical discipleship, Tenney, unlike many Free Methodists, was raised in a decidedly upper middle class family who owned a cabin on Minnesota's Lake Pokegama where she often spent her summers swimming and fishing, and where she also indulged her passions for golf and tennis. When ill health forced her temporarily to leave Greenville's faculty in 1925, she recovered in part by vacationing in Florida and spent the summer of 1927 touring Europe with her sister and her brother in-law, noted University of Illinois Defoe scholar A. W. Secord (1891-1957). Beginning in the fall of 1927 she worked in upper Midwest sales for the Emile Vaughan Company, an upscale New York dressmaker. Her health restored, Tenney returned

---

[2]There is a vast literature on Thompson. An important summary is found in Alan D. Gilbert, "Religion and Political Stability in Early Industrial England," in *The Industrial Revolution and British Society,"* edited by Patrick O'Brien and Roland Quinault (Cambridge: Cambridge University Press, 1993), 79-99. See also David Hempton, *Religion and Political Culture in Britain and Ireland: From the Glorious Revolution to the Decline of the Empire* (Cambridge: Cambridge University Press, 1996), 25-27.

[3]See also Albert C. Outler, ed., *John Wesley* (New York: Oxford University Press, 1964). Outler's edition of Wesley writings, which has remained in print continuously since its publication, and the reprint editions of Wesley's writings by evangelical publishers like Moody and Baker also played a key role in the revival of interest in Wesley.

to Greenville College in the fall of 1930, serving as head of the English department until her retirement in 1955.[4]

Tenney did take leaves in 1936 and again in 1938 to work on her doctorate at the University of Wisconsin. She received her Ph.D. in 1939. Her dissertation "Early Methodist Autobiography, 1739-1791" argued that "Wesley...took over the argument used in support of reason and used it to press the claims of intuition." As Tenney insisted, it was Wesley's "effective interpretation of faith that most impressed romantics" such as Blake, Wordsworth and Coleridge. And even as Wesley rejected the "unorthodox sentimentalism of perfectionism," he affirmed the possibilities of a life lived more fully in tune with primitive Christianity.[5] Perhaps fittingly for a dissertation, her thesis reflected the influence of her mentor Helen C. White, the first woman to be named a full professor in the College of Arts and Letters at the University of Wisconsin, who was recognized for both her vast knowledge of English Literature and her devout Roman Catholicism. Noted for the attention she devoted to her students, White modeled both the religious devotion and sensitivity to her students that would characterize Tenney as well.

If some looked to Methodist experience and the Wesley precedent to save the world from fascist or Communist totalitarianism, others sought a more modest liberation. Among Free Methodist leaders, including Tenney, concerns about Holiness Movement experiential excesses and lifestyle compromises had a long history. For Tenney and many other Free Methodists with deep roots in the Burned-Over District radicalism of the New England Diaspora, "vital Christianity ... was [primarily] an all inclusive way of life."[6] Ironically for a movement that had once been described as containing "the wildest people history has ever known," Free Methodism had never felt completely at home in the larger Holiness Movement. Even Free Methodist founders B. T. Roberts and Ellen Stowe Roberts, who were lifelong associates of Holiness Movement matron Phoebe Palmer, were deeply troubled by the "pride and worldly conformity" they encountered in National Holiness Association circles.[7] This was natural for a people who had never been completely comfortable outside the regions of Yankee cultural ascendancy. As

---

[4]L. Marie Jett, "Prof. Mae A. Tenney," *Papyrus* 12 May 1932, 4. See also biographical files for Mae A. Tenney, Greenville College Archives.

[5]Mary Alice Tenney, "Early Methodist Autobiography, 1739-1791: A Study in the Literature of the Inner Life." (Ph.D. diss., University of Wisconsin, 1939), 5. On these themes see Richard E. Brantley, *Locke, Wesley, and the Method of English Romanticism* (Gainesville: University of Florida Press, 1984), 129-132.

[6]Mary Alice Tenney, *Blueprint for a Christian World: An Analysis of the Wesleyan Way* (Winona Lake, IN: Light and Life Press, 1953), 281. On the Burned-Over District see Whitney R. Cross, *The Burned-Over District: The Social and Intellectual History of Enthusiastic Religion in Western New York, 1800-1860* (Ithaca, NY: Cornell University Press, 1950).

[7]On the Free Methodists as the wildest people in history see Frederick A. Norwood, *The Story of Methodism* (Nashville: Abingdon Press, 1974), 297. On Roberts and Palmer see Howard A. Snyder, *Populist Saints: B. T. and Ellen Stowe Roberts and the First Free Methodists* (Grand Rapids: William B. Eerdmans Publishing Co., 2006), 596.

late as 1916 and even after years of extensive mission work in the South and West, the vast majority of American Free Methodists resided in the so-called Second New England in Upstate New York, the Third New England in Michigan, and the Western Reserve of Ohio and Yankee dominated areas of Northern Illinois, Southwestern Wisconsin, and portions of Kansas. Growing up among transplanted New Englanders in Iowa, Tenney shared this cultural heritage, a heritage reinforced by her education at Greenville College, also a Yankee island in the Southern sea that is South Central Illinois.[8]

For Tenney, one of the most troubling institutional expressions of the Holiness Movement was Cincinnati's God's Bible School (GBS). In class she warned students about the school's cult like character and hinted that the entire Holiness Movement, while containing much of value, was unlike the FMC, in that it lacked roots in authentic Methodism. Theologically she remained suspicious of not only the experiential emphasis of GBS but its doctrinal teaching as well. Like other Free Methodist leaders she was unenthusiastic about the last two elements of the school's much emphasized four-fold gospel of Jesus as savior, sanctifier, healer and coming king. In fact, Tenney's warnings concerning GBS may very well have had a very specific target, popular Free Methodist evangelist E. E. Shelhamer who lived at GBS from the early 1930s to the mid-1940s and whose ministry was largely beyond the borders of the FMC. As she wrote with GBS and other Holiness Movement ministries in mind, "Many have made a specific religious experience the end, even emphasizing its emotional content."[9]

While some Free Methodists, such as popular radio preacher Myron Boyd who served two terms as president of the National Holiness Association, continued to be active in the larger interdenominational Holiness Movement, most Free Methodist leaders remained aloof. Even Canadian born evangelist and later bishop Charles Fairbairn, who acknowledged reading GBS's magazine *God's Revivalist* and who had sought spiritual advice as a young Methodist minister from GBS patron W. B. Godbey, completely withdrew from the *Revivalist* network after joining the FMC in the 1920s.[10]

Tenney's interpretation of Wesley both shaped and reflected the views of the two most important mid-twentieth century Free Methodist leaders, bishops J. Paul

---

[8]On the regional basis of Free Methodism see William Kostlevy, "Culture, Class and Gender in the Progressive Era: The Social Thought of the Free Methodist Church during the Age of Gladden, Strong and Rauschenbusch," in *Perspectives on the Social Gospel: Papers from the Inaugural Social Gospel Conference at Colgate Rochester Divinity School*, edited by Christopher H. Evans (Lewiston, NY: Edwin Mellen Press, 1999), 160.

[9]This paragraph is based on conversations with my mother, Dorothy Stuve Kostlevy, a student of Tenney at both the University of Wisconsin and Greenville College. On the fourfold gospel see William C. Kostlevy, *Holy Jumpers: Evangelicals and Radicals in Progressive Era America* (New York: Oxford University Press, 2010), 20-22. The last quotation is from Tenney, *Blueprint*, 116.

[10]Charles V. Fairbairn, *I Call to Remembrance* (Winona Lake, IN: Light and Life Press, 1960). Fairbairn actually spells the name of George B. Kulp, an important GBS figure, with a "C" in his autobiography, suggesting how far from the GBS circle he had come by the late

Taylor and Leslie R. Marston. Suspicious of popular fundamentalism, Taylor insisted that, "A spiritually defunct fundamentalism could never cope with an intellectually scintillating modernism." Taylor located Free Methodist identity in the heritage of the Protestant and English Reformations, the writings and experiences of the Wesley brothers, and the writings of early Methodists such as John Fletcher and Adam Clarke. "The love of Christ," Taylor asserted "was the full head of steam that drove the wheels of spiritual commerce in early Wesleyanism."[11]

The single most important figure in shaping twentieth century Free Methodist identity was Bishop Leslie R. Marston. Although condescendingly dismissed, along with other evangelical leaders, by historian William McLoughlin, as "the social elite of the marginal middle class," Marston had received a Ph.D. in psychology from the University of Iowa, and served on the White House Conference on Child Health and Protection. He was only thirty-three years old when he was named president of his alma mater Greenville College in 1927. In 1935 he became a Free Methodist bishop. From 1947 to 1964 he was senior bishop of the Church. In 1956 he was asked to write the denomination's centennial history. Presented not inappropriately as an historical interpretation of Free Methodism's first century, a third of the work is devoted to Wesley and early Methodism. The FMC is not actually organized until page 250. In a work clearly dependent on Mary Alice Tenney's *Blueprint for a Christian World* and drawing heavily, if selectively, on the recently published work by Timothy L. Smith, *Revivalism and Social Reform*, Marston presents the FMC as faithful heirs of Wesley. In fact Marston goes out of his way to emphasize the failure of Phoebe Palmer and the larger Holiness Movement to confront racial injustice. Intent on defending the FMC from the charges of being sectarian, Marston highlights Free Methodist membership in the World Methodist Council and the National Association of Evangelicals while making only one reference to Free Methodist membership in the National Holiness Association. In support of Free Methodist ecumenical involvement he even identifies ecumenical precedence in the ministry of John Wesley.[12]

One of the great disappointments in Marston's life was the failure of the FMC to establish its own theological seminary, although in his centennial history Mar-

---

1950s. Fairbairn and FMC bishop Leslie Marston were both involved in the April 1940 and 1941 ministers' conferences at Greenville College that did include figures from the larger Holiness Movement such as Harry E. Jessop, Paul S. Rees and Peter Wiseman. See *The Wesleyan Message Bearing Fruit: Addresses Delivered at the 13th and 14th Sessions of the Ministers' Conference, Greenville College, April 1940-1941* (Winona Lake, IN: Light and Life Press, 1942.)

[11]J. Paul Taylor, *The Music of Pentecost* (Winona Lake, IN: Light and Life Press, 1951), 92, 111, and J. Paul Taylor, *A Goodly Heritage* (Winona Lake, IN: Light and Life Press, 1960), 70.

[12]The McLoughlin quotation is from William C. McLoughlin, Jr., *Modern Revivalism: Charles Grandison Finney to Billy Graham* (New York: Ronald Press, 1959), 475. Leslie R. Marston, *From Age to Age a Living Witness: A Historical Interpretation of Free Methodism's First Century* (Winona Lake, IN: Light and Life Press, 1960). Marston's use of Timothy L. Smith's *Revivalism and Social Reform in Mid-Nineteenth Century America*

ston does put the best face possible on the church's decision to support a foundation for Free Methodist students on the campus of Asbury Theological Seminary. Always alert to the corrupting influences of Southern Methodism, even in its Holiness expression, Marston tried without success to convince Free Methodists on Asbury's faculty to make the personal financial sacrifices that teaching at a denominational seminary would require. For their part, Free Methodist faculty members who had experience working for notoriously low salaries in schools such as Wessington Springs College on the South Dakota prairie had no desire to return to servitude in righteous but poverty stricken academic institutions. Marston's unfortunate involvement in a divisive theological debate at Asbury owes much to his concern that authentic Methodism, especially Free Methodism, was poorly served by Southern Methodism's cultural, experiential and ethical deficiencies.[13]

Tenney's Vision and the Point of Christianity

For Marston and other Free Methodist leaders the centennial mission of the FMC was the recovery of the experience and teaching of original Methodism. This vision was built upon the edifice constructed by Mary Alice Tenney. For Tenney early Methodism was not merely a phenomenon of the eighteenth century, it was a return to the faith of early Christianity itself. As she wrote in her remarkable, if brief, spiritual classic *Living in Two Worlds: How a Christian Does It*, "They [Methodists] were convinced that the radicalism of the New Testament was essential to true Christian living." Fittingly for her interpretation, and with roots going back to Free Methodism's New England heritage, Tenney insisted that the larger point of Christianity transcended personal religious experience. It was the "glorious vision of a Christian world."[14]

This in fact had been the point of the August 24, 1744 message that resulted in Wesley's not being invited back to speak at the Church of St. Mary the Virgin in Oxford. It is here, and not at Aldersgate or with organization of the Holy Club or with the advent of Wesley's outdoor preaching, that Tenney begins her interpretation of the Wesleyan way. As Tenney notes, Wesley's message was similar in content and point to his controversial 1741 Oxford sermon "The Almost Christian" that had charged his audience, which included church dignitaries, university officials and students, with being only "half-Christian." In effect, behind Wesley's bold statements was an assumption that many of his contemporaries, especially church leaders, found to be the "most dubious" of his many irregularities, "that

---

(Nashville: Abingdon Press, 1957), 129-134, 211-212 is especially telling. Marston rejects Smith's view that Free Methodists were mistaken when arguing that Holiness teaching and experience were under attack in New York's Genesee Conference but highlights Smith's criticism of Phoebe Palmer for her indifference to the plight of slaves.

[13]See Kenneth Cain Kinghorn, *The Story of Asbury Theological Seminary* (Lexington, KY: Emeth Press, 2010), 161-187.

[14]Mary Alice Tenney, *Living in Two Worlds: How a Christian Does It* (Winona Lake, IN: Light and Life Press, 1958), 48.

God may be known as a living reality by every man, whatever his social status. The eighteenth century," Tenney noted, "had no liking for supernaturalism, free emotional expression or social leveling."[15]

In 1744 Wesley was back and asking a very basic question: "Why after all these centuries was the world still so unchristian?" Why, asked Wesley, had Christianity failed to fulfill the promises of the great Hebrew prophets that war would cease and righteousness, justice and mercy prevail? As Tenney notes, Wesley probably would have escaped censure if he had stopped his message with this largely rhetorical question, but he proceeded to indict Oxford itself and its magistrates, university leaders, instructors and even its students for failing to model Scriptural Christianity. Wesley, Tenney insisted, was placing blame for the failings of eighteenth century Christianity, "its humanistic theology... its moral compromises and its tolerance of social injustice" on English Christians themselves.[16]

Tenney, far more than her Free Methodist colleagues Bishops Taylor and Marston, saw Wesley's restoration of authentic Christianity as going far beyond the failed attempts of the Protestant Reformation itself. As Tenney noted, Wesley rejected the reformers' "restriction of perfection to perfection of faith." For Wesley "no branch of Protestantism had as yet explored the full implications of the Christian ethic." In fact, Tenney was convinced that a false emphasis upon conversion, especially a conversion experience, failed to grasp Wesley's real point that conversion was "the gate to a rich country of Christian experience, and further the manner of entrance might vary considerably with different individuals." Wesley, Tenney believed, united doctrine and experience for a very specific purpose, the creation of "a living fellowship with God, which will produce Christian character and express itself in Christian living."[17]

The point of authentic Methodism or real Christianity went far beyond conversion. It called for a distinctive way of life. Jesus' Sermon on the Mount was not an impossible command but "a precious promise." Tenney identified this "far reaching promise of the gospel" as the actuality of perfect love or Christian perfection. Christian perfection was the end or goal of the Christian enterprise. It was the point of Christianity itself. "Perfect love," she wrote, "is not static...nor is it primarily a religious experience. It is essentially a way of behaving." Tenney is hardly unique in this insistence. Behind Tenney one always senses the hovering presence, not of Wesley, but of her contemporary E. Stanley Jones. Christianity is not an experience; it is "the way." But Tenney is, of course, echoing Wesley, Edwards and especially Charles G. Finney as well when arguing that contrary to much popular preaching, Christianity is, after all, proved or disproved by the behavior of so-called Christians. As Allen Guelzo has argued, it was not in Wesley's ideas but in Finney's "demand for a holiness which would be visible and pub-

---

[15]Tenney, *Blueprint*, 15-16.
[16]Ibid, 18-22. Background material on Wesley's Oxford sermon is found in Albert Outler, ed. *The Works of John Wesley, Volume 1, Sermons 1-33* (Nashville: Abingdon Press, 1984), 109-116.
[17]Ibid, 108, 97.

lic rather than privatized and sentimental" that finds expression in later Holiness Movement social teaching and emphasis. But Tenney would have been less sure than Guelzo that the Holiness Movement was a conveyer of an authentic Christian social engagement. "Vital Christianity," Tenney concluded "is far more than a mystical experience, far more than devotion to a historic institution, far more than creedal correctness. It is a distinctive, all-inclusive way of life which has been shaped by dominant principles."[18]

In the years immediately following her 1955 retirement Tenney devoted much of her time to promoting her vision of the nature of authentic Christianity to lay audiences, especially among Free Methodists. In her truly neglected spiritual classic *Living in Two Worlds* she argued that Wesley's much neglected "General Rules" provided a model "for ways and means of living in two worlds while one worked at the task of Christianizing the present order." Intent on defending the heritage of Free Methodism, Tenney wrote, "The only mention many people ever make of the principles of their denominations is accompanied by an apology." During a time period of record church attendance and mass evangelism, Tenney reminded her readers that "for half a century the secularized church has sought for numbers, not Christians." "We have invidious terms," Tenney noted "which we apply contemptuously to efforts made by converts to become disciples: Fanatical, Puritan, and Pietistic." And with the mass revivalism of Billy Graham in mind she reminded Free Methodists that Wesley had never preached a sermon devoted to personal evangelism. "Evangelism," for Wesley she noted "was implicit not explicit."[19]

For Tenney, popular evangelism and compromised established Christianity had failed to make real disciples out of so-called "Christians" for a simple reason. As Tenney noted, "Can any Christian be a light to the world if he is unwilling to live permanently by principles and disciplines outlined in the Sermon on the Mount?" For Tenney, the key to the success of Methodism was the willingness of its members to accept discipline. If modern Christians hoped to have the same success, they needed to embrace a similar life of radical nonconformity to the world. Along with this emphasis on personal discipleship, Tenney insisted, as had Wesley, that Christianity was a social religion. For Tenney this social dimension could be recovered by a renewed emphasis on the traditional Methodist class meeting.[20]

---

[18]Ibid, 108, 119. Also see Allen C. Guelzo, "Oberlin Perfectionism and Its Edwardsian Origins, 1835-1870," in *Jonathan Edwards's Writings: Text, Context, Interpretation*, edited by Stephen J. Stein (Bloomington, IN: Indiana University Press, 1996), 170. The similar views of Donald W. Dayton are also subtle and nuanced. See Donald W. Dayton "The Holiness Churches: A Significant Ethical Tradition," *Christian Century* 26 February 1975, 197-201 and Donald W. Dayton, *The Theological Roots of Pentecostalism* (Grand Rapids: Francis Asbury Press, 1987), 160-167. The last quotations are from Tenney, *Blueprint*, 281.

[19]Tenney, *Living in Two Worlds*, 56, 92, 72-73. On the relationship of Edwards and Wesley see William Kostlevy, "Not Concerning the Heart but the Life: Jonathan Edwards's Treatise and John Wesley's Plain Account," *Christian History* Issue 116 2015, 36-37.

[20]Mary Alice Tenney, "The Origin and History of the Methodist Class Meeting," in Samuel Emerick, *Spiritual Renewal for Methodism: A Discussion of the Early Methodist*

But even here her emphasis remained deeply rooted in the personal ethical rigorist heritage of the FMC or perhaps better in the transplanted Puritanical culture of the New England immigrants. This is no place more evident than in many of the points of emphasis in her magnum opus, *The Blueprint for a Christian World*. In a work with a title that bears telltale signs of such popular New England immigrant social causes as the formal attempt to have the Constitution of the United States amended to officially acknowledge Christ as a formative influence in American society, Tenney, unlike modern students of Wesley, devotes an entire chapter to the Methodist response to dancing and pays special attention to the Methodist role in the revival of Sabbath observance that accompanied the rise of evangelicalism in British society. In fact many of Tenney's later writings focus on the corrupting influence of the cinema and television upon popular culture, and even more pointedly, the Christian church. At one point Tenney even suggests that the presence of slavery in "Christian England" during Wesley's lifetime was the result of the same kinds of Christian cultural compromises that allowed Hollywood to flourish in a not so Christian America. How many Christians, Tenney observed, have confessed "the guilt of church members for supporting pagan institutions" that have created a culture where materialism takes precedence over spiritual and moral values even at the expense of gullible young people without a sense of values like the recently deceased Marilyn Monroe? "All religious movements which have been virile and effective," Tenney wrote, "have examined their environing culture and assumed responsibility for change." In a world where some evangelicals were attempting to engage new and evolving cultural mediums themselves, Tenney found certain mediums beyond redemption. Personal vices such as drinking, smoking, Sabbath desecration and indulging the senses in forbidden cinema were the focus of her Christian social vision. In her conclusion Tenney noted, "even more than we fear the infiltration of communism should we fear the inner rot which has destroyed institutions and civilizations when Christians become insensitive to the infiltration of paganism." But this is probably the natural conclusion for a tradition that actually taught that Christian perfection was not a subjective religious experience but a way of behaving.[21]

It is hard not to conclude that part of the failure of Tenney and other Free Methodists, such as her student and disciple George A. Turner, another son of Yankee immigrants from New York's Burned Over District, to have the same effect as Donald W. Dayton, who they anticipate in many ways, was their failure to transcend the prudential culture of Free Methodism. Dayton's timely tract, *Discovering an Evangelical Heritage*, focuses on social causes that seem amazingly contemporary and ingeniously dismisses puritanical proclivities of evangelical-

---

Class Meeting and the Values Inherent in Personal Groups Today (Nashville: Methodist Evangelistic Materials, 1958), 11-19.

[21]For a discussion of the Christian Amendment Movement see Foster Gaines, *Moral Reconstruction: Christian Lobbyists and the Federal Reconstruction of Morality, 1865-1920* (Chapel Hill: University of North Carolina Press, 2002). Mary Alice Tenney, "The Disappearance of Moral Sensitivity," *Light and Life* 30 April 1963, 6-7.

ism in its introduction. Sadly, Tenney would live to see the day when Greenville College students would openly enter the Greenville theater through the front door. However it should also be noted that another of Tenney's students, Gilbert James, a GBS alumnus no less, would be honored in the dedication of the first edition of *Discovering an Evangelical Heritage*.[22]

In a certain sense Tenney may have anticipated some of the problematic implications of proposing a blueprint for a world unaware of its Yankee inspired city on a hill destiny. For the same Tenney who found the prudential rules of the FMC liberating also wrote "Why does separation from the world often become more important than witnessing to the world?" Fittingly, in her last book, *Adventures in Christian Love*, a series of sketches primarily of Free Methodist women, Tenney argues that love and not obedience "is the core of Christianity." In a work enriched by the perspective of Smith's *Revivalism and Social Reform*, Tenney did continue to insist that the "earnest Christianity" of Free Methodist founders B. T. and Ellen Stowe Roberts was intended in part "to interpenetrate the national culture with Christian principles." Nevertheless Tenney even here continued to insist that "evil individuals" rather than "evil institutions" were "the cause of a bad world" and faith in the "power of God, not educational or cultural betterment" was the hope of the world. In a work written for and highlighting Free Methodist women Tenney holds back few punches. As she notes, Free Methodism had failed to embrace the egalitarian vision of its founders. Noting that the FMC's real objection to the Pentecost Bands, a Christian renewal movement birthed by the FMC but not under church authority, was the role of women evangelists in the bands, Tenney argued, a church that refused to erase the limitations of "country, race, color or sex" was a hopelessly compromised institution unable to face the challenges of the mid-twentieth century. In effect Tenney, a child of the egalitarian vision of B. T. and Ellen Stowe Roberts, was anticipating the social vision and egalitarianism of Gilbert James and Donald W. Dayton.[23]

---

[22]A typical Free Methodist example of uniting the problems of racism and personal behavior is George A. Turner "Holiness and Social Tensions," in Kenneth E. Geiger, compiler, *The Word and the Doctrine: Studies in Contemporary Wesleyan-Arminian Theology* (Kansas City: Beacon Hill Press, 1965), 413-421. Dayton's *Discovering an Evangelical Heritage* should probably be read with Wallace Thornton, *Radical Righteousness: Personal Ethics and the Development of the Holiness Movement* (Salem, OH: Schmul Publishing Company, 1998) which highlights the role of lifestyle issues in Methodism and the Holiness traditions. Interestingly E. Stanley Jones, whose roots are in the Southern Holiness tradition and not the cultural peculiarities of Free Methodism, avoided the reduction of Christianity to a few personal vices.

[23]Mary Alice Tenney, "Widening Your Witness," *Light and Life* 30 June 1963, 5. Mary Alice Tenney, *Adventures in Christian Love* (Winona Lake, IN: Light and Life Press, 1964), 8, 18-19, 123-126.

Chapter 10

David P. Denton: Evangelist of Truth

William Snider

In the fall of 1955, Glenn Griffith pitched a gospel tent in Caldwell, Idaho that would initiate a secession group from the Church of the Nazarene that took the name Bible Missionary Union, later Bible Missionary Church.[1] This action precipitated two decades of realignment in the four major holiness denominations: the Church of the Nazarene, the Wesleyan Methodist Church, the Free Methodist Church and the Pilgrim Holiness Church. Coalescing around the Interchurch Holiness Convention (IHC), the emerging denominational groups were the product of post World War II changes in American religious culture. Eager to fulfill the Biblical mandate of evangelism, principles of separation from the world were revisited and revised with precept interpretation giving way to a more subjective understanding and enforcement. Proponents of change described the events as "Evangelism vs. Legalism."[2] Persons troubled by this process protested in the press, pulpit and with parliamentary procedural efforts in their respective conference/district assemblies. Since both groups were theologically similar it became necessary to differentiate between them. The protesting group became known as the Conservative Holiness Movement. Despite a common historical and theological background, the two groups traveled in different directions in their interpretation and practice of lifestyle and worship.

Troubled times call for heroic measures, and heroic measures call for persons temperamentally equipped to sustain lines of demarcation both defensively and offensively. Out of the mountains of East Tennessee came such a man. Rocked in the fundamentalism of the 1920s and nurtured in the drama of the Red Scare, he flowered into leadership in the protesting 1960s and then faded in the grip of the same personality characteristics which had propelled him into the public eye. Abhorred by some and admired to the point of worship by others, he rode the crest of controversy until the wave crashed on a isolated beach. When he died in 1994,

---

[1] For early history of the Bible Missionary Church, see Timothy A. Carr, *For Such A Time as This: The Story of the Bible Missionary Church, The Beginning Years* (Shoals, IN: Country Pines, 2011).

[2] Lee Haines and Paul William Thomas. *An Outline History of the Wesleyan Church.* 4th rev. ed. (Indianapolis, IN: Wesley Press, 1990), 112-115.

some wondered if anyone would take notice. But he had been true to himself and his God. A quarter century later, his story deserves to be told and explored. In its own unique way, it is a profile in courage.

David Pile Denton[3] was born June 15, 1914 in the east Tennessee town of Dayton. His father, Fred B., was understood to be a Methodist minister with a local preacher's license. It is reported that he operated a theater in Dayton and later a small grocery store in Chattanooga, Tennessee.[4] Fred and his wife Maluvea, a homemaker, had seven children, four sons and three daughters of whom David was the fourth child. In 1940, Fred deserted the family for another woman.

David attended local schools in Dayton without particular distinction, although he did enjoy the honor of having his elementary poetic efforts complimented by the famed Helen Keller. When David was eleven, his hometown, the Rhea County seat, was awakened with the invasion of the national press. The state of Tennessee had passed legislation prohibiting the teaching of evolution in the public schools. In 1925, John Scopes, a substitute teacher, was arrested for violating the statute and what followed was the famous Scopes Monkey Trial. The trial became a national contest waged in the press between the Fundamentalists defended by three time presidential candidate William Jennings Bryan and the Modernists/Evolutionists represented by the agnostic and celebrated defense attorney Clarence Darrow. Scopes was found guilty and was fined $100 only to have the verdict subsequently overturned on a technicality. Denton knew Scopes personally and as a young man sat on the steps of the courthouse to listen to the debate. He would later write,

> [I] heard the trial. I saw and heard the infamous, agnostic lawyer, Clarence Darrow, and his actions and attitude convinced me, as a boy, that he needed God even though he denied that there was one. I also saw and heard that great orator and 100% American, William Jennings Bryan, both as a lawyer in the trial and as he preached to the crowds on the courthouse lawn each Sunday. His kindly attitude and evident sincerity made a deep impression on me, as well as his tremendous ability as a speaker and his grasp of spiritual truth.[5]

Denton was deeply convinced of the validity of the creation story and commented rather humorously, "Even though there is not one iota of proof that man evolved from a lower form of animal (monkey or otherwise), they (supporters of evolutionary theory) certainly proved that many people are making monkeys out of themselves."[6] His conviction of the truth of the Biblical creation account

---

[3]The spelling of the middle name is disputed. The Social Security Application and Files Index spells it "Pile." Entries on ancestry.com list it as "Pyle." Whatever the spelling, Denton abhorred the middle name, refusing to divulge it. He was known as "David P." or "D.P."

[4]David Denton told me that his father operated the theater. Other family members did not recall that detail but did supply the information that he was a minister and operated the retail grocery store.

[5]Orbie Denton and David Denton. *It Happened in the Valley* (Concord, TN: Denton Publications, 1977), 4.

[6]Ibid.

became representative of his commitment to Bible truth in propositional form. It is impossible to measure the influence of the greater Fundamentalist-Modernist controversy on his young mind, but it is apparent that his convictions were set at a young age. It would appear that the atmosphere of that historic event was the cradle for the formation of propositional truth as he saw it.

In 1927 the Denton family moved to the Cumberland Plateau and the village of Crossville, Tennessee. Here he graduated from high school and here he met the love of his life, Orbie McLarty. When he left for college and subsequent ministry, he told her he would come back for her. In the next four years he saw her five times but on a Monday, unannounced, he arrived to claim his bride. She was ready and they were married in Albany, Kentucky on April 9, 1934.[7] David Denton could never have found a bride who would be more loyal and devoted to her husband. Through good and bad, known and unknown, little and much, she stood steadfastly at his side for fifty-three years until she died 1987 after a quarter century bout with cancer. David and Orbie Denton had three sons, David Edward, Roy and John, all of whom obtained earned doctorates and taught in universities in the South.

Upon high school graduation Denton left home for college. He left little record of his college education, although he indicated that he had attended Vanderbilt University in the early 1930s, and he held a permanent Tennessee teacher's certificate in both elementary and secondary education.[8] In later years, when many conservatives were blaming denominational educational institutions for the loss of purity of doctrine and passion for souls, Denton never despised education *per se*. While he expressed his concerns, he was a faithful supporter of Bible school education including the IHC's efforts to establish a graduate school called the Aldersgate School of Religion.[9]

In 1931, he experienced a unique and powerful conversion experience. He recounted that while traveling as a hitchhiker, he encountered bad weather and bad luck. He wrote,

> I was out on the road; no top coat; no protection; no place to go; no ride; and no God. Finally, late at night, I sought shelter where there really was none–under an electric tower by the side of the road. There was still a drizzle of rain; the grass was soppy wet; and I was totally exhausted and sore and sick. But, I laid down in the wet grass, tried to cover my head with what little clothing I could use; and tried to go to sleep. Of course, I was a miserable mess; and real sleep never came. Some-

---

[7] For the biography of Orbie McLarty Denton, see David Denton. *It Happened to Orbie* (Knoxville, TN: Evangelist of Truth, 1987).

[8] Orbie Denton and David Denton. *It Happened on the Mountain* (Concord, TN: Denton Publications, 1975), 55. David Denton, *It Happened to Some Young People* (Knoxville, TN: Evangelist of Truth, 1984), 19.

[9] In 1966-67, plans were formulated for Denton's own Bible school in Knoxville, Tennessee to be housed in the Stair Avenue Wesleyan Methodist Church. Furniture was acquired for the effort, but it was aborted by schism within the conference. This writer, who had promised to enroll, was given Denton's blessing to attend Hobe Sound Bible College in Florida.

time in the wee hours of the morning, I aroused . . . I began to wonder why I was in that shape and what I was doing there anyway. Eventually something seemed to say to me, "If you continue to go on like you have been doing, and refuse to mind God, this will be about all you can expect." Lying there in the wet grass I purposed to live differently. It wasn't but a few days, until I begged God to forgive me and keep me out of hell, and I promised Him that if he would–I would do anything that He told me to do. The burden left my heart, and I knew that God had forgiven me and saved me. I immediately began to mind Him, and until this very day, can truthfully say that I have never knowingly disobeyed His voice.[10]

That obedience would include a call to the ministry to which he humbly submitted. In fact, he testified, "I knew I had to preach and so began the next day."[11]

His conversion testimony shines a clear light onto the ministry of David Denton. Per his own experience, there would forever be a clear and focused emphasis on a definable moment of conversion. It would include a radical departure from sin and an uncompromising obedience to the will of God. It would always be a heaven or hell decision with no possible middle ground. These parameters of Christian experience were fixed in his mind and ministry, leaving him little appreciation for any conclusion that seemed to placate sin. Whatever the circumstances of life, conversion and Christian living were seen in absolute terms. This Fundamentalist (and some would argue Methodist) perception of experiential truth would mark his life. If the word "radical" could ever be applied to him, it flows out of this encounter with God.

Despite being a Southerner, Denton joined the Methodist Episcopal Church because "I thought that its Discipline was nearer to what the Bible teaches than the others."[12] He accepted his first pastorate in 1932 in his hometown of Dayton, and until 1944 he followed the pattern of Methodist ministers under the appointment system.[13] His philosophy of pastoral ministry was precise and colorfully stated.

---

[10]Orbie Denton and David Denton. *It Happened on the Road* (Concord, TN: Evangelist of Truth/Denton Publications, 1978), 5-7. Denton testifies to a 1936 sanctification experience in the same volume, 33-34.

[11]Denton. *It Happened in the Valley*, 47.

[12]David P. Denton. *It Happened while Building Churches* (Concord, TN: Denton Publications, 1990), 5.

[13]Establishing a chronology of Denton's ministry during the years in the Methodist Church is not easy. It must be deduced from isolated references in his writings. An attempt at such is as follows:

    1) Dayton, TN – one year (1932)
    2) ? – Decatur Circuit – one year (1933?)
    3) Graysville, TN – two years (1934-35)
    4) New Tazewell, TN – three years (1936-1938)
    5) Baileyton, TN – two years (1939 -1940)
    6) Greenville, TN – Conference Evangelist (1941)
    7) Church Hill, TN – eight months (1941-1942)
    6) McFerran Chapel – one and half years (1942-1943/44)

> When I was pastoring Churches, I always sought to win folk to the Lord and help them to get really established, I believed then, and still believe that the job of a minister . . . is to win souls to Jesus Christ. I never subscribed to this idea that all a pastor was supposed to do was to look after a few disgruntled sheep that act more like goats. If one is saved . . . they have a real concern for the lost. God commands all of His people to be witnesses and if one will not follow His command they are not worthy of His call.[14]

While not an imposing physical specimen at 5'9", 160 lbs., D. P. Denton was nothing if not a personification of energy and passion for the kingdom of God. He was a prolific preacher and seeker of souls. Upon assignment to a location he would usually extend his ministry by opening preaching points in abandoned churches and school buildings. Often his circuit became six or seven such venues.[15] At one assignment, he traveled many miles a month (sometimes walking because of impassable roads) to reach a secluded mountain village that had not had a pastor for an extended period of time. Such was his passion for the lost. He was never intimidated by anyone since seeking the lost was his divine mission. Businessman, politician, farmer or moonshiner--it did not matter. Often in his life he offended peers and religious leaders, but to his last day, he was respected by the common man.

David Denton was not only a preacher but he was also an editor/printer/publisher of Christian literature. In 1934 he began publishing the *Evangelist of Truth*, a religious/patriotic magazine that he would continue until his death. Operating under the motto "Proclaiming the Whole Bible Truth for God's Glory and for Our Country" the magazine was a literary voice for holiness and pro–American views.[16]

Denton also founded Denton Publications, which printed and distributed millions of books and tracts throughout the world. His philosophy of publishing mirrored his understanding of evangelism–a simple message simply, linguistically and stylistically presented for the common man.

In the early 1960's Denton began publishing Sunday school literature to combat what he viewed as the dangers of liberal offerings from the National Council

---

[14]Orbie Denton and David Denton. *It Happened at the Altar* (Concord, TN: Denton Publications, 1983), 5.

[15]Denton, *It Happened in the Valley*, 47. He says that in eleven years in the Methodist Church he started or reopened twenty-five rural churches that had been closed for lack of funds during the Depression.

[16]At the time of Denton's passing the *Evangelist of Truth* was held in the trust of a Board of Managers with Paul Bates, Indianapolis, as Chairman and David Turner as editor/printer. Dissatisfaction with Turner's published views prompted Bates to seek control of the publication. The matter was contested in court with Bates securing legal right to the magazine and the inventory. Currently Larry Warren, Washington, Indiana is the editor with the inventory of titles and tracts having been purchased by Bible Missionary Institute, Rock Island, Illinois. There is a strong probability that a complete publication run of the *Evangelist of Truth* does not exist, and even more unfortunate is the probability that Denton's files have also been lost.

of Churches. He was a strident promoter of holiness, securing publication rights for the writings of Free Methodist evangelist E. E. Shelhamer. Combining pen and pulpit, Denton became an aggressive force for values he held dear.

Among his publishing ventures was a book published in 1972, titled *The Reverend Spy*, the manuscript for which Denton said "came to me in a very unusual manner which I need not discuss...accompanied by a signed statement giving me the full rights of publication." He claimed that he was publishing it with only a "small amount of editing."[17]

The *Reverend Spy* recounted the activities of a young pastor who, after being rejected for military service for health reasons at the beginning of World War II, was recruited by a secret operative to spy for the United States government. Since many elements of the principal character's life paralleled those of Denton, including the initials of the protagonist and the locations of the action, many believed that the story was a true accounting of events in Denton's life. When questioned, Denton would neither confirm nor deny the truth of the story.[18]

It would be helpful to assess this "mountain man" at the end of World War II. First, he is a Southerner. Living in the aftermath of the Civil War and in the grip of the Great Depression, life was tough and much could be attributed to "northern Yankee" influences that were beyond Denton's control. Area poverty was countered by illegal whiskey traffic and government agents became the objects of suspicion. Even as Denton worked in the mountains as a Methodist minister, he encountered antagonism that had to be broken down before he could minister effectively. While the grace of God is a powerful force, someone has said "we are the sum total of the experiences through which we pass." Could this southern mountain man be expected to carry some of these scars into a larger world? Perhaps he could. In summary, we have a Holiness Fundamentalist specializing in antagonism to sin and passionate about evangelism working against the backdrop of a native geographical suspicion, the disappointment of a compromising church, and the reality of sinister forces seeking to undermine the values he holds most dear.

In July of 1944 Denton joined the Wesleyan Methodist Connection of Churches (WMC) and accepted the pastorate of the Bristol Tennessee Wesleyan Methodist Church.[19] He remained there until 1948 when he was elected President of the Tennessee Conference of the WMC, and he relocated to Knoxville. As a "Connection of Churches," the WMC tended to emphasize local church autonomy in contradistinction to the strong episcopal government that characterized the Methodist Episcopal Church. Second, particularly after 1888, the WMC had purposefully

---

[17]David P. Denton. *The Reverend Spy* (Knoxville: Evangelist of Truth, 1972), 7.

[18]According to United Methodist minister Billy Gillespie of Kingsport, Tennessee, one of Denton's sons (probably David Ed) in a letter denied that events reported in *The Reverend Spy* were possible based on his memory of his family during the period covered by the book. Billy Gillespie, report to the Holston Conference Historical Society, Rutledge, Tennessee, April 28, 2007.

[19]Tennessee Conference of the Wesleyan Methodist Connection of Churches. *Conference Minutes,* 1944, 18–19.

identified with the emerging holiness movement and emphasized a second work of grace as taught by John Wesley. Third, the WMC had a strong emphasis upon ethical conformity as reflected in lifestyle issues. The General Rules of the 1947 Wesleyan Methodist Discipline highlights areas of concern, particularly with regard to dress:

> It is further expected of those who are admitted to our churches that they should continue to evidence their desire of salvation: First, by doing no harm–by avoiding evil of every kind, especially that which is not generally practiced such as . . . the putting on of gold and costly apparel . . . [and] the wearing of apparel which does not modestly and properly clothe the person.[20]

This affirmation was further supported by a statement in the "Special Rules" which stated,

> Let none be received into the church until they have left off the wearing of gold and superfluous ornaments and have adopted modest attire . . . if the mature men and women of the Church do not have a conscience on this matter it will be impossible for the Church to maintain its testimony against worldliness in the younger years.[21]

The Tennessee Conference affirmed this emphasis in its 1947 Conference Resolutions and Laws by adding further interpretation.

> In view of our disciplinary stand on the matter of jewelry and our interpretation of the Scriptures in regard to it, we do not think it consistent with our standards for a Wesleyan Methodist minister to use the ring ceremony in performing a wedding. Therefore preachers of this Conference shall be asked to refrain from performing a ring ceremony involving a member of the Wesleyan Methodist Church.[22]

This was the WMC as Denton found it when he transferred from the Methodist Church in 1944. In this fellowship, he could shake the disappointments of a compromising denomination for an organization that stood for holiness and separated living. Here he would find peace of mind and heart. Here his heart would be at rest. And for this he would contend, should that be required. The changes that would follow often led to the general affirmation "I didn't leave the church, the church left me."

In 1952, the Resolutions and Laws were significantly amended to read as follows:

> We shall continue to interpret the teachings of the Scriptures and the Special Rules of the Discipline in accord with the standards held by the early Methodists and the Wesleyans of the past generations. To this end we reaffirm our stand against the reception of any member as a full member who wears jewelry, including the wed-

---

[20]*Discipline of the Wesleyan Methodist Church of America* (Syracuse, NY: Wesleyan Methodist Publishing Association, 1947), 30-31/Paragraph 46.

[21]Ibid., 31, 33, 35/Paragraphs 46, 51, 56.

[22]Tennessee Conference of the Wesleyan Methodist Church of America. *Annual Journal 1947*, 14. In the 1948 statement, the specification of excluding "members" was expanded to "all." Tennessee Conference of the Wesleyan Methodist Church of America. *Annual Journal 1948*, 14.

ding band or other unnecessary ornaments, and declare ourselves in favor of higher standards of dress, and other worldly manifestations on the person. Our ministers are asked to refrain from performing wedding ceremonies using the ring, and to be positive in their declarations regarding this entering wedge of worldliness.[23]

This resolution remained in the Minutes of the Tennessee Conference of the WMC through the 1966 conference year.

Denton took a dim view of the denominational name change from "Connection" to "Church," which occurred in 1947. In fact, he always insisted that he had not submitted the conference charter for the name to be altered, maintaining that he was the only conference president in the denomination not to do so. To critics he commented, "If you think that we feel too strongly along this line, please, be patient with us and remember that we spent twelve years in the ministry of one of the most highly organized ecclesiastical machines to be found in the Protestant world."[24]

In 1951 he was asked to present a paper on "Meeting our Modern Menace." Expected to comment on the evils of Roman Catholicism and Communism, favorite topics of his, Denton responded with a three-point outline "Super State, Super Church, Super Crime."[25] Narrowing his concerns from the pattern of a monolithic Roman church, Denton warmed to his subject.

> An ecclesiastical hierarchy within Protestantism would be just as deadening and devastating as the Roman version... The church today is afflicted with numbers of "little Hitlers" who usurp authority that is not theirs and imagine themselves a law unto themselves. The old, old story is that men with big ideas, abundant resources, high sounding titles and large memberships are not satisfied to follow the good shepherd as he seeks the lost sheep, but they would rather spend their time making resolutions and writing laws about the sheep, or else seem interested only in building packing houses so that they can enjoy the income from the flock... to invest in or allow too much authority to any leader has produced evils that always worked to the detriment of nations and churches...[26]

Fearing that tightening organization would compromise the "main line of endeavor–the salvation of precious souls," Denton warned that misplaced denominational priorities such as size, money, and bureaucracy would bring disastrous results.

> Our doctrines will be compromised to suit the whim of men; our standards will be lowered to accommodate the unregenerate; our services will become an avenue

---

[23]Tennessee Conference of the Wesleyan Methodist Church of America. *Annual Journal 1952*, 11.

[24]David P. Denton. *Meeting our Modern Menace* (Crossville, TN: Evangelist of Truth, 1961?), 3.

[25]Denton. *Meeting our Modern Menace* , 1-5.

[26]Denton. *Meeting our Modern Menace* , 12, Introduction, 18.

for mere ritualistic formalism rather than revival fires; our leaders will be selected by political maneuvering rather than by Holy Ghost direction and our distinctive reasons for existing will be lost forever.[27]

These were hardly words to endear him to a denomination that characterized the organizational change as a period of "Centralization and Maturity."[28]

In 1951, the Ohio Wesleyan Methodist Conference passed legislation giving further specificity to the Wesleyan Methodist Discipline statement regarding jewelry to include the disallowing of the wedding band in the requirement for membership. The legislation was appealed to President Roy Nicholson who ruled at the 1955 General Conference that such legislation was "unconstitutional" on the grounds that only the General Conference had the prerogative to set terms for church membership. He was sustained by the General Board of Review. We have already noted that the Tennessee Conference with Denton as president had passed similar legislation, and Tennessee did not rescind its action. In 1952, Denton resigned the presidency of the Tennessee Conference for health reasons.

By 1956 the Tennessee Conference, under the leadership of President M. L. Arnold, had added a paragraph to the Resolutions and Laws regarding television. It read,

> As television is a satanic miracle to wreck the Christian Faith, our ministers are asked to take a stand against it, preach against it, and condemn it, and that no minister or delegate be elected to office who has a television set or who is in favor of it. And, we recommend the local churches hold the same standard.[29]

The following year the Knoxville First Wesleyan Methodist Church under the leadership of pastor S. D. Herron sought to enforce such a requirement for their local church officers. The effort was appealed to the General Church, and the 1959 General Conference overruled the action. Denton, who had returned to office in 1958, did not relent.[30]

WMC officials were wearying of the struggle. At the 1963 General Conference, thinly veiled legislation was introduced and passed to provide that

> The General Conference or, during the interim, the Board of Administration by a two thirds vote of all its members, shall be empowered to transfer the supervision of the ministers and churches of a Mission Annual Conference to the related Executive Secretary or to one of the General Superintendents for a specified period of time if such action is deemed to be in the best interest of the work of the Conference. This action must be reported promptly to the president of the Conference.[31]

---

[27]Denton, *Meeting Our Modern Menace*, 13.

[28]Haines and Thomas. *An Outline History of the Wesleyan Church*, 105.

[29]Tennessee Conference of the Wesleyan Methodist Church. *Annual Minutes, 1956*, 11.

[30]For a more explanation of the conflict between the Tennessee and Ohio Wesleyan Methodist Conferences and the WMC, see Wallace Thornton. *Radical Righteousness: Personal Ethics and the Development of the Holiness Movement* (Salem, OH: Schmul Publishing, 1998), 151-158.

[31]Wesleyan Methodist Church of America. *General Conference Minutes*, 1963, 184.

The Tennessee Conference was a Mission Conference and, in accordance with this provision, action was taken to appoint C. Wesley Lovin, General Secretary of Church Extension, as Tennessee Conference president. The action was resisted by a large majority of the conference ministers and laity, and Denton remained the titular head. In 1964, the Tennessee Conference passed a "Resolution of Non-Cooperation" with the mother church until such time as peace could be restored, but there would be no peace. Men with administrative responsibility and legislative fiat had collided with persons of conviction based on the Word of God as they saw it. With no resolution in sight, on October 9, 1964 the WMC filed suit in Chancery Court, Knoxville, Tennessee asking the court to declare C. Wesley Lovin president of the Conference and to secure the Conference monies and property to the general church. The General Conference of 1966, which Denton did not attend, refused to seat delegates from Tennessee until matters were resolved to the satisfaction of the denomination.

After much verbiage and jockeying for position on both sides, in 1968 the matter was settled out of court with seceding churches paying a percentage of the value of their property and those who were organizing under the name Tennessee Bible Methodist Connection of Churches providing payment for the campground.

Unbowed, Denton emerged from the circumstances strong and unscathed with those who appreciated his stand for truth as he (and they) understood it. Through the pages of the conference periodical, *Tennessee Tidings*, and through a series of letters and specially called meetings, Denton maintained the Biblical basis for their stand for separation from the world and condemned the General Church for oppressive regulations and compromising values. In his mind, his fears had been realized, and there were many who agreed with him. Arguing in the pulpit and the press for the preservation of "the old fashioned way" he remained in office until 1987 when he resigned due to his wife's health.

While Denton was hardly popular among WMC leaders, he was a cause célèbre in the emerging Conservative Holiness Movement. Popular in their pulpits and admired in the partisan press, he was welcomed by those who shared his concerns. In the years 1955-1968 what J. Gordon Melton has called "the Glenn Griffith movement"[32] had grown, finding elements of support in each of the major holiness denominations.[33] These dissidents would find aid and comfort in the yearly gathering of the IHC led by Allegheny Wesleyan minister Harold Schmul.[34] The Convention was the result of concern among conservatives over the direction of their respective holiness denominations.[35] Harold Schmul (Wesleyan Method-

---

[32] J. Gordon Melton. *The Encyclopedia of American Religions* (Wilmington, NC: McGrath Publishing Company, 1978) Vol. I, 236-242.

[33] See Brian Black. *Holiness Heritage: Tracing the History of the Holiness Movement* (Salem, OH: Allegheny Publications, 2003).

[34] For a survey of the IHC, see Harold E. Schmul, Ella Fruin, Leonard Sankey and Rebeca Rundell. *Profile of the Interchurch Holiness Convention: A Retrospect of 40 Years of IHC Ministry* (Salem, OH: IHC, 1987).

[35] "Contending for the Faith" in *Valiant for Truth: Compilation of Sermons by Holiness Preachers and Writers*, ed. H. E. Schmul (Rochester, PA: H. E. Schmul, n.d.), 193-220.

ist), H. Robb French (Wesleyan Methodist) and R. G. Flexon (Pilgrim Holiness) together called the first meeting in 1950 in Salem, Ohio.

Subsequently gathering at God's Bible School (Cincinnati, Ohio), and at Huntington, West Virginia, and Dayton, Ohio, some ten thousand would join to express their concerns over what was perceived as a spiritual decline, reflected in forms of piety, worship and separation from the world. For many years Denton served on the governing committee of the IHC and preached almost annually. Executive Secretary of the IHC, Harold Schmul, offered this observation about Denton:

> He was one of the Conservative Holiness Movement's best preachers proclaiming the wonders of the Word without fear or favor . . . when in the pulpit he spoke with authority and finality, urgency and passion. He spoke with the eloquence of fire and love. He would not fudge. He would not budge. He stood tall and true to God and His Word. Truth never wanted a defender when David Denton was standing guard.[36]

Denton's judgment was clear and sometimes surprisingly objective even to those among whom his ways and opinions were not always appreciated, even within IHC circles. The Tennessee mountain man with a unique accent, an amazing collection of stories and the victim of perceived ecclesiastical abuse was received with open arms. The days of the Fundamentalist-Liberal controversy lived again in this champion of the narrow, but straight, way.

The October 1964 WMC court action was Denton's high-water mark. The immediate crisis had passed, and responsibility now changed from something that approximated guerilla warfare to the grueling task of church administration. Now the returning soldiers from the campaign for truth must be rehabilitated into the cause of evangelism, discipling and cooperative effort, and it would not prove easy to do. Those whom he had trained for battle found it difficult to submit to Denton's authoritarian leadership when shot and shell had largely ceased. Having resigned his conference position, Denton was lonely. The evolving movement did not always meet his expectations, and the leadership of his successor, a North Carolinian with whom he had fought shoulder to shoulder, now did not satisfy the old warrior.

In 1990, Denton withdrew from the Tennessee Bible Methodist Connection to join a few compatriots in a smaller and more obscure group.[37] By this time the pen that had served him well in battle was taking aim at targets perhaps of his own imagination. Persons who had enjoyed and cheered his literary broadsides when directed at a common foe now winced when they felt the vitriolic blasts directed their way. Gradually, Denton faded from public view, and he died on December 4, 1994. A relatively small group of mourners gathered in Crossville, Tennessee

---

[36]Harold Schmul, editor. "David P. Denton," *Convention Herald*, January-February, 1995, 3.

[37]Wallace Thornton insists that the members of the withdrawing group were contending against the possession and use of the VCR. (See Thornton. *Radical Righteousness*, 157-158.)

to pay their respects, and then his remains were laid beside his beloved Orbie in a small cemetery within one hundred yards of a church he had established. He became part of the Christian past.

History can be kind or cruel. Assessments made out of context are as skewed as exposition without appreciation for linguistic, cultural and historic background. So we step back to the turbulent sixties when the holiness churches were as strife ridden as the streets of the United States. In that setting, who was David Denton? He could be kind, and he could be brusque. He could be social, and he could be remarkably aloof. He could be fair, and he could be judgmental. He could be compassionate, and he could seem to be insensitive. He seemed always to be suspicious, with an eye for impending conflict, and yet he was never radical for the sake of staking out an extreme position. Always–whether preacher, agent or administrator–he sought for truth. He lived as an old soldier who had "done his duty as God gave him the light to see that duty."[38]

David Pile Denton was considered by some to be at the very least a demi-god and by others the reincarnation of the demonic. Those who knew him were rarely neutral, and, to be honest, this man of the mountains tended to view and assess the world around him in much the same light as it had cynically or adoringly viewed him. Perhaps he can be better understood in the words of presidential nominee Barry Goldwater, speaking in 1964, a year crucial to both the speaker and to David Denton, "Extremism in the defense of liberty is no vice; moderation in the pursuit of justice is no virtue."[39] David Denton would have substituted "verity" for "liberty" and "justice" in order to satisfy his conscience and, as such, today he kneels before the only God and our Saviour as a faithful servant having performed to the best of his ability–an unapologetic and uncompromising "Evangelist of Truth."

---

[38]Words taken from the speech of General Douglas MacArthur upon his last appearance before Congress on April 19, 1951.

[39]Barry Goldwater, in his acceptance speech for the Republican nomination for President of the United States, San Francisco, CA , July 16, 1964.

Chapter 11

Born in the Fire

Edwin Woodruff Tait

When my grandmother, Lillian Harvey, was in her eighties, looking back over a long and stormy life, she often summed up her sense of alienation from contemporary religious life with the phrase: "those who are born in the fire cannot live in the smoke."[1] For Lillian and her husband Edwin, the spiritual intensity of their early years in the Burning Bush set the standard for the rest of their long and active lives of ministry. Throughout their often stormy careers as evangelists, teachers, organizers, writers, and publishers, Edwin and Lillian Harvey sought to keep the "fire" alive in the midst of the "smoke" of what they saw as an increasingly worldly and lukewarm twentieth-century evangelicalism. This is their story, and my own, making this essay at least as much personal reminiscence as scholarly study.

As readers of Bill Kostlevy's 2010 *Holy Jumpers* know, the "Burning Bush" was the informal moniker of a radical "come-outer" Holiness denomination, the Metropolitan Church Association (MCA). Founded in 1894 as the "Metropolitan Methodist Mission," by 1900 the MCA had become an independent Holiness church, formally withdrawing from the Rock River Conference of the Methodist Episcopal Church in the fall of that year.[2] In 1904, the MCA embraced an eschatologically informed communal theology, teaching that in the "last days" God was calling believers to give up private property as part of entire consecration. In 1905, the church purchased a large hotel, the Fountain Spring House in Waukesha, Wisconsin, and began the complex process of moving the entire community and its various activities to Waukesha.[3] By 1912, there were more than five hundred people in residence, living an intense but, by many later accounts, rewarding life of study, worship, and manual labor.[4] At the same time, the MCA continued

---

[1]The phrase "when you are born in the fires of revival, you cannot live in the smoke of denominationalism," occurs in an autobiographical fragment by my grandfather, included in the book *Let My People Go* (Harvey and Tait, 1997), 13, ascribed to "the president of a Welsh Bible College" who had lived through the great Welsh revival of 1904-5.

[2]William C. Kostlevy, *Holy Jumpers: Evangelicals and Radicals in Progressive Era America* (New York: Oxford University Press, 2010), 59.

[3]Kostlevy, *Holy Jumpers*, 112.

[4]Kostlevy, *Holy Jumpers,* 113.

135

its evangelistic activities throughout the United States, and established missions in Britain, Scandinavia, India, South Africa, Latin America, and the Caribbean.[5]

My grandfather, Edwin F. Harvey, was born in 1908 at Waukesha to Henry L. Harvey and Beatrice Foster Harvey. Henry L. Harvey was the younger brother of Edwin L. Harvey, who was one of the founders and principal leaders of the MCA. Both Harvey brothers had been successful hotel owners in the 1890s who along with several other wealthy businessmen had given up their property in order to establish the community at Waukesha. Since Edwin L. and his wife Gertrude had no children, my grandfather, his brother Henry, and his sister Irene were the closest thing to aristocracy the Burning Bush had during its first decade in Waukesha. They grew up with the knowledge that the eyes of the entire community were on them (my grandfather used to tell me that as a teenager he took pride in driving the manure wagon in full view of the many windows of the Fountain Spring House in order to demonstrate his humility), and that they would be expected to carry on the Church's legacy.[6]

My grandmother, on the other hand, born Lillian Johnson in Pittsburgh in 1911, came from working-class German parents, both of whom had come to America as children and had grown up in the Midwest, meeting and marrying in the MCA. Lillian grew up in ramshackle apartments in a series of cities--Pittsburgh, Detroit, and Chicago--at one point living next to a morgue and across from a brothel. Her father, John Johnson, was one of the MCA's most committed preachers. According to my grandmother, Edwin L. Harvey used to refer to him as his "war horse." Johnson was a stern but devoted father who did not allow his children to play, keeping them busy out of school hours with piano practice and, of course, nightly meetings. Lillian was the oldest of nine children (two of whom died in childhood) and according to her later reminiscences she often felt neglected by her mother, who devoted her time to mentoring other young women.

In 1926, E. L. and Gertrude Harvey handed over leadership of the MCA to W. S. Hitchcock. E. L. Harvey died shortly afterwards. Hitchcock's main achievement, at least in Kostlevy's narrative, was to eliminate the MCA's debts. He did this by slashing radically the number of people resident at the Waukesha headquarters, leaving only those whose activities directly supported the church. Other members were expected to go back into the world they had abandoned by "giving up all" and work for a living like anyone else. Hitchcock also closed the Church's home for the elderly. As a result, many people who had given their property to the Church with the expectation of being cared for were turned out to fend for themselves.[7]

For Hitchcock, this ruthless restructuring was spiritually as well as financially necessary. As Kostlevy puts it, Hitchcock was convinced "that the community's indebtedness was the result of spiritual lethargy and as such demanded

---

[5]http://metrochurchassn.com/history4.html, accessed May 13, 2016; Kostlevy, *Holy Jumpers,* 147.

[6]Kostlevy, *Holy Jumpers,* 150-151.

[7]Kostlevy, *Holy Jumpers,* 155.

repentance."[8] Accordingly, in 1926-28 a religious revival swept through the MCA. Senior leaders such as Henry L. Harvey publicly repented and acknowledged that they had lost their sanctification.[9] At the same time, members of the younger generation came to the fore, professing the new birth and/or entire sanctification for the first time. Both the repentant elders and the newly awakened young expressed their experience of the Holy Spirit through the sorts of dramatic physical demonstrations that had accompanied the early days of the MCA. But whereas the early MCA had latched onto the doctrine of "giving up all" as an outward sign of total consecration, and had directed their polemic toward other Holiness groups who allegedly failed to do this, the Hitchcock MCA took a more inward turn. While obedience to church authorities was seen as a *sine qua non* for Holiness, it was obviously not enough. A continual self-examination, and a continual effort to re-evangelize those who were already part of the movement, became central to the revised self-understanding of the MCA.

Among the young people who rose to prominence as a result of the revival were the two sons of Henry L. Harvey, Edwin F. and Henry L. Jr., and their friend Howard Bitzer. And among the young people who watched from the pews was the teenaged Lillian Johnson. My grandmother often claimed that she had never really noticed Edwin until he was filled with the Holy Spirit. My grandfather was, temperamentally, an introverted, bookish person who was always nervous when speaking in public. Yet the experience of sanctification transformed him into a dynamic, enthusiastic proponent of Hitchcock's redefined Holiness radicalism. And watching him and others, Lillian felt the pull of this kind of religion as well.

At the same time, her parents were moving in the opposite direction. John Johnson was removed from the board of trustees in 1928, and according to family accounts, Hitchcock and those loyal to him began interfering in Johnson's evangelistic work, accusing him of not being "hot" enough. Kostlevy interprets this primarily in terms of a power struggle, with Hitchcock seeing Johnson as a "threat." And certainly it seems hard to define just what about Johnson's ministry had been deficient. Johnson drifted away from the MCA and spent years unaffiliated with any church, before eventually joining the Church of the Nazarene, the embodiment of the moderate, conventional version of Holiness that the MCA had always opposed. Henry L. Harvey Sr., in contrast, accepted his similar treatment by Hitchcock and remained a member of the MCA, although his loyalty would be tested by the conflict between Henry Jr. and the Hitchcock leadership.

Her parents' perceived rejection of the Church forced Lillian to make both a religious choice and a career choice. She considered pursuing a career as a teacher, and according to family tradition, her father encouraged her in this. But Lillian believed that God wanted her to enter the MCA's Bible School instead and become a missionary, and she persisted in this choice even when her family urged her to leave the Church due to the treatment of her father. This was, by her later account, one of the most difficult choices of her life. To choose Hitchcock's MCA

---

[8] Kostlevy, *Holy Jumpers*, 156.
[9] Kostlevy, *Holy Jumpers*, 157-158.

over a family that had been disciplined by the Church and was in the process of rejecting it was practically to disown her family, since the MCA discouraged contact with fallen-away or worldly relatives. From now on, the MCA would be her family and Hitchcock her spiritual father.

But the "outward" choice to put church over family was not enough to bring spiritual peace, or to satisfy what Hitchcock understood as total consecration to God. As my grandmother later described it, Hitchcock urged her over and over again to give herself wholly to God, muttering "it's spiritual suicide" when she told him that the price was too great. The "price" at this point seems to have been psychological--the total inner consecration that Holiness theology demanded, and which the Hitchcock MCA was determined to define as rigorously as possible. Too glib and easy a claim to place "all on the altar" raised suspicions of "Nazarene religion."

One specific area of difficulty about which my grandmother spoke later was her sexuality. She saw herself as a very moral person and prided herself on not flirting as other girls did. However, while working in a secretarial capacity at the MCA headquarters, she realized with shame that she always managed to time her visit to the mail room just as the classes full of young men (including my grandfather, who was teaching at the Bible School) were letting out.[10]

Marriage was a particularly difficult issue in the MCA under Hitchcock's leadership. The *Discipline* published in 1930 explicitly required the consent of "the godliest persons in the association" before any member of the church could marry.[11] As Kostlevy points out, this meant in practice that entire sanctification was a prerequisite for marriage.[12] And yet, of course, one of the prerequisites for sanctification was a willingness to put "all on the altar," which included a willingness to forgo marriage. From the fact that her eventual experience of sanctification followed a commitment to celibacy, expressed in a written vow found among her papers after her death, it seems clear that part of the price would have involved renunciation of marriage.

In Lillian's own account of her spiritual struggles during these years, however, the single symbolic action that had come to represent the price she was unwilling to pay was jumping up and down on the sidewalk and praising God in public. Upon her refusing to obey what she believed was God's command to do this, she entered "five years of darkness" (1930-35) which only lifted when she obeyed a similar command and publicly testified on a trolley bus. She often described this as "living in hell." While outwardly devout, she experienced no sense of God's presence and, in her later judgment, was a terrible witness to her siblings and oth-

---

[10] I do not know the exact chronology of this story, which was one she told frequently as a key moment in her spiritual journey. I know that she studied at the Bible School, and that my grandfather was one of her teachers, but I don't know if this incident preceeded, coincided with, or followed her own time as a student.

[11] Kostlevy, *Holy Jumpers*, 159.

[12] This attitude persisted in my family to some extent--my grandmother frequently exhorted me as a teenager to make sure I was totally consecrated to God before I seriously thought about girls.

ers because her piety was entirely legalistic and mechanical, lacking in love and joy. For the rest of her life, she believed that if she ever deliberately disobeyed God she might experience this same horrific withdrawal of the divine presence.

During these years, like other young workers in the MCA, she spent most of her time canvassing--selling cards and calendars with Bible verses on them. The MCA maintained teams of workers (most of them, apparently, female) in various American cities, whose main job was to raise money for the Church through canvassing, although they also taught Sunday Schools for disadvantaged children and engaged in other evangelistic work.[13]

The spiritual logjam finally broke in early 1935, when Lillian committed herself to overcome her natural shyness and obey the impulse to testify publicly. At this point she professed to be born again but not yet sanctified. Her written vow of celibacy dates from this year, but it is not clear whether it predated or postdated her experience of sanctification. This came during a visit to the Boston mission during the summer of 1935, where one of the other young heroes of the revival, Arthur Bray, prayed with her and exhorted her to receive the blessing before returning to Long Island, where she was stationed. As she drove back to Long Island, ecstatic with the presence of the Holy Spirit, she found herself frequently speeding--behavior inappropriate for a newly sanctified person. But as often as she reduced her speed, she would start to think, "I have what the Apostles had on the day of Pentecost," and inadvertently her foot would begin to press down on the accelerator once again.

The exuberant joy she experienced in Boston carried her through a difficult few years in New York and Philadelphia. As a team leader, she was responsible for the spiritual welfare of other women, many of whom were older than she was. Fundamental to her experience of the Holy Spirit was the willingness to face conflict for what she believed was the Biblical standard of Holiness: "back there in Boston I settled it to face the battle that people who have been filled with the Holy Ghost have had to face all down through the ages, and there is no regret in my soul whatsoever. In fact, I mourn over the years spent without waging this glorious strife."[14]

Meanwhile, others had noticed the change in her. Henry L. Harvey Jr., after meeting her at the annual camp meeting after her sanctification (probably in 1935, before he departed for India), remarked that "Lillian shook hands with me like a man" (i.e., she was now able to relate to men without her fear of her own sexuality getting in the way). But Henry's brother Edwin was even more impressed with the change in her. Shortly before leaving for Scotland in 1937, he wrote her a proposal of marriage--or at least, as he phrased it, a proposal for a friendship possibly

---

[13]Evangelism was not supposed to be part of the canvassing itself, and in general the canvassing seems to have taken priority over evangelism, although my grandmother's letters from the later 1930s indicate that she put a lot of energy into her Sunday School teaching. For an overview of the importance of canvassing in the MCA under Hitchcock, see Kostlevy, *Holy Jumpers*, 156.

[14]Letter to Creo Peter, March 7, 1936.

leading to marriage. Lillian rejected this proposal because of what she believed was God's will that she remain unmarried, but Edwin's belief that God had other plans for her clearly made an impression (and by her own admission, she had admired him greatly ever since she had first noticed him at the 1928 camp meeting). After more thought and prayer, she wrote back to him expressing a willingness to correspond, and in September 1938 they were married with the approval of both families and the Hitchcocks (although Lillian did not invite her parents to the wedding owing to their break from the Church).

Thus, the children of two of the first-generation MCA leaders whom Hitchcock had sidelined became leaders of the MCA's mission and Bible School in Glasgow. Meanwhile, Henry L. Harvey Jr. had become the leader of the mission in India after the tragic death of his colleague Howard Bitzer. Furthermore, the MCA under Hitchcock experienced a surge in foreign missions, contrasting with its relative stagnation in domestic evangelism. While the MCA's workers in America were largely relegated to selling calendars and greeting cards, the Indian--and, increasingly, the Scottish--missions were engaging in tireless evangelism that replicated to some extent the energy of the early years of the movement. Edwin Harvey, in a 1937 sermon, drew on his experiences visiting his brother's work in India to challenge the idea that the "great apostasy" of the last days made evangelism pointless: "The night is truly coming when no man can work, but thank God there are still a few beams of the setting sun shining across the golden fields. Arise, let us reap!"[15]

One of the difficulties faced by the Harvey brothers was the proper relationship between evangelism directed at bringing in new converts and concern for the spiritual condition of their own workers. If the evangelists themselves were not truly sanctified--and by Hitchcockian standards very few were--then how could they be used to bring people into a living relationship with God? Here Edwin and Henry eventually took very different paths. In 1936, shortly after arriving in India, Henry Harvey announced that many of the workers were "inert" and "immune to fire" and needed "an injection of dynamite."[16] In 1937, visiting the mission in South Africa, he criticized one worker for using "the vocabulary of 20 years ago," and another for praying in a way that showed him to be "unbelievably out of it."[17] But by 1943 he was arguing to his brother that continual focus on the spiritual renewal of his workers made effective evangelism impossible, especially after the death of Howard Bitzer, who was the "specialist" in such work. Henry was convinced that God had told him to "launch out into the deep" in active evangelism and reject Hitchcockian authoritarianism as well as the endless introspection that, he believed, paralyzed evangelistic work.[18] Henry's path soon took him out

---

[15]In *Message of Victory* 13.6 (June 1937), 4-5, 14, cited at 14.

[16]Letter to Edwin Harvey, August 10, 1936.

[17]Letter to Edwin Harvey, Sept. 27, 1937.

[18]Letter to Edwin Harvey, April 1, 1943: "Howard was the specialist supreme in rebuilding wrecked lives. And God convicted me beyond a shadow of a doubt when he died that the time had come for a turn over. In the first place I had to choose then and there

of the MCA, after a failed attempt to rally the younger members of the Church in opposition to Hitchcock. Henry would go on to join the Church of the Nazarene and to serve as the second president of the evangelical charity Compassion International.[19]

Edwin and Lillian took a different path, which also led them out of the MCA, but not toward the Church of the Nazarene or any other conventional evangelical denomination. They remained convinced that a focus on the spiritual transformation of their workers was vitally important. At the same time, like Henry, they became dissatisfied with the failure of Hitchcock's MCA to practice evangelism, and they began to question the MCA's unremitting hostility to other Christian churches. In a 1939 sermon, Edwin Harvey described visiting a mining village and walking around the town on a Sunday morning hearing the various churches sing about the Cross, while it was obvious from the cars parked outside the churches and from the look and demeanor of the people that they really knew nothing about the crucified life.[20] By the 1950s, while living in the Lake District, he was making a habit of attending the local Anglican church with his daughter Trudy, and this habit of attending local churches even if he disapproved of many things about them persisted to the end of his life. Although he condemned official ecumenism (especially involving Catholicism) as "the hell-hatched scheme of amalgamation"[21] and "the unity of death,"[22] both he and Lillian became increasingly committed to a vision of the "invisible church" as the union of all true believers, and to seeking for and fostering unity with anyone in whom they detected a spark of spiritual life, no matter their church affiliations.[23]

In an autobiographical fragment published posthumously, Edwin Harvey pinpointed the Scottish MCA's 1947 annual convention as the point where these changes came to a head. After days of prayer preparing for the convention, Edwin and Lillian decided that they needed to change their methods, and in retrospect my grandfather pointed to this as the catalyst that led to a great move of the Holy Spirit, with people confessing their sins and experiencing the new birth and sanctification. From then on, the Scottish mission turned away from the canvassing model and toward more active evangelism, and away from traditional MCA

---

whether I would hold a series of revival meetings lasting ad finitum [sic] among our own people or whether I was going to launch out into the deep. God told me to launch out and let the dead past bury its dead. From that moment I ceased to be a dictator on this field, although I pray God that I shall never cease to be a leader of men."

[19] http://www.compassion.com/about/history/1960s, accessed May 13, 2016.
[20] "The Glory of the Cross," in *Message of Victory* 15.2 (Feb. 1939), 8-10, 15.
[21] Harvey, *Let My People Go*, 194.
[22] Harvey, *Let My People Go*, 71.
[23] In a letter to her mother from May 1953, Lillian Harvey responded to her mother's statement that she was "glad she was a Nazarene" by saying that this no longer bothered her as it would have formerly, "for, I know the body of Christ is not built around one separate organization--although I believe some have grown so large that the discipline and depth of piety greatly varies."

sectarianism and toward the vision of promoting Holiness through interdenominational witness.

In 1950, W. S. Hitchcock was removed from leadership by the board of trustees. By this time Henry Harvey Jr. had already decisively broken with the MCA, leaving Edwin and Lillian as the primary heirs of their parents' legacy. The new president, Charles Sammis, seems to have enjoyed little confidence, especially among the younger members of the church, many of whom wished to replace him with Edwin Harvey. In the meantime, Edwin was invited to return to America and given a position at headquarters. The Harveys, however, found the atmosphere in Waukesha stultifying, as described in a 1953 letter from Lillian Harvey to her parents and brother Jim, explaining why they had chosen to separate from the parent church. The MCA continued to expect all members to contribute physical labor, and this, from the Harveys' perspective, made it impossible to do serious evangelism. Edwin had no stenographer, and Lillian was expected to do housework and child care and carry out preaching activities in the time left over. The Harveys swapped child care responsibilities so that they could both preach on alternate nights, but they looked back fondly to the Glasgow mission with its "willing people who have not all the advantages in the world, who are glad to relieve us of our temporal burdens, so that we--Eddie and I--can concentrate on our work of leading others." This leadership, furthermore, needed to be concentrated on evangelism and teaching rather than administration: "Life is too brief to sit behind a desk and administer directives to canvassers, and help decide who should move to the second floor, and how many rooms they should be allowed in the Bible School." By 1953, the Harveys had come to see the basic problem as the "community system" and the financial activities necessary to support it: "We do love our dear friends and early co-workers, but our whole aim is varied. They still wish to maintain a community and naturally a canvassing system which will support it. We desire to break up everything that savours of community, and utilize only those who are not called particularly to preaching, teaching, but are rather helps, to do the cooking, office work, etc. But, any regardless of how young who show vision, spiritual life and a 'divine call' to put them into harness."

The transition was not an easy one. As recently as 1946, on an earlier visit to America, Edwin Harvey had written sternly to his parents, at that point themselves at odds with the Church, exhorting them to submit to Hitchcock and the authority of a "Holy Ghost Church," and defending his refusal to come and visit them at Henry Jr.'s home in Grand Rapids, because to do so would be "countenancing your action which is at present Scripturally untenable."[24] In diary entries from the period after their return to Scotland in 1951, Lillian wrote of her fears that she was confusing her husband by her own changes of opinion, and confessed that she sometimes hoped for death. My mother describes walking in on her father one day and finding him flat on the floor sobbing.

The wrenching decision to leave the MCA shaped the rest of my grandparents' lives. They would never again fully trust any religious organization, even one they

---

[24]Letters of June 19 and 24, 1946. The quotation is from the second letter.

themselves led. If the MCA, a "Holy Ghost Church" born in the fires of revival and characterized by the demand for total consecration to God, could become a stagnant pool of empty authoritarianism, then no church was safe.

But as traumatic as the decision to leave the MCA was, it was only the first step in a long journey toward a radically anti-institutional stance. For several more years, the Glasgow MCA functioned as an independent Holiness mission under the leadership of the Harveys. They had become increasingly frustrated with the older workers' complacent acceptance of a perpetual pattern of "seeking sanctification" without ever "getting through." Then, in 1956, Edwin and Lillian left Glasgow with some of the younger workers and established a new organization, Message of Victory Evangelism or M.O.V.E., named after the Scottish MCA's magazine, the *Message of Victory*, which the Harveys took with them as part of their severance agreement with those who remained behind. Their goal was to establish a mission that would be entirely free from the sectarian and communitarian trappings of the old MCA, and would be able to function as a purely interdenominational body rather than as a rival church over against other churches.[25] And they hoped, with this small cadre of young, enthusiastic followers about 15-16 at its height, to be able to build a community of people who were truly consecrated to God.

From 1956 to 1962 the M.O.V.E. was based in a farmhouse in the Lake District, before moving to the industrial city of Blackburn. They continued the outreach efforts that they had begun in Glasgow, travelling all over Britain to establish "bands" (an echo of early Methodist terminology) that would spread the message of Holiness without forming new churches. They were particularly successful in Shetland, the most northerly islands in the British Isles, where they established a bookshop and where they gained several recruits for the full-time mission. In the industrial cities surrounding their Lake District base, they began "late night meetings" for young people who didn't want to go home when the pubs closed at 11 p.m. They began visiting pubs all over Britain to sell copies of the *Message of Victory*, which by this time had become differentiated into an evangelistic version and a less frequently published "Deeper Truths for Christians." They also began writing and publishing books, beginning with a devotional reader collected from the "Deeper Truths" issues of the *Message of Victory* and published in 1954 while they were still in Scotland.

But in the midst of all this activity, Lillian was still dissatisfied. In spite of her declaration in 1953 that she and her husband intended to "break up all that savours of community," the mission continued to be run on largely communal lines, with the workers, mostly women, living together with the Harveys. This allowed very little privacy, and in 1962 the Harveys and their daughter Trudy moved into a cottage by themselves for two years, while moving the primary headquarters of the M.O.V.E. to Blackburn. Thereafter, the M.O.V.E. adopted a policy of scattering its

---

[25]In a letter of June 1953 to her brother Jim, Lillian Harvey laid out her vision for a Bible School in Glasgow, a vision that would three years later lead her and her husband to abandon the Bible School altogether and found the M.O.V.E.

workers around the country in small groups rather than keeping them all together in one large community.

The bigger problem, however, was theological. Lillian's spiritual experience did not match what her theological tradition told her ought to happen. After sanctification, her sinful nature was supposed to be eradicated. But, in fact, she continued to feel sinful impulses, and the tensions and stresses of community life no doubt exacerbated her sense of her own inadequacy. Her personal and theological crisis reached a head in 1967, and she spent several months in France sorting out just what she believed about Holiness and what God's will was for the rest of her ministry.

This would turn out to be yet another turning point in her life. "What God showed me in France" would be the basis for the theology she taught and lived for her last forty years. The fundamental insight was a reorienting of the concept of Holiness from an emphasis on the experience of sanctification to an emphasis on an ongoing personal relationship with Christ. She found ample justification for this shift in John Wesley, who frequently said things like "the moment I stop looking to Christ, I become a devil." Gertrude Harvey, furthermore, had preached in a sermon printed in the *Message of Victory* in 1937 that a profession that has lost its joy and power has become like a sinking ship and should be abandoned for the lifeboat, which is Christ.[26] Oswald Chambers was also a major influence. But the single biggest influence, possibly, on her new understanding was Watchman Nee's *The Normal Christian Life*. Nee brought the Plymouth Brethren emphasis on identification with Christ into Lillian's Wesleyan theology, and it would never quite be the same again.

In the summer of 1967, after her recuperation in France, Lillian and Edwin returned to the United States for the first time since their break with the MCA. Their letters to their co-workers in Britain, mostly written by Lillian, reflect some of the exuberance and release of her new spiritual insights. She expresses regret for having tried to control people too much, and an awareness that the fear of compromise may have hindered her from engaging lovingly with other people. Her relationships with her relatives seem to have improved greatly at this point, and the Harveys even considered forming a joint book-publishing endeavor with Lillian's younger sister Mary, who had begun writing children's books. The most important fruit of the 1967 trip from a personal standpoint was her reconciliation with her sister Gerry, who was now living in Mexico and dying of cancer. Lillian made a special extension of the trip to go to Mexico City and visit Gerry, who (like her brothers Dan and Johnny) had abandoned evangelical Christianity altogether. At the same time, this was also when the Harveys first made contact with the "conservative Holiness" movements in America--people who had either left the Nazarenes or otherwise sought to continue the strict lifestyles and doctrinal emphases of the turn-of-the-century radical movements. In particular, Lillian

---

[26]*Message of Victory* 13.4 (April 1973): "Take to the Lifeboat," 4. 4.

wrote back to Britain enthusiastically about the work of Methodist Holiness evangelist Lela McConnell in Eastern Kentucky.

Back in Britain, the Harveys continued their evangelistic work for seven more years, before officially retiring as leaders of the M.O.V.E. in 1974. In that year they rented a farmhouse in rural Staffordshire and moved into it with their daughter Trudy, their son-in-law Barry Tait (a young Australian of Shetland origin who had come to the mission in 1967, while they were in America, and had been converted), and their six-month-old grandson Edwin Tait. Here they increasingly devoted themselves to the publishing endeavors that they had begun in 1954. Besides devotional readers such as the *Christian's Daily Challenge* and the two-volume series on prayer, *Kneeling We Triumph,* and reprints of nineteenth-century works, they had begun a series of biographical sketches called *They Knew Their God.* This series, eventually growing to six volumes, introduced readers to a wide range of evangelical hagiography, focusing on the inner lives of its subjects. At the same time, the Harveys (and Taits) continued to be involved to some degree in the work of the M.O.V.E.

The most distinctive aspect of the six years in Staffordshire, however, was the Bible study that the Harveys established in their home. Rather than wide-ranging evangelistic work, they focused on sharing their teachings with a small group from the nearby villages, mostly Methodists. A number of dramatic conversions followed. Some of the Methodist converts then went back to their local chapel and began testifying to what they had experienced, questioning the faith of other members of the chapel who had not had a similar experience or whose lives seemed too worldly. Although my grandparents and parents were serving as local preachers, they were not formally members of any church, and the local Methodist leaders came to view them as a menace. The fact that one of the conversions led to a divorce, with the unconverted husband leaving his newly converted wife, further created mistrust of the strange American intruders.

In the fall of 1980, my parents and I visited America, in part in order to find a possible property to which to move, although my family had not ruled out the possibility of moving elsewhere in Britain or Northern Ireland. We did live in Northern Ireland for several months before moving to Indiana in February of 1981. The move to America was due to a number of factors beyond the immediate problems we faced in Staffordshire. One was a fear of Communism and a belief that as the last days approached, America might hold out longer and thus offer more room for ministry. On a less apocalyptic level, my grandparents were correct to note the increasing secularization of Britain. They were exhausted from decades of evangelism which had produced relatively little fruit. They were increasingly coming to focus on a "deeper life" ministry to evangelical believers, especially through the growing list of books they published. The United States, in the throes of its "evangelical moment" with the election of Ronald Reagan, seemed like a more attractive harvest field. And my grandparents were, no doubt, nostalgic for their native country, to which they had always intended to return eventually.

We were, in many respects, very much like Rip Van Winkle, returning to a country whose religious landscape had changed dramatically. The "conservative

Holiness" groups with which my grandparents had made contact in 1967 found our acceptance of wedding rings for women too worldly, and in general my family had moved outside the sphere of strict Holiness theology due to their years of interdenominational ministry. For all the common ground in an abhorrence of worldliness, we did not understand worldliness in quite the same way and tensions soon arose. At the same time, my family was in very little sympathy with mainstream neo-evangelicalism, which they found shallow and worldly. We briefly attended a Nazarene church whose pastor was reputed to be "old-fashioned." While we liked his preaching, the fact that the youth group was advertising a trip to the King's Island amusement park was less appealing, and we never joined that congregation. The Holiness denomination with which we found most common ground was the Evangelical Church in North America (ECNA), largely consisting of Holiness elements of the former Evangelical United Brethren but also including followers of W. S. Hitchcock who had left the MCA when he was removed from power. The ECNA, however, was at once a bit too lax in its lifestyle requirements and too conventionally Holiness in its doctrine. Meanwhile, disagreements both spiritual and financial with the British couple who had followed us to America in order to work on the books together led to my family abandoning the publishing work to them temporarily (they eventually moved back to Britain and we purchased it back from them) and moving to the mountains of East Tennessee in the fall of 1982.

East Tennessee was, in many ways, a strange home for us, with very little Holiness presence, although we had initially been invited there by an old MCA friend. But by this time my grandparents' focus on writing and contemplation had led them to welcome the seclusion of the Appalachians and the freedom not to try to fit into the complex configurations of late twentieth-century Wesleyanism. There was a Nazarene church in town which we attended sporadically, but more often we were chronic visitors in local Baptist churches, never joining any of them formally and getting into a doctrinal conflict in the one church in which we became heavily involved. (I became the argumentative theological nerd I am through defending Wesleyan doctrine against my AWANA leaders.)

My grandfather's death in December 1983 devastated my grandmother (and indeed all of us), but it also shifted the spiritual balance in our family considerably. My grandfather had always been the more conventionally Holiness of the two, but also the more stable and charitable in his relationships with others. My grandmother had a more eclectic and mystical spirituality, drawing from any author who seemed to have a spark of interest in the inner life. But in her relationships with living people she was highly sensitive and often harsh. Typically she welcomed new acquaintances generously, but over time tended to become increasingly demanding of them spiritually, often leading to conflict and a severing or cooling of the acquaintance. The legacy of the Hitchcock years and her youthful commitment to follow God rather than her family always haunted her. She remained convinced that if she ever failed to "take a stand" when needed, God's presence would depart from her, and without my grandfather's moderating influence this fear became increasingly obsessive. At the same time, she developed a wide network of disciples through the books, many of whom called her regularly or came to visit. Our contacts varied from Holiness people to Charismatics to fundamentalist Baptists to neo-Calvinists to neo-Anabaptists, with one or the other group dominating at different times. The common thread was usually that the people who appreciated my grandmother's ministry were people dissatisfied with their own churches (this included many pastors, unsurprisingly) and/or with the institutional church generally. My grandmother came to believe that the "Church Age" was drawing to an end and that a new wave of large-scale revival or reform was unlikely. The spiritual decay, as she saw it, of evangelicalism in the country where it was strongest was one of the signs of the End. What was left was for true believers to gather in small groups and informal networks and keep the fire burning, gathering out a faithful people in expectation of the Lord's return. She was born in the fire--she refused to live in the smoke.

In 2002 she suffered a series of strokes which left her speech severely impaired and brought on evident dementia, including paranoia. After several years in a nursing home, the paranoia abated and my parents were able to take her home, where they cared for her until her death in August 2008. She was buried beside my grandfather on top of a mountain overlooking Lake Watauga.

Compared with the grand spectacle of the MCA's annual camp meeting, or even their earlier years of busy evangelism in Britain, the last years of my grandparents were a story of retreat and defeat. Time and again they withdrew from situations of conflict, turning ever inward in their search for more complete consecration to God. They were never successful in building a community of people whom they believed to be filled with the Spirit. They were over and over again disappointed in coworkers with whom they hoped to collaborate, and by the end of their lives they had completely lost confidence in the spiritual value of institution-building. One Charismatic pastor derisively referred to my grandmother in the 1980s as "an old guru sitting on top of a mountain," and there was some accuracy in the gibe.

And yet, right up to my grandmother's strokes in 2002, dozens of people around the world sought her spiritual counsel, and after her death they still speak of her with reverence. There was fire in her, and in my grandfather. At times it seemed that the fire was one of destruction rather than purification--that it devoured everything in its path and consumed its own children. But those of us who have been touched by it find it hard to accept either conventional religion or conventional worldliness. My own vocational and spiritual restlessness bears witness that I too have been touched by that fire. To be burned by it is better than living without it. May it never go out.

Chapter 12

Reckoning with Babylon: G. T. Bustin and Radical Holiness Interaction with Roman Catholicism

Wallace Thornton, Jr.[1]

G. T. Bustin

One of the major developments in recent American religious history is the rather sudden dissipation of traditional evangelical anti-Catholicism in the 1970s.[2] This

---

[1] Unless otherwise indicated, all works cited were written by G. T. Bustin.
[2] William Kostlevy, conversation with author, March 31, 2016.

has resulted in shifting attitudes among participants in the Holiness Movement, leading some to advocate rapprochement with Roman Catholicism, or at least partnering "together for the kingdom of God." While it is recognized that in some world regions Roman Catholics remain resistant to "conversation or shared mission with non-Catholics," it appears that some American holiness people feel that the issues resulting in division during the Protestant Reformation are so far removed historically as to be incomprehensible and irrelevant today.[3]

However, because the Holiness Movement, as well as Roman Catholicism, has a global presence, these issues remain significant and sensitive. In addition, it smacks of historical naïveté to suggest that important differences between Protestantism and Roman Catholicism ended four or five hundred years ago. Indeed, since its earliest days the Holiness Movement has had rich and varied interactions with Roman Catholicism. This complex exchange, involving both renunciation and appropriation, deserves exploration, rather than a gloss downplaying its importance. Perhaps no better window into this dynamic interface could be provided than recent developments in the South Pacific nation of Papua New Guinea (PNG) and their roots in the radical holiness ministry of G. T. Bustin.

Radical Holiness and Nation Building

In 2015 media pundits were overwhelmed by a veritable spiritual tsunami that swept over PNG, culminating in some of the largest and most dramatic demonstrations of Christian devotion in recent history.[4] Much of this centered around the gift of a rare first-edition 1611 King James Bible to the nation of PNG from Dr. Gene Hood (1937-2015), which fittingly marked the climax of a long and fruitful ministry since Dr. Hood passed away the very week that the Bible was presented to officials from PNG.

Indeed, this act culminated Dr. Hood's remarkable life that was distinguished by accomplishments in diverse areas including business entrepreneurship, especially in the healthcare and radio industries; financial leadership, including chair-

---

[3]Jeremy Scott, "Catholics and Nazarenes: Friends or Foes?" *Holiness Today* (March/April 2016), 8-11. On worldwide tensions, see Philip Jenkins, *The Next Christendom: The Coming of Global Christianity* Rev. and Expanded (New York: Oxford University Press, 2007).

[4]Will Higgins, "Hoosier's Bible creates a stir: Preacher donates rare King James first edition to Papua New Guineau," *The Indianapolis Star* (Tuesday, May 5, 2015), 1A, 4A. Cf. "Preacher's rare Bible stirs hearts, controversy," *USA Today* (Posted May 5, 2015). http://www.usatoday.com/story/news/nation/2015/05/05/gene-hood-bible-papua-new-guinea/26944301/; Liam Cochrane, "Thousands welcome arrival of 400-year-old King James Bible in Papua New Guinea," *ABC News* [Australian Broadcasting Company] (Posted April 28, 2015). http://www.abc.net.au/news/2015-04-28/thousands-greet-bibles-arrival-in-papua-new-guinea/6428856; Jack Lapauve Jr. "Christians Move 400 Year Old KJV Bible To Parliament," *EM TV News* (Posted September 16, 2015). http://www.emtv.com.pg/article.aspx?slug=Christians-Move-400-Year-Old-KJV-Bible-To-Parliament&. (All accessed March 29, 2016).

manship of the World Trade Center in Indianapolis; political activism, particularly with regard to the Christian school movement; and, nearest to his heart, pastoral ministry, especially a pastorate of over forty years in the Indianapolis area that also included administration of a thriving Christian school.

In addition, Dr. Hood's local ministry served as a springboard for numerous international activities, including distribution of over one million Bibles in Russia and disaster relief in Central America. Among those particularly dear to him was his energetic support of the various ministries initiated by G. T. Bustin (1903-1995) whose pioneering missionary endeavors led to the establishment of the Papua New Guinea Bible Church. In fact, as a "strong supporter" of G. T. Bustin,[5] Gene Hood actually served for a time as the "Assistant Director" of Christ's Ambassadors, one of the mission organizations that Bustin had founded. Dr. Hood's wife, Carolyn, also served as the organization's "secretary and treasurer," which involved considerable assistance with correspondence and proofreading.[6] After G. T. Bustin's death, Dr. Hood utilized his "extensive radio work" experience and business expertise to provide "logistic and monetary support to the ongoing work in PNG for many years. In recent trips to the country, Dr. Hood had been an inspiration to the people in urging them to continue to take the way of holiness."[7] The gift of the Bible was conceived during Dr. Hood's last trip to PNG (November 2014) as a way of commemorating the fortieth anniversary of the nation's independence from Australia and to celebrate the new direction of leadership indicated by the Speaker of the Parliament, Theodore Zurenuoc.

In an open acknowledgement of "urgently needed reformation and restoration" and "modernization" toward the goal of "National Unity,"[8] the Speaker invoked biblical imagery as he forecast his vision for the nation's future: "We have been in the wilderness these forty years, it is time to cross over to the Promise Land!"[9] To represent the changes he had in mind, the Speaker called upon the Parliament of PNG to approve the "removal and replacement of the carved images in the Grand Hall of the Parliament," notably a large totem pole with "three heads representing the god of witchcraft on the left, the god of immorality on the right and the god of idolatry in the middle."[10] The Parliament approved replacing this totem pole with a "National Identity and Unity Pillar," upon which the word "unity" is to be inscribed in each of the over 800 languages spoken among the over 1,000 tribes constituting the citizenry of PNG.

The symbolism projected for the new monument is indicative of a religious revolution. Rather than imagery glorifying the animism and cannibalism of the

---

[5] "A National Treasure: Papua New Guinea's Bible," *Convention Herald*, vol. 69, no. 1 (2016), 7.

[6] *Our Miracle-Working God* (n.p.: n.d.), 33. Carolyn Hood, conversation with author, April 25, 2016.

[7] *Herald*, 7.

[8] Theo Zurenuoc, *Removal and Replacement of the Carved Images in the Grand Hall of the Parliament* (Port Moresby, PNG: Office of the Speaker, 2014).

[9] *Herald*, 7.

[10] *Removal*.

past, the edifice is projected to exalt a new unifying principle for this formerly fragmented island nation, now welded together as a rapidly developing country.[11] Remarkably, this unifier is the Christian faith. Thus, the base of the monument will consist of jasper stone representing "the Word of God – The Foundation, the Eternal Source of Wisdom, Principles and Moral Conscience." Likewise, the eternal flame at the top of the forty-foot column will symbolize "the light that comes from the Word of God showing us the direction for PNG to follow, and representing the Holy Spirit as our ever present help."[12]

The gift of the 1611 Bible from Dr. Hood was envisioned to symbolize further the commitment on the part of PNG national leadership to government established on biblical principles. With its permanent resting place in the Parliament chamber itself, it was received with pomp and circumstance akin to the reception of royalty, likened to the ceremony employed for Queen Elizabeth's visit to the nation a few decades ago. When it arrived at the airport of the capital city of Port Moresby in April 2015, it was welcomed with a red carpet processional and military salutes as religious leaders representing the evangelical community in PNG conveyed it in a special contrivance evocative of the ancient Ark of the Covenant. It was greeted with speeches made by Prime Minister Peter O'Neill and Speaker Zurenuoc in the presence of over 20,000 spectators. Likewise, when it was introduced into the Parliament House and pronounced a "national treasure" on Independence Day, September 16, 2015, the attendant celebration garnered a crowd of around 100,000. At the ceremony's height, the Prime Minister declared, "This Bible is being placed in Parliament. There it will remain until our Lord returns to earth. It will guide us in every government decision." With the blast of a ram's horn, spontaneous shouts, and national and provincial flags waving in the breeze, "the very atmosphere was saturated with awe and charged with victorious praise"! Missionary participants Robert and Barbara Brock reported that "it was like living in the pages of the Bible itself!"[13]

These events suggest more than ephemeral displays. The Speaker views them as comprising "a defining moment" in the nation's history. Indeed, they represent a spiritual movement, from the grassroots to the highest echelons of PNG government, to place the Christian faith at the center of national life. For the Parliament, this involved "extensive research" into competing available ideologies with the determination that "the ideals of the Christian faith" offer the "best" foundation on "which we can truly unite our people and draw the virtues of integrity in order

---

[11] PNG recently ranked as the world's seventh fastest-growing economy. Elena Holodny, "The 13 fastest-growing economies in the world," *Business Insider* (Posted July 12, 2015). http://www.businessinsider.com/world-bank-fast-growing-global-economies-2015-6. (Accessed March 29, 2016).

[12] *Removal*.

[13] Report from Robert and Barbara Brock (New Palestine, IN: Independent Nazarene Church, December 26, 2015).

to manage our national affairs."[14] This conclusion was largely influenced by a nationwide revival that has transformed individual lives and societal structures from the tribal level up, helping to forge into a united nation a collection of "1,000 nations" which were often embroiled in intertribal warfare in the past. This new unity was evidenced on Independence Day 2015 by "tribal warriors" who were erstwhile "avowed enemies," rejoicing together "united"—"by the power of the Book of books, the Bible!"[15]

The resolve of the PNG government through its elevation of the Bible "to declare to the world that PNG is a Christian Nation,"[16] and the underlying revival helping to precipitate this determination, has not been without detractors. Among the most vocal of these critics have been the Roman Catholic bishops of PNG and the Solomon Islands. In a "Pastoral Letter," they linked recent strengthened ties between PNG and the nation of Israel with the attempts to remove the totem pole from the Parliament and suggested that PNG officials were conflating the "God of Israel" with the "state of Israel," thereby promoting the idea that "an alliance with the state of Israel can bring prosperity to PNG." In an ironic twist reflecting the syncretistic tendency of Roman Catholicism, the bishops defended the carvings of the totem pole as simply representations of "the diverse peoples of the many regions of PNG" and emphatically protested that the "images are not idols." Rather, they depicted the new emphasis on being a "Christian nation" as actually fostering a particularly insidious form of "idolatry"—that is making "material wealth one's goal." In effect, the bishops suggested that what has developed is "a new kind of cargo cult combined with a 'prosperity gospel'." They further implied that the rare 1611 Bible now in Parliament has become the object of this new "cargo cult" and the symbol of "a distorted presentation of Christianity."[17] This critique comes even though PNG leadership has made clear the nature of the gifted Bible as an unique historic representative of the Word of God, not as an end to be worshipped in itself.

The truth is that, rather than a "cargo cult," the spiritual groundswell leading to these celebrations which have perplexed Roman Catholic leaders in PNG represent instead a product of the radical holiness tradition. In fact, the revival that is sweeping PNG has been spearheaded by the Papua New Guinea Bible Church, one of the world's fastest-growing indigenous holiness denominations with over seven hundred churches and an average of over one hundred thousand participants in weekly worship. This fact may bring no comfort to Roman Catho-

---

[14]Theo Zurenuoc, *Statement of the Speaker on the Restoration, Reformation and Modernisation of the National Parliament: A National Unity and Identity Project* (Port Moresby, PNG: Office of the Speaker, 2014), 10, 12, 13.

[15]Brock.

[16]*Statement*, 13.

[17]Bishop Arnold Orowae, "Pastoral Letter of the Catholic Bishops of PNG/SI," *Catholic Reporter PNG* (Posted November 30, 2015) https://www.facebook.com/catholicreporter.papuanewguinea/posts/1073540406013080:0. (Accessed March 29, 2016). "Cargo" is a traditional PNG term for trade goods, thus "cargo cult" connotes a materialistic spirituality.

lic observers, but it helps to clarify the deeper issues involved. Indeed, a look at the missionary who pioneered the work leading to the Papua New Guinea Bible Church provides insights into just how complex the interactions between the Holiness Movement and Roman Catholicism have been and may explain some of the tensions existing today.

Ecclesiasticism and Independent Ministry

Green Tolbert Bustin became legendary among conservative holiness people in his own lifetime as an independent missionary who tirelessly pioneered works among "other sheep" largely neglected by established organizations.[18] H. E. Schmul, co-founder and longtime leader of the Inter-Church Holiness Convention, praised Bustin as "a peerless pioneer in mission evangelism" and "in adventures of faith."[19] Bustin's eldest daughter likewise acknowledged that "he was strictly a pioneer. He never stayed long at one place. He would struggle, work hard, and sacrifice to get a work started, then leave it for others to continue, while he set out upon a new venture."[20]

Bustin's career as a pioneer minister began in the United States as he established a series of "home missionary" churches throughout the South.[21] His ministry also began in denominational contexts, starting with evangelistic campaigns that he conducted while a student from 1922 to 1924 at Trevecca College, a Nazarene institution. After college, he ministered under the auspices of the Pilgrim Holiness Church, which he served as superintendent over the Arkansas-Lousiana District from 1931 to 1935.[22] However, it was not until a denominational crisis uprooted him that Bustin engaged in the work for which he is best remembered—foreign missions.

The significance of the denominational crisis that catapulted Bustin into independent work and helped launch him into foreign missions could hardly be overstated. It remained prominent in his mind throughout the remainder of his ministry, as evidenced by frequent references in his voluminous writings. Indeed, his severance from the Pilgrim Holiness denomination would forever mark Bustin's ministry and provides considerable insight into his perspective on Roman Catholicism.

---

[18]The "conservative holiness" movement emerged mid-twentieth century as an offspring of the radical holiness tradition blending traditional holiness emphases with Fundamentalist concerns. See Wallace Thornton, Jr. *The Conservative Holiness Movement: A Historical Appraisal* (Beech Grove, IN: Thornton Publications, 2014).

[19]H. E. Schmul, "Introduction" to G. T. Bustin, *The Man Christ Jesus* (Salem, OH: Schmul, 1987), 3.

[20]Claudine Bustin Chamberlain, "I Remember," *Mission Messenger* (August-September-October, 1995), 9.

[21]*Fresh Fuel for Missionary Fires* (Intercession City, FL: Intercession Press, n.d.), 15.

[22]*My First Fifty Years* (Intercession City, FL: Bustin, 1953) Digital Edition (Holiness Data Ministry, January 4, 1996).

In the mid-1930s, tensions developed in the hierarchy of the Pilgrim Holiness Church, and Bustin was caught in the crossfire. The controversy revolved around what denominational historians have dubbed the "Finch dissension," a splinter group centered in Colorado Springs and led by former general superintendent of foreign missions R. G. Finch.[23] When General Superintendent Walter L. Surbrook demanded that Bustin vote against Finch and those aligned with him, "or else," Bustin reported that "without one moment's hesitancy, my answer was, 'Then it will be "else." 'You can have my head, but I shall keep my heart.'" He later admitted, "Had I then known what I knew later, I might have obeyed; yet not knowing some facts at that time, I would have defiled my conscience had I voted to please the General Superintendent...."[24]

The price Bustin paid for his recalcitrance was immense—a series of "heart-bleeding blows"—he lost his position as district superintendent, had all his scheduled meetings in the denomination cancelled, and was "suddenly and ruthlessly torn" from his "beloved people in the southland" after "nearly nine full years of service."[25] Regardless, he testified, "I have never regretted for one minute having made the decision to obey God rather than man."[26]

Although some Pilgrim leaders pled with Bustin to return to the denomination, even offering another district superintendency, Bustin did not feel clear to return, nor did he feel right in mounting opposition to the denomination's leadership. Rather, after much prayer he believed that God had used the experience to thrust him into independence, concluding that Surbrook had unwittingly done him "a great favor": "He had set me free to give my life for the cause of missions in various parts of the world."[27]

About the time Bustin became disengaged from denominational connection, he began a series of independent mission ventures including an around-the-world evangelistic tour beginning in the fall of 1937, pioneering in 1939 a work in the Bahamas from which sprang the "greatest revival" he had yet witnessed,[28] and establishing a mission post in Haiti in 1945 that included a school, a medical clinic, and, eventually an "influential radio station." Of course, his "wildest" pioneer venture began in 1948 when he entered previously closed territory in the highlands of New Guinea and established a mission work there.[29]

---

[23] See Wallace Thornton, Jr. *Radical Righteousness: Personal Ethics and the Development of the Holiness Movement* (Salem, OH: Schmul, 1998), 96-101, as well as official Wesleyan denominational histories.

[24] *Miracle-Working*, 12.

[25] *Fifty*.

[26] *"The Lord Heard It"* (Avonmore, PA: West Publishing, n.d.), 70.

[27] *Abounding Life* (Beech Grove, IN: Gene Hood, 1988), 57. Although Bustin affiliated with the Immanuel Missionary Church led by R. G. Finch shortly after leaving the Pilgrim Holiness Church, this association was brief.

[28] *Miracle-Working*, 15-16.

[29] *Miracle-Working*, 17; "Obituary: Rev. G. T. Bustin," *Mission Messenger* (August-September-October, 1995), vol. LI, no. 4, 6.

Bustin was free to pursue these endeavors only because he had become a "free lance" or "independent," a status he highly valued, contending that "the world's most outstanding characters of all ages have been 'free lances'." Defining a "free lance" as "one who acts, speaks, or writes irrespective of any party," he suggested that among this "'notorious' minority" were Abraham, Daniel, Jesus, Paul, Martin Luther, John Wesley, George Muller, William Booth, Charles Cowman, "fifty million martyrs," and "some of God's little children today."[30]

As a consequence of the division in the Pilgrim Holiness Church, Bustin would thereafter have a strong suspicion of denominational loyalty and "ecclesiasticism."[31] He bombarded with equal vehemence both sides of this coin—hierarchical ladder-climbing on one side and heavy-handedness on the other. Regarding the first, he protested against using academic and ecclesiastical titles for posturing, lamenting that these are "sad times when even preachers of the Gospel, at least professedly so, have gone wild about flattering titles" to gain "a better standing among men."[32] He contrasted such affectations of superiority with the teaching of Christ:

> He had no place for trumped-up, vainglorious titles bestowed by men such as Rabbi, Master, Archbishop, and such blasphemous titles as Cardinals, Supreme Advocates, and Popes, all of which came into the picture later when supposed Christianity, then apostate, became identified with paganism. At this point don't throw me off altogether, but, in all honesty, where in the Word of God are found such appelations of dignity in relation to God's faithful servants, including the common title of Reverend and the coveted title of Doctor?

The list of titles offensive to Bustin obviously reflects his antipathy toward the Roman Catholic hierarchy. He feared that their posturing would be emulated even among holiness people: "Some of us have been grieved at heart by being informed that professed holiness leaders in relation to Bible Schools have now passed rules to the effect that all teachers must have degree titles."[33] The context of such protests makes it clear that Bustin's stance here was primarily antielitist rather than anti-intellectual.[34]

Bustin's opposition to ecclesiastical overreach likewise indicates concern lest Roman Catholic abuses of power make inroads into holiness groups. He even cautioned people against saying that they "belonged" to a denomination:

> You might be a member of some denomination, but if you love God in sincerity, you do not *belong* to the denomination.... In most cases, denominations expect their members to really and truly belong to their particular order, therefore your

---

[30]*The Soul of Jonathan* (n.p.: 1961), 2.
[31]*Secrets of True Success* (n.p.: n.d.), 7.
[32]*The Lamb and the Lion* (Florala, AL: Bustin, n.d.), 20.
[33]*God Glorifies a Gate-Keeper* (Summerfield, FL: Bustin, n.d.), 29-30.
[34]Bustin was quick to qualify such protests: "These prolonged punches are not made as a thrust at learning." *The Great American Tragedy* (n.p.: 1954) Digital Edition (Holiness Data Ministry, July 26, 2008).

time, talents, and treasures are considered the property of such orders. This is sad, for to belong thus to a denomination, God has no say over one's life. Of course, this type of dictatorial order teaches that "the voice of the church is the voice of God."[35]

Interestingly, this was the very argument that General Superintendent Surbrook employed in his demand to Bustin in connection with the "Finch dissension." Bustin's response was the most offensive charge he could muster against this "temptation to sell out to ecclesiasticism."[36] He told Surbrook, "That sounds too much like Roman Catholicism."[37] He elaborated about a year later:

> Every denomination tinctured with Roman Catholicism – and, though sad to say, almost all, sooner or later are – has in course of time adopted this theory. The fact of the case is this: in every denomination in the history of the Christian Church, outstanding saints, who have wholly followed the Lord, have had to choose between the voice of God and that of the church.[38]

For Bustin, then, Roman Catholicism represented the ultimate in ecclesiastical tyranny. While he recoiled with horror at "Mariolatry," "licentiousness" and other theological and moral ills he associated with Catholicism, for him the "paganistic leaven ... being disseminated by the unchristian and un-American principles of the Roman Catholic Church" was systemic as well as theological in nature. He asserted that "their system of teaching" does not harmonize with "American principles." In other words, it was undemocratic, and Catholic schools were "institutions of Babylon" foisting "idolatrous principles" on unsuspecting children. For him, one of the most egregious aspects of the "idolatry" it promoted was an idolatry of position, in effect exalting the ecclesiastical hierarchy so that, ultimately, "The Pope is their Master and their god."[39]

Bustin saw this hierarchical idolatry as one of the three contemporary "satanically inspired systems"—"Communism, Romanism, and Modernism."[40] He asserted that "Catholicism is [just] as damning as Communism, and in some respects more subtle, for it glides under the guise of Christianity, thus deceiving millions." Furthermore, "every country on earth dominated by this system of iniquity [is] blighted and cursed,"[41] because "every such country is given to idolatry, and idolatry is in God's eyes rated as the most hateful and hideous of all sins."[42]

---

[35]*The Lord Heard*, 69-70, original emphasis.

[36]*Secrets*, 7.

[37]*Abounding*, 56.

[38]*People of Purpose or God's Heroes* (Colorado Springs: Bustin, 1937) Digital Edition (Holiness Data Ministry, August 5, 2011).

[39]*American*.

[40]*Treasured Tears* (Weslaco, TX: Bustin, 1963) Digital Edition (Holiness Data Ministry, July 25, 2008).

[41]*American*.

[42]*Fifty*. On idolatry as the "primary definition of original sin," see Diane Leclerc, *Discovering Christian Holiness* (Kansas City, MO: Beacon Hill Press of Kansas City, 2010), 164-166. Cf. Richard Lints, *Identity and Idolatry: The Image of God and Its Inversion* (Downers Grove, IL: InterVarsity Press, 2015).

With such opinions in mind, every Roman Catholic proselytized for the "pure gospel" was a special trophy of grace in Bustin's ministry. He agreed with the assessment of his colleague C. J. Goodspeed that "if none other had been reached for God…, the salvation of" one such convert from Catholicism "is worth all our efforts." Accordingly, a special benefit of his radio ministry in Central and South America was that it was "hard for the wicked priesthood to keep people from hearing the Gospel by radio."[43] Such concern also lent special urgency to be first to enter new territories in New Guinea when they were opened for mission work, lest "the Roman Catholics, … would soon gobble up the whole area, and the poor natives would be left utterly without the Gospel."[44]

Another demonstration that Bustin's protest against Roman Catholicism was systemic in nature was the fact that he did not intend his polemics as a "thrust at individual Catholics."[45] Indeed, he admitted that "nice people can be found in Communism, Romanism, and Modernism, but the systems are of hellish origin."[46] He concluded that there were "many fine Catholic people" who were disillusioned with the system themselves: "Many of my friends are Roman Catholic in name. They are afraid to denounce it and yet they are disgusted with it."[47] Perhaps this explains how that, regardless Bustin's vigorous opposition to the Roman Catholic system, he could still find inspiration for his own spirituality and philosophy of ministry within that tradition.

Voluntary Poverty and Faith Missions

In fact, one of the most significant hallmarks of Bustin's ministry bore a deep impress from centuries of Catholic piety. This was voluntary poverty—the willing, intentional relinquishment of claims to property, positon, and prestige that might otherwise be in one's possession. This played such an integral role in Bustin's life that he considered it the key to any special measure of success he may have enjoyed:

> Why God has been so good to me I cannot tell except for one little trait in my life. From the beginning I have purposely chosen the hard way—the cross way. While others have played politics to pull themselves into the most pleasant positions the Lord has given me grace to purposely put myself in a position where I have had to trust Him.[48]

Indeed, this formed a pattern throughout Bustin's life. When he first began pastoral work, he had a choice between a relatively comfortable position offering a $100 monthly salary or "a new congregation of poor people" with no promised salary. He took the latter. Years later, he reflected, "There has never been a doubt

---

[43]*Fifty.*
[44]*My First Seventy-Five Years* (Florala, AL: G. T. Bustin, 1978), 205.
[45]*American.*
[46]*Tears.*
[47]*American.*
[48]*Fifty.*

in my mind as to the will of God in this matter, but have had reason to thank God many times for this decision to take the hard place and the way of faith rather than sight."[49]

This testimony reflects the connection in radical holiness thought between self-denial and reliance on God—the faith principle. Simply put, if believers would place all of their lives at God's disposal, they could "put complete trust in the faithfulness of God to meet their every need—divine *possession* assured divine *provision*."[50] Thus, if one will choose the "hard way" of voluntary poverty, it will afford greater opportunity for the Lord to demonstrate His faithfulness. At the forefront of such demonstrations would be missionaries like Bustin: "If any man on earth ought to be gloriously carefree and jubilant, it should be the 'Faith Missionary.' He should always speak with assurance, and without covetousness. He is more than a millionaire if he possess[es] true faith."[51]

Without doubt, G. T. Bustin's career provides some of the most dramatic illustrations in Holiness Movement history of this powerful conjuction between voluntary poverty and the faith principle. This began with his pioneer "home missionary" days during the depths of the Great Depression and continued throughout his itinerancy among the islands of the sea. His writings are filled with incidents illustrating divine provision in times of dire need and divine protection in the face of harrowing danger:

> Numerous experiences could be related which are incidental to island missionary life. We have often waded shark-infested waters in the darkness of the night with our clothes off and carried above our heads, we were in storms often, once on the coral reefs, many a sleepless night spent on a rough sea, and have walked scores of miles barefooted over sharp rocks and through marshy sloughs. Repeatedly the family has not known where the next day's food would come from. We made it a rule to tell no one of our personal needs, and to never borrow. We can never remember a day when we had nothing to eat. The Lord in some special way provided for us.[52]

The interface between voluntary poverty and divine providence not only worked out in connection with physical and financial hardships, but also in relation to social privations. Perhaps most obvious, the itinerant nature of Bustin's ministry frequently found him away from family:

> ... I have had occasion to know something of the sorrows of separation. Over and over as an evangelist, missionary evangelist, and missionary to different countries it has been my lot to go alone. On one occasion I was separated from my devoted wife and beloved children for seventeen months on a stretch.... Being a lover of children such a life to me has not been an easy cross.[53]

---

[49]*Fifty*. Cf. *How Great Thou Art!* (Westfield, IN: Bustin's Books, 1971), 73.

[50]Wallace Thornton, Jr. *When the Fire Fell: Martin Wells Knapp's Vision of Pentecost and the Beginnings of God's Bible School* (Lexington, KY: Emeth Press, 2014), 102.

[51]*Fuel*, 66.

[52]*Fifty*.

[53]*Tears*.

Even more painful was the criticism and opposition Bustin endured when "God's leadings became such that even some of God's dear children thought" him to be "foolish."⁵⁴ This was particularly the case when Bustin felt led to begin what became his around-the-world evangelistic tour with a venture to Australia, which he began when that country (as well as the United States) was still very much in the grip of the Great Depression. Other holiness people with considerable influence dismissed him as "a big fool." After the trip met with remarkable success, Bustin thought that his "foes, who were dead sure I had missed the will of God by going abroad without any promised support by any group, would be willing to admit that our Lord had graciously provided. However," he reported, "I was grossly mistaken."⁵⁵ Bustin acknowledged, "It would not have hurt so deeply had the world thus spoken, but such remarks came from those who professed the same as I." However, the intrepid pioneer refused to become "embittered," but rejoiced that "in God's overruling providence these merciless shafts of suffering were transmitted into tremendous values in my life." In fact, such opposition drove him to greater reliance on the Lord: "I needed the weaning from earthly dependencies that first of all I might learn to trust only in Him."⁵⁶

As these pains of his early foreign mission endeavors reflect, some of the strongest criticisms of Bustin's work came in the area of his self-denial (and the consequent privations it meant for his family) and his dependence on divine provision. Bustin responded, "It is understandable that some folk are not favorable toward such a course in life, and feel that no worker for God should venture forth without first having the assurance as to just how he and his would be provided for. This is man's way of thinking, but not God's way.... God delights in proving His faithfulness to those who depend only upon Him."⁵⁷

For inspiration and precedents for this lifestyle of austerity and aggressive faith, Bustin followed an approach strikingly familiar to pious Roman Catholics. He looked to saints of the past to validate his own practice and to bolster his faith. For example, elements of his around-the-world tour took on the aura of a pilgrimage, as he visited the Holy Land and several sites in Great Britain associated with prominent preachers and missionaries like Wesley, Knox, Moffat, and Livingstone.⁵⁸ He also relied heavily on hagiography, for his library "consisted mostly of biographies of great men of the past."⁵⁹ He was drawn especially to the stories of martyrs and others who experienced extraordinary suffering for the cause of Christ.⁶⁰ Of particular import to Bustin's own work was the story of James Chalmers, earlier missionary to New Guinea who had been killed and eaten

---

⁵⁴*Fuel*, 16.

⁵⁵*Miracle-Working*, 13-15.

⁵⁶*Fifty*.

⁵⁷*"...A Way in the Wilderness"* (n.p.: G. T. Bustin, n.d.), 64-65.

⁵⁸*Wilderness*, 25, 68-70.

⁵⁹Claudine Bustin Chamberlin, *Mambo* (Summerfield, FL: Evangelical Bible Mission, 2002), 186.

⁶⁰*"Our God Is . . . We Are"* Part 2 (Beech Grove, IN: Gene Hood, n.d.), 28-29.

by cannibals.[61] Bustin encouraged others to "read faith inspiring literature," and his own writings were lavishly laced with anecdotes and quotes from these heroes of the faith.[62] He found in them the "secret" of "revolutionary power," "remarkable fruitfulness," and "radiant beauty": "Their only ambition was to glorify God in sharing Christ with others. They loved not their lives to the death."[63]

Of course, direct antecedents to the radical holiness embrace of voluntary poverty are located in its Methodist forebears, such as early American circuit riders led by Francis Asbury, who "gave away nearly all the money that came his way."[64] In addition, Bustin personally located inspiring examples of voluntary poverty in the work of earlier faith ministries, both radical holiness and others, whether home or foreign.[65] However, Bustin's inspirational models also included prominent Roman Catholic monastics and mystics from the past, reflecting continuity between their commitment to self-renunciation and Bustin's own.

For example, Bustin extolled the practical piety of St. Francis of Assisi who was famously married to Lady Poverty.[66] The implication of an indebtedness of the radical holiness impulse to Roman Catholic monasticism is not overdrawn. Korean scholar Yeon-seung Lee has suggested that "the Radical Holiness Movement displayed the characteristic combining modern-day monasticism and missions. The possession of property and all secular entertainments were voluntarily relinquished, while monastic spirituality was translated into promotion of foreign missions as an ultimate form of self-denying piety."[67]

In addition, the resonance of Holiness spirituality with Roman Catholic mysticism has been demonstrated by scholars including Melvin Dieter and Patricia Ward.[68] Bustin himself elevated Madame Guyon as a model of purity and self-denial who served as a repudiation of the corrupt Roman Catholic hierarchy of her day.[69] However, the greatest similarity between Bustin's radical holiness commitment to voluntary poverty and the Roman Catholic ascetic ideal may actually appear in Bustin's view of Christ Himself.

---

[61] While cannibalism was common in pre-evangelized New Guinea, it was not ubiquitous. "The facts are that by far the majority of New Guineans are not cannibals, and never have been" (*The Heart of Heathendom* [n.p.: n.d.], 3).

[62] *Secrets*, 20.

[63] *This Is Life Eternal* (Summerfield, FL: Bustin, n.d.), 20.

[64] John H. Wigger, "Where Have All the Asburys Gone?" in Henry H. Knight III, ed. *From Aldersgate to Azusa Street* (Eugene, OR: Pickwick Publications, 2010), 66.

[65] See Klaus Fiedler, *The Story of Faith Missions: From Hudson Taylor to Present Day Africa* (Oxford: Regnum Books, 1994).

[66] *"As He Is"* (Westfield, IN: Bustin, 1967), 24.

[67] Yeon-seung Lee, "Native Initiative in the Transnational Holiness Movement: American Bible Schools and the Oriental Missionary Society in Asia, 1900-1911," *World Christianity and the Fourfold Gospel* (September 2015), vol. 1, no. 1, 85.

[68] Patricia A. Ward, *Experimental Theology in America: Madame Guyon, Fénelon, and Their Readers* (Waco: Baylor University Press, 2009), 166.

[69] *He Careth For You* (n.p.: n.d.) Digital Edition (Holiness Data Ministry, April 14, 1998).

While the martyrs and other saints throughout the ages provided inspiring models, Bustin's piety and theology remained thoroughly Christocentric. Thus one of his largest books, *The Man Christ Jesus*, delineated the human character of Christ as a model of practical piety. In particular, Bustin's commitment to voluntary poverty rested on a Christological foundation. For him, Jesus remains the epitomy of love, humility, and denial of self.[70] Since Christ chose to empty Himself and suffer, we should follow His example: "For even hereunto were ye called: because Christ also suffered for us, leaving us an example, that ye should follow His steps" (I Peter 2:21). Bustin asked, "Why should any true lover of our Lord find it in his heart to feel that he should be exempt from trials and tears while his Redeemer suffered and sorrowed so greatly?"[71]

In Bustin's thinking, Christ and the saints have demonstrated the necessity of suffering.[72] Indeed, "all the great saints ... were incessant sufferers. Every one of them passed through God's school of testing and suffering before they were qualified to do God's work." The term "school" was used purposefully by Bustin in connection with suffering. Bustin explained its instructional function: "The principle of obedience is planted in the heart by the Spirit of God, but the unfolding and application of this principle are learned in God's school of suffering."[73] Again, this applied to even Christ:

> Jesus suffered as no other person on earth has ever suffered, yet not without a purpose, even while He lived down here. We are told that 'He learned obedience by the things which He suffered.' These words do not infer that He was ever disobedient, for we know He was not. By His suffering He was trained in obedience, or oriented in obedience. He was schooled in suffering as is true concerning all of God's children.[74]

The application of this principle to the practice of voluntary poverty logically follows. Since poverty entails suffering, one of the surest ways to enter the "school of suffering" is through self-renunciation. As his mission work expanded, Bustin continuously sought for "young men and women ... prepared to frown on the follies of life's easy way" and "accept the challenge of the ranks of trailblazers in the western highlands of New Guinea to fight for King Jesus."[75] He saw the great hindrance of world evangelization to be the lack of Christians "willing to voluntarily enter God's school of private and personal instruction."[76] He admitted, "I am constrained to feel ashamed when I try to compare the victorious lives and jubilant deaths of these mighty giants for Christ back there with most professed believers in our day of carnal comforts and luxurious ease."[77]

---

[70] *Man Christ*, 156.
[71] *Tears*.
[72] II Timothy 3:12; Romans 8:17; and Philippians 1:29, 2:5-7.
[73] *Mountains of Grace in Valleys of Tests* (Intercession City, FL: Bustin, n.d.), 7.
[74] *Christ's Likeness* (Avonmore, PA: West Publishing, n. d.), 45.
[75] *Gospel Trail Blazing in the Jungle of New Guinea* (n.p.: n.d.), 66-67.
[76] *Mountains of Grace*, 7.
[77] *Wilderness*, 46.

Bustin recognized certain conditions for self-renunciation and reliant faith to be effective. Negatively, it must be undertaken without solicitation of assistance for personal needs. He testified of his own practice extending back to his home missionary days, "It was our privilege—a blessed one too—to trust God for all needs. We found Him ever faithful. This does not mean we had it easy. We were—and are yet—in His school. School life is not easy. We purposed to stay out of debt, and to tell no one our personal needs. The Lord had a chance to prove Himself again and again."[78]

Gene Hood said that one of the key passages that Bustin cited to support this approach was Psalm 50:12, "If I were hungry, I would not tell thee: for the world is mine, and the fullness thereof."[79] For precedent, Bustin again looked to Christ where he was enthralled with the "silence of the Lamb of God" when suffering during His trials.[80] Bustin concluded, "Love suffers silently. Divine love never makes any fuss about its sufferings...." This love is now to be reflected in silent suffering by Christ's followers: "Love never grumbles and growls about its lot in life. The lone worker in a strange land may suffer from loneliness, but the world never knows it. His sufferings are internal."[81] As others observe such suffering without complaint, it provides a poignant witness: "What is more beautiful than the silence of saints in the midst of extreme sorrow and suffering?"[82]

Positively, another condition for the conjunction of voluntary poverty and faith missions to be successful was the participation of supporters as well as workers. (Apparently, Bustin saw no problem with publicizing needs of a ministry, so long as they were not of a personal nature.) Bustin recognized the necessity of "the 'rope holders,' the unseen and unsung heroes and heroines behind the lines":[83]

> It is true that the Lord has not called all to go to the other side of the world to labor, nor does He call all to be preachers in the ordinary sense of the word, yet all are called to serve for Him. If He has not called you to go, then he has called you to support those who do go.

A key component in Bustin's understanding of this responsibility brings it into contrast with the Roman Catholic system which relegates voluntary poverty to a responsibility of the especially pious, such as monks and nuns. Rather, in Bustin's ideal, voluntary poverty reinforces the radical holiness commitment to egalitarianism. Simply put, not only ministers—but lay persons as well—have a responsibility to practice self-renunciation. Bustin emphatically asserted, "He has not called the missionary to deny himself to a greater extent than He has called you to do so." Indeed, mutual self-denial (for worker and supporter) is the *only*

---

[78]*Fuel*, 15.
[79]Conversation with author, March 2015.
[80]*Lamb*, 22.
[81]*Fuel*, 56.
[82]*Lamb*, 23.
[83]*Adventuring with God in the Wilds of New Guinea* (Intercession City, FL: Bustin, n.d.), 59.

way the radical holiness confluence of voluntary poverty and the faith principle will work. Bustin elaborated,

> Some of the missionaries may be thrown into circumstances where their lot will be more disagreeable than yours at home, but this is nothing.... If we are faithfully filling God's place for us in life it will not be too easy for us anywhere. In this writer's judgment, some of the greatest missionaries he has ever met have not placed a foot on foreign soil.[84]

In fact, Bustin's writings are replete with examples of sacrificial supporters who enabled him to venture into new expeditions of faith. Especially dear to him was the story of three ladies and a Baptist church whose combined gifts enabled him to pioneer the mission work in New Guinea. He gratefully acknowledged, "I could not have gone had it not been for these dear souls to whom the Lord spoke and they readily responded."[85] Highlighting their importance, he contended that "those who stay and support are entitled to all the promises and rewards of those who go forth and serve."[86]

Bustin's commitment to this egalitarian approach to voluntary poverty became inculcated in his New Guinea mission from its inception. His first Sunday in their new building at the Mele Station, he "explained something of what it meant to give, and that [he] wanted them to learn to give to the work of God from the very beginning, even though at that time very few had turned to the Lord." The results were astounding. The following Sunday the first offering resulted in over seven hundred pounds of food being donated and "eight dollars in money," even though standard wages were "twelve cents a day."[87] The New Guineans learned their lesson well, developing a sense of responsibility to support gospel work in their own land that helped lay the groundwork for a strong indigenous church.[88] Furthermore, their desire to share the burden for others led to aggressive outreach to other countries as far away as Nigeria.[89] In effect, Bustin had combined the radical holiness egalitarian impulse and its faith principle with a monastic-like stress on voluntary poverty to help fuel a revival with global influence.

---

[84] *"As He Is"*, 66.

[85] *Abounding*, 25.

[86] *Give Me This Mountain* (Westfield, IN: Bustin, 1971), 303.

[87] *Mary's Memorial* (Weslaco, TX: Bustin, n.d.), 11-12.

[88] Gerald Bustin, "The Papua New Guinea Bible Church: A non-dependent national church – alive and thriving," *The African American & Missions* (March-April 2000), cited in *Mission Frontiers* (http://www.missionfrontiers.org/issue/article/the-papua-new-guinea-bible-church. (Accessed June 22, 2015).

[89] In 1989, the Papua New Guinea Bible Church made missions news by sending the Pilipo Miriyo family as missionaries to Nigeria. See timeline in *Mission Messenger* (November-December 1999) vol. LV, no. 2, 7.

Conclusion

Little wonder that Roman Catholics and American holiness people alike are astounded by the transformation occurring in PNG. Rather than a "cargo cult" that makes "material wealth one's goal," what has bewildered the Roman Catholic hierarchy in PNG is an egalitarian revival that has adeptly employed one of their own ideals of piety—voluntary poverty. Indeed, the revival has produced unprecedented interaction between the grassroots and the upper levels of civil government there. However, among American holiness proponents, the ideal of shared commitment to self-renunciation has not fared so well. Indeed, loss of commitment to sacrificial living and involvement in ministry among American holiness people may give them more in common with an embattled Roman Catholic hierarchy than either they or the Catholic bishops would want to admit.

In the 1950s, Bustin himself bemoaned the materialism of many Americans: "We are a selfish people. We have 8% of the world's population and possess 69% of the world's wealth. We are given to feasting, drinking, frolicking, and hoarding, while half the world suffers with hunger, and from a thousand to thirteen hundred million are perishing in their heathen darkness. How can we say we love God?" In a denunciation that belies Roman Catholic charges of materialism, Bustin asserted, "We idolize our [jobs], our business, our homes, and our habits. We are cursed with covetousness. God says covetousness is idolatry."[90]

What has often resulted in America among holiness churches with an erstwhile commitment to egalitarianism is another system of inequity, in which ministers are expected to embrace poverty while others pursue the American dream. In effect, what is left may be more accurately described as "involuntary" poverty, summed up in the deeply entrenched attitude of some churches toward pastors with the glib slogan, "Lord, you keep him humble, we'll keep him poor." Consequently, ministers and their families have been relegated to near monastic austerity in some cases, outreach-oriented ministry has been stifled, and faith ministries have often been crippled because the "rope-holding" part of the equation has been neglected.[91]

Bustin decried such self-absorption with a pathos fueled by his missionary zeal:

O Lord, awaken us, have mercy upon us, and help us to repent of our wicked selfishness. We profess to follow Thee and walk as thou didst walk; but we are found liars. Thou didst give Thine all for us and for those "other sheep." We have profited

---

[90] *American.*

[91] See Christian Smith and Michael O. Emerson with Patricia Snell, *Passing the Plate: Why American Christians Don't Give Away More Money* (New York: Oxford University Press, 2008). On clergy compensation for the largest American holiness denomination, see Richard Houseal, *Picture of Bivocational Pastors in the Church of the Nazarene: What are the Implications for Clergy Preparation?* http://nazarene.org /files/docs/Picture%20of%20 Bivocational%20Pastors%20in%20the%20Church%20of%20the%20Nazarene.pdf. (Accessed April 9, 2016).

by Thy poverty, and have been saved by Thy sufferings, but we have clogged the channels by our selfish living, and have stopped the flow of Thy free salvation to all the wide world.[92]

Hopefully the revival in PNG will produce heart-searching among those who claim to follow the Christ whom G. T. Bustin loved and emulated. This revival's genius may be best expressed in that pioneer missionary's prayers shortly before his death: "I've been asking God to forgive me for doing so little for Him, and I've been praying that God would make me more like Christ."[93]

---

[92] *Fuel*, 9-10.

[93] "Challenge given by Gerald Bustin at G. T. Bustin's funeral," *Mission Messenger* (August-September-October 1995) vol. LI, no. 4, 3.

Contributors

Michael Avery. President, God's Bible School and College.

David Bundy. Research Professor of World Christian Studies, New York Theological Seminary.

Kenneth J. Collins. Professor of Historical Theology and Wesleyan Studies, Asbury Theological Seminary.

Donald W. Dayton. Author of *The Theological Roots of Pentecostalism* and *Discovering an Evangelical Heritage*.

Barry W. Hamilton. Emeritus Professor of Historical and Contemporary Theology, Northeastern Seminary (Rochester, NY).

Paul L. Kaufman. Professor, Hobe Sound Bible College.

William Kostlevy. Director, Brethren Historical Library and Archives.

Gari-Anne Patzwald. Independent Scholar and Editor, Elgin, Illinois. Author of *Waiting for Elijah: A History of the Megiddo Mission*.

Priscilla Pope-Levison. Associate Dean for External Programs and Professor of Ministerial Studies, Perkins School of Theology, Southern Methodist University.

William Snider. Pastor, Krome Avenue Church, Miami, Florida.

Howard A. Snyder. Visiting Director, Manchester Wesley Research Centre, Manchester, England.

Edwin Woodruff Tait. Consulting Editor, *Christian History*.

Jennifer Woodruff Tait. Managing Editor, *Christian History*.

Wallace Thornton, Jr., Independent Scholar, Indianapolis. Author of *Radical Righteousness* and *When the Fire Fell*.

www.ingramcontent.com/pod-product-compliance
Lightning Source LLC
Chambersburg PA
CBHW020803160426
43192CB00006B/417